The Science and the Profession of Libraries
A Visionary's Perspective
(A collection of 20 papers)

125th Anniversary Commemoration Volume

The Five Laws of Library Science

1. Books are for use
2. Every reader his/her book
3. Every book its reader
4. Save the time of the reader
5. Library is a growing organism

The Science and the Profession of Libraries
A Visionary's Perspective

(A collection of 20 papers)

125th Anniversary Commemoration Volume

Sarada Ranganathan Endowment for Library Science, Bangalore

and

Ess Ess Publications

2018

S.R. Ranganathan Classics-1,
The Science and the Profession of Libraries - A Visionary's Perspective
(A collection of 20 papers)

A 125th Anniversary Commemoration Volume - Edited by Dr. A.Y. Asundi,
Dr. B.M. Meera

Published by Ess Ess Publications, New Delhi
On Behalf of
Sarada Ranganathan Endowment for Library Science, Bangalore

Edition 1, 2019

Bibliographic Description

2*x*RAN P18

S.R.Ranganathan Classics-1, The Science and the Profession of Libraries -
A Visionary's Perspective. (A collection of 20 papers): A 125th Anniversary
Commemoration Volume/Ed. by A.Y. Asundi and B.M.Meera
Ess Ess Publications, New Delhi.

Pagination, Size, HB

Library Science, Scholarly Communication, Ranganathan

ISBN: 978-93-87698-09-3

Printed and Bound in India

Foreword

Dr S. R. Ranganathan is widely recognized by the library and information profession world over as one among the leading giants of the 20th Century like Melville Dewey, Charles A. Cutter, W. C. Berwick Sayers, Paul Otlet, Henry E. Bliss. The celebration of birth anniversary of such giants should be an occasion for the present generation of the profession to revisit their ideas and contributions, and to chart the way forward for the profession and the discipline of Library and Information Science.

Ranganathan was a profound thinker and a prolific writer. He had written 60 books and around 2,000 articles covering all aspects of Library Science, library organization and management, tools and systems for knowledge organization, reference service, public library legislation, academic and special libraries, etc. They are now considered as classics. His ideas are still sought after, relevant, thought provoking and continue to inspire and influence thinking and research in Library and Information Science in the 21st Century. To cite an example, Ranganathan's idea of *Facets* and *Facet Analysis* continue to find applications in the digital environment. Steve Papas, co-founder of Endeca, which uses Ranganathan's system in its software says, "Facets are all about manipulating multidimensional space". "You can't do that in the physical world. But Ranganathan was ahead of his time. The constraints of the physical world didn't inhibit his imagination."

Ranganathan's books are available in print form and some have also been digitized for easy access. However, his articles published in various journals are difficult to access, but they carry nascent thoughts. Sarada Ranganathan Endowment for Library

Science (SRELS) will bring out compilations of useful articles as a book for easy accessibility.

The articles presented in this volume have been carefully selected for their classic value. They cover a wide range of topics in the field of Library and Information Science presenting an insight into the vision and fore thought of Ranganathan.

I am sure this effort by the Endowment will be well received by the profession.

S. Parthasarathy
Former Head, INSDOC (CSIR), New Delhi
Member, Board of Trustees,
Sarada Ranganathan Endowment for Library Science

Preface

1. INTRODUCTION

Shiyali Ramamritha Ranganathan, born on 9th August 1892, is widely acknowledged as the father of library science and library movement in India. His birth centenary was observed in 1992. In the same year the International Society for Knowledge Organization (ISKO) and the IFLA had their international conferences in India to celebrate his birth centenary. The Department of Posts of the Government of India released a commemoration stamp with the first day cover in his honour.

The year 2017 marked the 125th birth anniversary of this giant. The Sarada Ranganathan Endowment for Library Science (SRELS) organized an international conference in association with the Indian Institute of Technology Madras, the Ranganathan Centre for Information Studies, Informatics (India) Ltd., NASSCOM Foundation and a few other organizations in October 2017[3] to mark the 125th birth anniversary. The conference titled "Revisiting Ranganathan" looked at the relevance of Ranganathan's tools, techniques and ideas in the context of the digital environment and the emergence of Web as the primary channel for information sharing, communication, dissemination and retrieval. The idea was to chart the way forward. The ISKO (Singapore Chapter) also held its annual event, *'Innovations in Knowledge Organization'* (IKO 2017) as a pre-conference event in association with SRELS.

Even earlier there have been events in India (and elsewhere) that have attempted to re-visit Ranganathan's ideas, such as the International Conference on Ranganathan's Philosophy organized by the Indian Library Association in 1985. More recently, an OCLC research sought to reorder the Five Laws of Library Science of Ranganathan in the context of shifting user behaviour[1]. Ranganathan's ideas and tools continue to be relevant and find application even in the digital environment. To quote David Weinberger in an article he wrote in *Forrester*, "It's as if Ranganathan designed Colon Classification in 1933 specifically for the kind of instant reshuffling that computers made feasible decades later"[2]. Clearly, Ranganathan and his ideas continue to attract attention as there is hardly any aspect of librarianship, information work and service that Ranganathan has not touched upon.

Ranganathan's legacy can be seen in libraries and academic institutions all over India. His passion for public library system continued till the very end. The model library bill that he published continues to serve as a reference document for Indian states in drafting their own public library bills. Ranganathan continued to be the honorary chair of the FID (International Federation for Documentation) till he passed away in 1972. His contributions as the Chair of the Documentation Sectional Committee of the Indian Standards Institution (now, Bureau of Indian Standards) for developing standards in areas related to libraries and documentation are significant. His report as Chairman of the committee to review "Library Science in Indian Universities," of the University Grants Commission, (UGC, 1965)[3] prepared a road map on education programmes in LIS. His report as Chairman of the UGC Review Committee(1965)[4] on University and College Libraries still continues to be seen as a guide even 50 years after it was submitted.

Given the depth and range of Ranganathan's contributions, we, at the Sarada Ranganathan Endowment for Library Science, realised that it is indeed a very tall order to assess the relevance of Ranganathan's ideas in a two-day event such as the one we had organized in October 2017[5]. Hence, we thought it necessary and useful to expose the profession, particularly the present generation of library and information professionals to some of Ranganathan's less known writings. We decided to bring out a series of Volumes titled *S.R.Ranganathan Classics,* containing collections of selected papers of Ranganathan that appeared in periodicals. The present volume, *The Science and the Profession of Libraries - A Visionary's Perspective* is the first one in this series.

2. CRITERION FOR SELECTING PAPERS

This volume contains 20 papers of Ranganathan on a wide range of themes and subjects. The selection of papers for this volume was indeed difficult. We looked at "An *Essay in Personal Bibliography"* compiled and edited by A. K. Das Gupta(1967)[6], as a companion volume to Ranganathan Festschrift, *'Library Science Today'*. A few published journal articles of Ranganathan were selected from this bibliography. To this some more papers were added after checking several periodical sources, both print and online. One criterion that was employed in selecting the papers for inclusion in the present volume was that they continue to be cited even several decades after they were published.

3. HIS UNIQUE STYLE

Ranganathan has adopted a unique style to drive home his ideas. Sections of some of his papers are seen to be in the form of a dialogue between him and someone else, resembling a Blog on today's Web. An example could be found in one of his papers "Documentation, Computer and Classification" (1967)[7], included in this volume, which explains to a professor in a Scottish university the importance of classified arrangement of documents on library shelves for effective browsing and retrieval. Ranganathan has effectively employed this style of presentation in many of his writings to drive home his views.

The second unique feature of his style of presentation is the effective use of illustrations. This is vivid in his paper "*Documentation: A Vital Link in Communication*" (1962)[8], included in this volume, which presents a logical view of the link between documentation and communication.

The third unique feature of Ranganathan's style of presentation is the use of analogies especially from ancient Indian scriptures and writings from writers of different countries and also from different subjects and linking them to the concepts in library and information science. His book on Documentation (1973)[9] linking it to *Kurmavatara* is an example.

4. SPECIALISED TERMINOLOGY AND REFERENCING

An important characteristic of Ranganathan's writings is his use of specialized terminology. Ranganathan did more than anyone else in Library and Information Science to develop a standard terminology especially in the areas of classification and cataloguing. Ranganathan was equally particular about consistent use of terminology for representing concepts, e.g. in the schedules of *Colon Classification*. While his *Prolegomena* had only a limited number of Canons for the Verbal Plane, an examination of the schedules of *Colon Classification* clearly displays his emphasis on consistent and standard use of terminology; it is difficult, for example, to come across a single instance of use of plural form of a noun to represent a concept in the schedules of *Colon Classification*! Many of his papers would also begin with a glossary of technical terms employed in the text.

Ranganathan also adopted a unique referencing style for bibliographical references in his writings. This style was later adopted and published by the Indian Standards Institution (now, Bureau of Indian Standards) as the Indian standard for bibliographical references. The most significant characteristic of this style is its two-way linking; linking a section of the text to related references and linking references to appropriate portions of the text. To realize this, he would extensively number the sections of the text. The pagination of the texts was also distinct as he used two sequences for pagination – continuous serial numbering and section and sub-section numbers on each page to facilitate easy retrieval of the needed portion of the text by the reader.

This volume, *The Science and the Profession of Libraries - A Visionary's Perspective* contains 20 papers of Ranganathan published in Indian and foreign journals. Ranganathan also published a few papers in *Current Science* founded by Sir C.V.Raman.

5. CONCLUSION

The papers in this volume indicate the very wide range of topics on which Ranganathan wrote. The Sarada Ranganathan Endowment for Library Science, founded by Ranganathan himself, thought it appropriate to bring out this collection as part of its efforts to '*Revisit Ranganathan*' and, more particularly, to introduce the present generation of LIS professionals to some of Ranganathan's ideas on different aspects of librarianship and Library and Information science. The Endowment will continue its efforts to '*Revisit Ranganathan*' and carry forward his ideas, tools and techniques.

6. ACKNOWLEDGEMENT

The Sarada Ranganathan Endowment for Library Science would like to place on record their deep sense of gratitude to Ms. Kavitha Kumar of M/s Informatics (India) for her assistance and support in various stages of planning this volume and its preparation for printing. The Endowment also places on record its deep sense of appreciation for the excellent work done by the editors, Prof. A.Y. Asundi and Dr. B.M. Meera in selecting the articles and editing them for the volume. The Endowment expresses gratitude to publishers of all the source journals for permitting the Endowment to reprint the papers in this volume. Our gratitude to Mr. N. V. Sathyanarayana, CMD, Informatics (India) Ltd., for all the support and assistance in preparing this volume.

K. S. Raghavan
Member-Secretary, Sarada Ranganathan Endowment for Library Science

REFERENCES

1. Connaway, Lynn S. and Faniel, Ixcehl M. (2015) Reordering Ranganathan: Shifting User Behaviours, Shifting Priorities Abridged by K. S. Raghavan (*In* The Library in the Life of the User: Engaging with People Where They Live and Learn / Compiled by Lynn Silipigni Connaway.) Dublin, OCLC Research, pp. 1-32 (First Published in SRELS Journal of Information Management)
2. Weinberger, David. Rediscovering Ranganathan. Forrester. http://semanticstudios.com/pdfs/forrester.pdf
3. University Grants Commission (UGC, 1965). Library Science in Indian Universities. New Delhi, UGC.
4. University Grants Commission (UGC,1965). University and College Libraries, Containing the Report of the Library Committee of the University Grants Commission, and the Proceedings of the Seminar on "From Publisher to Reader" held on March 4-7, 1969. New Delhi, UGC.
5. Sarada Ranganathan Endowment for Library Science-SRELS(2017). Revisiting Ranganathan: International Conference on Knowledge Organisation, Library and Information Management. Celebrating 125th Birth Anniversary of S.R.Ranganathan. October 23-25, 2017. IIT Madras, Chennai. [unpublished proceedings]
6. Das Gupta, A.K. (1967). An essay in personal bibliography: a bibliography of the writings on and by Dr S.R. Ranganathan

Festschrift Volume 2 /Compiled by A.K.Das Gupta. Asia Publishing House, Bombay

7. Ranganathan,S.R.(1967). Documentation, computer and classification. Library Science with a slant to Documentation. 4(3): pp. 197-225.
8. Ranganathan,S.R.(1962). Documentation: A vital link in communication. Annals of Library Science, 9 (4), pp.176-181,
9. Ranganathan, S.R.(1973). Documentation: Genesis and development. Delhi, Vikas Publishing House: pp.56-57.

★★★

CONTENTS

Libraries and Library Movement

S. R. Ranganathan
(University Library, Madras)

On the 5th of November 1940, the Public Library at Bangalore celebrated the Silver Jubilee of its installation and the event may be used as an occasion for reviewing the library movement in India.

The sister State of Baroda had already made a name in library matters when the Bangalore Public Library was established. For as early as 1907 the late Gaekwad had instituted public libraries in the State. In 1910 he secured the services of Mr. W. A. Borden, an American librarian, to work out a library system, for his State. Mr. J. S. Kudelkar was the first Indian librarian to take charge of this library system. In collaboration with Mr. M. N. Amin he developed the Central Library, the numerous local libraries and the travelling library system.

The example of Baroda did not take long to stimulate Mysore. In 1914 two public libraries of the modern type were established, one in Mysore and the other in Bangalore. These libraries were formally opened to the public in 1915. They were managed directly by the Government till 1921 when they were transferred to the care of mixed committees of officials and non-officials.

The first British Indian province to think of a library system was the Punjab. In 1915 its university engaged the services of Mr. A. D. Dickinson, an American librarian again, to reorganise its library on modern lines. Fortunately for Punjab he went beyond his scheduled work, organised a library training class, wrote the

Reprinted with permission from Current Science, 10(1), pp. 1-10, 1941.

Punjab library primer and initiated the library movement in the province. Thus again 1915 turns out to be an important date in the library history of India.

Taking our stand on that year let us have a look backwards and forwards. Isolated libraries had existed all along from very early days. But they do not constitute library movement. The apex of such isolated libraries in the provinces was constituted at Calcutta with the name Imperial Library by the Curzon Act I of 1902.

On the non-official side the Andhradesa has done pioneering work. The first Andhra library is said to be the one started about the year 1898 in the village of Kumudavalli in the West-Godavari district by Ganjam Venkataratnamgaru. The library workers of Andhradesa had also been actively sponsoring an All-India Library Conference during the twenties, as one of the many auxiliary conferences associated with the Indian National Congress.

Work through non-official library associations has now become a regular feature. The Madras Library Association was founded on the 30th January 1928 and the Punjab Library Association on the 30th January 1929. The Andhradesa Library Association and the Bengal Library Association had come into existence a few years earlier. An All-India Library Association was formed in 1933 and is holding biennial conferences. Since that date provincial library associations have been formed in some other areas like the United Provinces (1935), and Bihar (1939).

The Andhradesa library workers have the credit of having started the first library periodical. It was called the *Indian library journal*. It sent out a few issues at irregular intervals and it seems to have now gone into suspended animation.

The Punjab Library Association inaugurated the *Modern librarian* in November 1930. It began first with the ambition of being a monthly. After the first two issues it was put to the necessity of issuing double numbers in alternative months. Now it has avowedly declared itself a quarterly. It has completed ten volumes of considerable value.

The Bengal Library Association has been issuing a Bulletin at regular intervals. The combined numbers 1 and 2 of volume 2 which came out in 1938 appear to be the latest ones.

The Andhradesa Library Association started a bilingual quarterly entitled Andhra granthalayam early in 1939. It has just now completed the first volume by clubbing issues 3 and 4 into a double number.

The Madras Library Association has inaugurated an annual periodical with the title *Memoirs of the Madras Library Association*. The first volume came out in April last.

Of all the different Library Associations of the country it is the Madras Library Association that is most prolific in its publications. It has inaugurated three important series of publications: Everything About Something Series; Bibliographical Series and Publication Series.

The first is an attempt to bring out books on current thought in modern Tamil, as such books are not easily forthcoming in the book-market of the province. Two books have come out in this series till now.

Sixteen items made up of book-selection lists in South Indian languages, library companions to certain text-books and bibliographies in certain subjects have appeared in the bibliographical series.

The volumes of the publication series form the most considerable contribution of that Association to the world's library literature. Nine volumes have come out so far. Three more are in preparation. The intention is to cover all branches of Library Science. The basic book is the *Five laws of library science* (1931) which in the words of Sir P. S. Sivaswami Iyer "reduces everything connected with the libraries to five cardinal principles from which all the rules of library organisation and management are developed as necessary implications and inevitable corollaries". The other volumes cover the fields of classification cataloguing, administration, reference service and bibliography. Another publication of some value on reference service was published this year by Mr. Fazl Elahi. Library movement cannot flourish in our land unless substantial treatises come out continuously from all parts of India.

The Madras Library Association has also the credit of having made two outstanding contributions which have received international recognition. They relate to classification and cataloguing.

The Colon Classification sponsored by that Association has many novel features of which its composite nature is the outstanding one. The *Library Association record* (London) estimates it with the words "The result is almost perfect." A new subject creates its own number in the notation". The Year's *work in librarianship* pronounces it to be the best exercise in synthetic classification. On account of its composite nature and the eight devices it has developed, it carries the individualisation of ideas and subjects to a far greater degree than any other scheme.

The Association has also sponsored what is perhaps the only complete code in book form in the English language for the preparation of a classified catalogue. The *Library Association record* (London) estimates the Code as one of considerable value.

The credit of having started the first school of librarianship in India goes to the Punjab University Library. It was inaugurated in 1915 and is still being continued as a six months' course every alternate year.

The second school of librarianship was founded by the Madras Library Association in 1929 as an annual summer school for three months. This was taken over by the University of Madras in 1931. In 1938 the course was converted into a full-timed one year one leading to the University diploma. About 130 persons have been so far trained by the Madras school.

The third school of librarianship was begun by the Andhra University in 1934 on a rather ambitious scale out of all proportion to what was warranted by the library conditions of the country. It had to be suspended from 1937.

Another school of librarianship is being conducted in alternate years by the Imperial Library at Calcutta.

The Bengal Library Association is also giving occasional short courses.

The outstanding library buildings of the modern type that were completed during the last few years are those of the Central Library at Baroda and the University Libraries of Lahore, Benares, Madras, Waltair, Annamalainagar and Lucknow. In most of these libraries the buildings are designed to suit the open access system, Most of them are also provided with artificial lights so as to make it possible for the libraries to work during nights. The longest hours are kept by the Madras University Library which works on all the days of the year without exception, for 13 hours from 7 a.m. to 8 p.m.

The above resume of the recent history of Library Movement in India significantly omits mention of any considerable State action, in particular, of library legislation, which forms the basis of continued library development in other countries of the world. The first attempt at promoting library legislation was made at the Library Service Section of the First All-Asia Educational Conference held at Benares in 1930. A Model Library Act with compulsory clauses was presented to that Conference. This Model Act was made the core of the *Five laws of library science*.

Munindra Deb Rai Mahasai had the Model Act adapted to the conditions of Bengal and sought to introduce it in the Bengal Legislative Council. But it was disallowed by the Viceroy. The Madras Library Association promoted a public library bill on the lines of the Model Act but converting all the compulsory clauses into optional ones to avoid opposition from government. The Viceroy's consent was received and the support of most of the district boards and municipalities who were to be created library authorities was also obtained. The bill was introduced into the Legislative Council by Mr. Basheer Ahmed Sayeed in October 1933. It came out of the Select Committee stage in 1934, but all further progress was blocked by the unfriendly attitude of the then Finance Member. Though it was not formally withdrawn the bill lost its life by the dissolution of the Legislative Council in 1936. On the reconstitution of the legislature under the Government of India Act, 1935, Mr. Basheer Ahmed Sayeed gave notice in October 1937 to introduce the bill in the Madras Legislative Assembly. But it was not permitted by His Excellency the Governor.

It is a matter of experience all the world over that Library Movement cannot take root and thrive, if it is made to depend purely on private philanthropy or the enthusiasm of private individuals. Nor will it receive the necessary attention of the local bodies simply because libraries are mentioned in a schedule of the Local Boards Acts among the various purposes on which a local body may spend any money that it may occasionally spare. Local bodies will go the whole hog in the matter only if there is a separate public library act implemented by a department of public libraries presided over by a professional librarian.

The experience of several countries points to the need for even a more drastic step with compulsory clauses in the public library acts which empower penalties being imposed upon local bodies which do not exercise their library function with sufficient vigilance and to a prescribed standard.

Library legislation will be required if the country is to be filled with a co-ordinated network of live public libraries capable of functioning as efficient instruments of universal education. That, as we have seen, we are yet to have in India. But so far as the needs of the intellectual aristocracy go, it can be said that India is well provided by its university libraries and the libraries of the various departments of the Government of India and of the several Research Institutions. Before the last world depression, money was easily forthcoming and many libraries were well provided for. It was this fact that brought their resources to an adequate level. But of late the finances of most of the libraries are being crippled. If a more generous and far-sighted policy is not inaugurated it will not be long before even the combined resources of all such libraries prove inadequate to the requirements of the nation-building research activities.

Will it be too much to hope that the Government and universities will strive their very best to continue their library policy along liberal lines? Will it be too much to hope that they will realise that money spent on libraries is not money thrown away for ever, but on the other hand every pie spent on increasing the resources of the libraries and on improving their man-power and their service to the public will come back to the community in the form of extended literacy and efficient citizenship.

It is true that the war in which the country now finds itself entangled and the political abnormality that prevails in the land make the present moment inopportune to speak of library reforms, library legislation and above all finance for libraries. But surely the war is not going to be a perpetual feature of the world. Similarly the present political impasse is not going to be permanent. It is not asking for too much if we appeal to those who now wield the power that the libraries should not be starved at least for the obvious economic reason that the gaps now created will cost far more than now to get filled up later. Countries which are in the thick of the fight have not developed any serious indifference to the library needs of their people. Again thanks to the activities of library associations a good deal of popular enthusiasm has been created for libraries. If the enthusiasm is made to die out by a stingy policy, it would be far more difficult to whip up enthusiasm a second time.

★★★

Newton, Mathematics and Ramanujan

Rao Sahib S. R. Ranganathan, M.A., L.T.,F.L.A.
(*Librarian, Madras University Library, and Secretary, Madras Library Association*)

Abstract

SEPARATED by an interval of about two centuries and a half, the mathematical heritage of mankind was enriched by two remarkable men - Newton born in Britain on 25 December 1642, and Ramanujan born in India on 22 December 1887. They had just a little in common; but they differed widely in most matters - even in the force that pulled them to mathematics.

DISSIMILARITIES

Newton spent his early years in fairly comfortable circumstances, in spite of his father dying before his birth and his mother remarrying before he was three; Ramanujan's parents, though both were living, could not keep him above want till he began to earn. Before entering adulthood, Newton had passed through the University of Cambridge, learned virtually all that could then be learnt in mathematics and contacted the eminent mathematicians and natural philosophers of his days, either as teachers or as friends; but till his twenty-fifth year Ramanujan could not come across any who would understand him or his language and still less teach him, nor could he finish the university course nor know the then state of mathematical knowledge. Notwithstanding his anxiety to avoid 'contention' of any kind, Newton's discoveries involved him in frequent and bitter controversies and much tension prevailed between him and his peers; it was, on the other

Reprinted with permission from Current Science, 11(12), pp.11-18, 1942.

hand, an atmosphere of uniform and spontaneous admiration, love and respect that surrounded Ramanujan after he was discovered. Newton was long-lived; Ramanujan died prematurely.

SIMILARITIES

And yet they had just a few things in common. Mathematics was the meeting ground of the two geniuses, though they approached it from different directions. Their life's work was done by the time they were thirty, though one lived for half a century thereafter and the other gave up his mortal coil almost immediately. Newton wrote down his results in diaries, letters and note-books, most of which are still preserved in some British libraries and had been all published in his own days though it was a job to make him release them for print; Ramanujan too wrote down his results systematically in a note-book which he left behind in England, where I was fortunate to pick it up in 1925 though it was in a tattered state; and it is now the most precious possession of the Madras University Library, still awaiting publication as a whole. The Royal Society elected both of them as its fellows before they passed thirty.

INTEGRAL CALCULUS

Newton's boyhood had been rich in hobbies of a mechanical sort like making kites, sundials and windmills. Kepler's *Optikas* is said to have been the first book to engage his serious thought. Consistently with this, one of the important books that Newton himself published was his *Opticks*(1704). He would grind lenses and if the telescope could not be made achromatic, he would invent a new type of telescope, the reflecting one. Consistently with this if a mathematical tool was wanting or defective, he would improvise a new tool or sharpen what existed. When his theory of gravitation led him to calculate the attraction of a sphere, which he could not do by the then known mathematical tools, he invented a new tool - the integral calculus. Particular problems of finding lengths, areas and volumes had been solved before him by special devices; but a general tool applicable to all similar problems was invented only by Newton and that because his preoccupations with his theory of gravitation needed it. The *Tractatus di quadratura curvarum* first appeared as an appendix to his *Opticks.*

CONICS

The determination of a central orbit as a conic involved Newton in facing the problem of finding the conic when a focus and three other conditions or any other five conditions were given. These were fully investigated in the *Principia*(1687).

PROBLEM OF THREE BODIES

The phenomenon of tides challenged Newton for an explanation on the basis of his theory of gravitation. While Proposition 66 of Book I and 24 and 26 of Book III of the *Principia* were turned on it directly, the foundations of the profound problem of three bodies were also laid incidentally.

CALCULUS OF VARIATIONS

In considering the form of ships, Newton was obliged to determine the shape of bodies of revolution that will experience the least resistance when moved in the line of its axis. He improvised in 1686 a new tool to do this job and showed it to Fatio Duillier who published it in the pamphlet *Investigatie geometrica solidi rotundi in quod minima fiat resistantin*(1699). This tool, the calculus of variations, was lost sight of, until it was rediscovered by Lagrange in 1762.

CALCULUS OF FINITE DIFFERENCES

Proposition 40 of Book III of the *Principia* is followed by Lemma 5 which gives a general solution of the problem: "To describe a geometrical curve which shall pass through any given points" - the fundamental proposition of the calculus of finite differences.

Methodus differentiates (1711) which gives- another solution of the same problem was first translated into English in the pages of the *Journal* of the Institute of Actuaries in 1918.

CUBICS

The Enumeratio *linearum tertu ordinis* which appeared as an appendix to *Opticks* was the first systematic contribution to the theory of higher plane curves, 72 species of cubics were enumerated. As many propositions were without proof, this became one of the most commented of Newton's works. His method of classifying cubics appears to have inspired Waring to apply it to the quartic of which he obtained 84,551 species. To evaluate Newton's contribution to this field, we should remember that the modern tool of projective geometry had not yet been forged.

CALCULUS OF FLUXIONS

The most discussed of Newton's tools from the point of view of priority of discovery is the calculus of fluxions. This again was forged to meet a definite situation in the determination of orbits. In fact he first invented the binomial theorem and then this calculus. The *Principia* had given its substance without the name in certain propositions of Book I. Evidently influenced by his dynamical interests, Newton regarded all variables as functions of time and all variation as primarily happening as time flows on. He, therefore, invented a calculus to determine the rate of change of any magnitude regarded as a function of time. These rates were called fluxions. They were with respect to time. The rate of change of a magnitude x with respect to another magnitude y he defined as the ratio of the fluxion of x to the fluxion of y. In spite of Newton's fluxional approach providing the beginner with an intuitive and familiar illustration of the concepts of calculus and in spite of time having been appropriately basic in the specific problem that led Newton to its discovery, it was soon felt that it was needless to drag in time where it was not concerned; and Leibnitz produced a calculus unobsessed by the spirit of time. But insularity kept out for long the more fertile calculus of Leibnitz from the home of Newton. It was not till 1812 that the sterile calculus of fluxions was deposited in the museum. In that year the Analytical Society of Cambridge was founded to adopt Leibnitz in place of Newton; or as Babbage, one of its founders, put it, "To promote the principles of pure D-ism in opposition to the Dot-age of the University". Non-mathematical readers can see the pun if they are told that the notation for the differential coefficient of *x* was *x* (*x* dot) in Newtonian calculus and D*x* (Dee *x*) in Leibnitzian calculus.

NEWTON'S APPROACH

Thus Newton's approach to mathematics was from the side of physics and the phenomena of the material universe and for the purpose of employing it as a tool. Concrete phenomena are ever so complex and there is no end to the variety of tools which they call for. Even to-day mathematics is being enriched by new tools demanded by newly discovered phenomena in physics; witness the calculus of operations, the calculus of tensors and the theory of Wave Function. Green, Kelvin and Poincare are some of the later mathematicians who enriched mathematics in this way. The Indian mathematicians of the Vedic age had enriched geometry similarly, i.e., by the urge to solve a concrete problem.

RAMANUJAN'S APPROACH

But Ramanujan's approach to mathematics was from another side, the side of form - its beauty and potency. Euler, Galois and Riemann had done so before. The Greek mathematicians of the classic age had enriched geometry similarly. We saw that Newton's boyhood-experience registered with his mode of approach to Mathematics. It was so with Ramanujan too. His boyhood was spent in making patterns of magic squares, playing with the formulae enumerated in Carr's *Synopsis* and listening to *puranic* discourses on the infinite attributes of God. Two intimate friends who were with him virtually all through, except during his sojourn in England, assure me that his sensitiveness to form was unusual and that, as they could not follow mathematics, he used to entertain them till late in the night with interpretations of the *Ramayana* and the *Mahabharata* based on certain patterns of thought which were exquisitely beautiful and the mathematical correlates of which he would occasionally indulge in expounding.

FORCE OF FORM

Hardy's reminiscence about the taxi-cab No. 1729 is significant. Hardy's remark that it was 'dull' elicited a prompt reply from Ramanujan: "No, it is a very interesting number;it is the smallest number expressible as a sum of two cubes in two ways." Hardy asked for the corresponding number for fourth powers and Ramanujan replied, after a moment's thought, that the first such number must be very large. The fascination and force of form may be traced behind most of Ramanujan's work on the theory of numbers and of modular functions. We witnessed a pretty manifestation of the same in a mathematical social evening at Madras in 1914 in which Ramanujan pierced, as it were, through the traditional integer-garb of the Leibnitzian form for the differential coefficient of the nth order and utilizing the Eulerian generalisation of the factorial into the gamma function entertained the audience with the beauty of fractional differentiation.

COMPLEMENTARY APPROACHES

Both the approaches are necessary to disclose the potency of mathematics. But the illumination from Ramanujan's side of approach is more subtle and visible only to a select few; while that from Newton's side is more extensive and lights up many a path in many a field of knowledge.

★★★

Library Responsibilities of Independent India

S. R. Ranganathan
M.A., D.Litt, L.T., F.L.A.

INTRODUCTION

India's independence implies freedom to develop her library system on a nation-wide basis and obligation to develop her library personality so as to become a peer of other nations in the international library sphere. During the last century of her dependency and inaction, the world has re-evaluated libraries and made them social institutions charged with the duty of working as an agency for the perpetual self-education of one and all. India did not have the freedom to fall in line with this world-trend. A few isolated book collections have: no doubt been built, mostly in universities. But they have not yet been vitalised as fully as they can be, but even book collections have not yet been formed at the levels of public, business and national libraries. Indeed it is not far wrong to say that India has yet to realise, how much her progress in governmental, industrial, educational, cultural and international matters has to depend on a well-planned national library system.

THE POTENCY OF BOOKS

The success of the life, to-day and in the future of India will depend on the facilities she builds up for the creation and absorption of new ideas. These facilities should include among other things a plenty of reading materials. Their supply will

Reprinted with permission from Indian Librarian, 3, pp. 19-30, 1948.

depend on authors, printers and publishers. But their effective distribution will depend on libraries. All these must work together to step up India to a high level of efficiency, to make her catch up the world in the least possible time and to keep her abreast of other nations thereafter. In the service of books and periodicals, new standards must be forged and the tendency to imitate outmoded foreign standards or to perpetuate the hesitant methods of the dependent past must be avoided. In particular fatalistic determinism and indifference derived from the absorption of a wrong presentation of her values of life during the last century by western scholars and a pseudo-cheerful and foolhardy acceptance of anything that comes along on-board the ship, born out of political protection and subjugation should be avoided. The tendency to live for the moment only, though the next moment may see one hurled into perdition, and the tendency to live for selfish ends and sell the larger and lasting interests of the nation for a mess of pottage, must be given up. It is in the power of books to cure these pathological attitudes. The book-trade and the library profession must influence for good the thought of today. The mood to turn to serious books, tuned to India's advance, must be induced in the people. Catch penny books, morally subversive literature and self tultipying thought, must be avoided so much as to disappear altogether. The generation of India's adults brought up by the imperialists will raise a false alarm and call this a danger to freedom of the press and the advent of censorship. They may call it impracticable, idealistic and uneconomic. But is it so? Whether we like it or not, private profit should no longer be allowed as the sole or primary motive in running a business as it has been with alien exploiters. Vocation and service should hereafter rank as equal and complementary partners. Then only can the potency of books be utilized by independent India. The total book-stock in the libraries of India should be rapidly stepped up to 10 millions.

THE POTENCY OF LIBRARIES

The library is in a key position to encourage or discourage the spread of ideas conducive to a better way of life for the community. It is a recognition of this fact that has set up in the United States the drive for "distribution of books by the million" and the establishment of a network of libraries. Libraries have a wonderful chance to take a special and constructive part in the attempt to build a better standard of values in the life of people. The standard of public taste should be improved. Those who do not read should be encouraged to read, those who read, and yet read indifferently should be handed something that would give them a better idea what books should be and a chance of unconsciously improving their civic, moral and spiritual outlook. The business of serving books should therefore become a vocation and a real profession with jealously guarded standards to which all must conform. The potency of the library should be fully utilised by independent India. The pubic library system of India should soon include 14,000 Travelling Libraries calling once in a fortnight at 3,00,000 Delivery Stations, 5,000 Branch Libraries, 144 City Central Libraries, 321 Rural Central Libraries, 24 State Central Libraries and 1 National Central Library.

LIBRARIES AND INDUSTRIES

India has gained her independence at a time when 'manufacture' had given place to 'machino-feature' development of hydro-electricity and the supply of energy to villages is introducing machinery even into the so-called cottage-industries. Skill in improving machine-production is not mere manual skill. Muscular nimbleness and deftness improved by practice, though forever necessary are not longer sufficient. Thinking, and for this purpose the enrichment and stimulation of one's thought by that of others, have become necessary. It is not merely the gross physics of materials but also their chemistry, bio-physics and bio-chemistry that have to be mastered, to meet the demands of modern industry—including agricultural industry. These subjects are explored and extended from day to day in response to the demands of industry. More traditional knowledge proves to be utterly inadequate. The men in the industry have to be kept informed about up-to-the-minute phases in the development of knowledge. These developments take place in all parts of the world. India can no longer escape their incidence. On the other hand, independent India must go forward to meet and invite these developments to step-in without any further delay. Our protected life-hitherto has induced indolence in us. One of the first acts of India should be to shake off this indolence and reinforce manual skill by new thought. New thought means cultivation of intellect. This needs the service of books. Libraries are needed in all the industries to serve books with expedition and discrimination. About 1,000 Business Libraries will have to be established to feed our industries.

LIBRARIES AND ADMINISTRATION

With the rapid growth in the complexity of life and the economic interlacing of the countries of the world, government itself has become problem calling for serious research as a basis for legislative, executive and administrative action. To discharge its duties in, peace as well as in war, government has to enter upon scientific research—not only in social and applied sciences but even in fundamental sciences. Research is impossible without efficient book-service. Administration itself has become impossible without books. But India's governments—whether at the Union Centre or in the States—have yet to realise that the men in their departmental libraries should be taken as equal partners by the heads of the departments. India should cease to regard them as clerks, even to enable, the officers expect and accept all the help they need from the printed sources of knowledge. She should give the departmental librarians the status, the salary and the freedom due to the men of any other technical service as engineering, technology, agriculture, forestry or archaeology. As many as 600 Departmental Libraries should soon begin to irradiate the rooms in the Secretariates.

LIBRARIES IN SCHOOLS

To induce in her adults the ability to use libraries intelligently and purposively, India has the responsibility to promote library habit even at school stage. An unfair abuse had been levelled against Indians by the Hartog Committee that they had no reading habit. It was unfair because an educationist with the experience of Hartog should have known the school-conditions in his own country and in India and of the absence in India of the special efforts which the Board of Education and the schools of England make to cultivate the habit of purposeful reading and to make the library a live part of the school. Independent India can not delude herself that children will of their own accord take to books. Books are artificial entities. A collection of a considerable number of them in a library becomes bewildering even to the initiated reader. He finds it difficult to walk through the highways and byways of the book-world and get all which the books can give. Nor does it occur to him that he can ask for help. Initiation at the adult stage is difficult and ineffective. Indian must start the initiation as all other countries do, even at school.

To make the initiation pleasureable and far-reaching in its effect, the library should become the hub of every school and college, from which all the activities of the pupils radiate and get irradiated. India's academic library system should soon have 15,000. School Libraries, 321 School District Libraries, 1,000 College Libraries and 30 University and Research Libraries.

NATIONAL CENTRAL LIBRARY

The libraries of the country—public, industrial, departmental, special and academic—should all work in unison. They should be integrated into a single system. To co-ordinate their work, to establish standards for materials, procedure and service, to effect national economy by centralising the technical treatment of books such as classification and cataloguing, and the preparation of bibliographies and to act as the medium for India's library contact with the other countries and the World Organisations for the promotion of library service and documentation, India should immediately find and develop a National Central Library. Her blue-print for this institution and for the library system as a whole, of which it should be the apex, should be electric. About 44 countries of the world have already established their National Central Libraries. They show all kinds of variations. Most of them suffer from the handicap of long established tradition. Some of the recently established ones suffer by too great a dose of imitation of the older ones. In planning her National Central Library, India should not commit that mistake. She must look ahead. Her ambition should be to leap ahead of others. This must be the advantage she should reap from her entering the field after 44 countries had established themselves. It has been observed that in spite of her having won political independence, India has not yet shed her mental dependence. If this be true of the leaders, it would prove fatal. If this be true in educational matters, it would blight the future. If this be true in the design of the National Central Library, India's Library personality will become stunted and this will effect her personality in every other sphere. Independent India should beware of these dangers. She must bring out her National Central Library whole as an egg. She must at once invest it with every possible function which the most progressive thinkers in the field could conceive of. She must make it worthy of her cultural heritage. She must make it an effective lever to lift her cultural, academic, industrial, political and international status to an eminence that is second to none. She must make it the central station for thought energy, which could activate her future life to its best.

FOREIGN LIBRARY CENTRES

The National Librarian should also be charged with the duty of establishing and maintaining Indian libraries in all other countries. The function of these libraries should have little to do with the diplomatic relations. Its objective should be to make available to the foreigners correct information about India not through special organs improvised for the purpose, but by the service of books and periodicals that get created in India spontaneously without any propaganda motive. It should work through its classics, ancient as well as modern, which are the outpourings of the best of her sons and daughters. Promotion of cultural contact, true understanding and well-informed friendship, should be its aim. The National Librarian should send to the foreign libraries the best representatives of the Indian Library profession. Independent India should recall to mind how she used to send out, in her ancient days, her best books as messengers of light into all her neighbouring countries—into Turkestan, Tibet, China, Japan and South-East Asia. She had then known that the most potent planes of contact between two nations were spiritual and intellectual ones. Accordingly she sent some of her best sons abroad for the spread of spiritual light and copies of her best books for the dessimination of advanced thought. Let awakened India be glad that her ancient method of using books as ambassadors has not been out-moded but is being vigorously used by the modern countries. Let her now take advantage of the cheap mechanical multiplication of copies of books invented when she was asleep and send out and serve personally her books more plentifully than in the past and thus revive her library contact with the world.

LIBRARY MANPOWER

To man this vast library grid and to keep it in an efficient state of service, India will require about a library profession 1,20,000 strong, apart from clerical and unskilled workers. These will fall into four groups when viewed from the angle of responsibility and the ability needed for it.

The top group may have to about 900 strong. They must be the best of the men which India can find. They must be men of highly integrated personality, capable of creative thought, leadership, and daring vision and above all endowed with single-minded devotion to their calling, application and industry. 30 such men should be trained each year. They cannot be trained in isolation in the different States. Wisdom will be in the Union Government maintaining in its own University at Delhi an advanced All India School of Library Science to produce these path-finders and the Governments of the States sending their chosen men to this school for getting fitted up. These men should finish off their training with a doctorate.

The second group, which will consist of the librarians of the smaller cities and the heads of sections in the Central Libraries of the Nation, the State, the Rural Areas and the bigger cities, may have to be about 1,200 strong. These must be able men. 40 of them must be produced each year. They must have an intensive post-graduate course of two years and earn a degree, in Library Science. India will need only one Central College of Library Science for these people. It is but appropriate that this college must be in the care of the University of Delhi.

About 50,000 men will have to be trained to work under direction in the various libraries. A one-year post-graduate Diploma Course should prove sufficient for them. To produce 1,700 such men each year, each of the universities will have to maintain a College of Library Science.

The remaining 66,000 men will have to work in very small libraries. They must be able to do their work with the aid of a carefully written *Manual for library work*, provided they are initiated to their use and to a 'proper library outlook in a rapid three-months' course conducted in each State. 2,200 should be so trained in all the states taken together.

LIBRARY LITERATURE

Another library responsibility of independent India is the production of literature in Library Science. The Madras Library Association has already published basic books on most of the branches of the subject. But they are all too advanced. There is urgent need to write books in a lower key. Again the Madras books are all in English. They should all be relayed in the different regional languages of the country. The schemes of classification, the code for catalogue and the manual for administration should all be revised and brought up to date from time to time.

The library opportunities and responsibilities of India are thus very vast indeed. The library profession in general and the Indian Library Association in particular are ever ready to serve the State in the due development of the library personality of India.

★★★

Special Librarianship - What it Connotes?

S. R. Ranganathan
Delhi University Library, Delhi, India

Abstract

Special librarianship is a puzzling term. It is causing some confusion in the all-too-meagre body of Indian librarians. The ineffability or the ambiguity—whatever it may be — of this is almost reducing it to a slogan. Like all slogans it induces some vague but powerful feelings. Those under the spell of a slogan resent being asked what exactly the slogan means. *Special librarianship* is no exception to this rule. I found this inconvenient question raised in some of the meetings and conferences which I attended in Europe and America last year. There, too, I witnessed the usual resentment and evasion. When, what is perhaps the first Special Libraries Association in the world was organized in the United States in 1909, its founders undoubtedly had something definite to denote by the term *special libraries.*

In those days the term, *library,* commonly meant a collection of books, rather than the activity of bringing them into intimate relation with a group of readers by the librarian. Used in that sense a special library can only mean a library of special books. One of the implications of the first law of library science is that it is the soul or the thought-content embodied in books which makes them of value in a library. This means that it is specialization in a subject that can make a library a *special library*. The fourth international edition of the *Universal Decimal Classification* confirms this meaning; on page 51 of volume I, part 1, it defines *special libraries* as "Libraries and

Reprinted with permission from Special Libraries, XL, p. 77-90, November, 1949.

collections of books devoted to special subjects or sciences. Eg., medical libraries".

Can *special librarianship* be taken to mean the art of running a special library? Whether this definition is significant at all will depend upon the meaning of the term *librarianship* considered by itself. *Librarianship* may be defined as the art of fulfilling the laws of library science, that is:

1. Promoting the use of books
2. Finding his book for every reader
3. Finding its reader for every book
4. Saving the time (subjective as well as objective) of the reader
5. Doing all these, whatever be the manner and the rate at which the library grows.

The chief items of work involved in this art are book-selection, book-acquisition, book-classification, book-cataloging, book-display, book-circulation, reference-service and librametry or a statistical evaluation of the efficiency of the library. None of these can vary in quality from subject to subject, to such an extent as to call for a change in the technique of the art. To use a familiar mathematical mode of expression, if we regard the subject as the independent variable and librarianship as the dependent one, librarianship is constant. Confining the books of a library to a special subject does not, therefore, lead to *special librarianship*. If we insist on linking *special librarianship* with special libraries, though the latter has a meaning, the former has none.

1. A LIBRARY REPRESENTS A TRINITY OF BOOKS, READERS, STAFF

To give it a meaning, we should regard some other factor in the library as the independent variable. For this purpose let us recall that a library is a trinity consisting of books, readers and staff. As librarianship is the art practised by the staff, we shall be begging the question if we regard the staff as the independent variable.

2. "READERS"

Let us examine the result of making "readers" the independent variable. What is the result of varying the readers? They may be varied in several ways. They may vary in their vocation or profession. This will lead to special libraries such as architects' libraries, medical libraries and librarians' libraries. This result is the same as the one we already had by varying the subject and we have seen that this does not lead to *special librarianship*.

Readers may vary in age. This will lead to special libraries like children's libraries, libraries for adolescents and libraries for adults. The technique of acquiring, classifying, cataloging, displaying and circulating books and librametry will be the same in all these classes of libraries. Even in book-selection, it is not so much the technique of selections as the type of books that will vary. But the technique of reference service is bound to vary with the psychology of the class of readers served. Child-psychology differs from adolescent psychology, and both of these, from adult-psychology. There is, therefore, some justification to regard children's librarianship, adolescents' librarianship and adults' librarianship as *special librarianship*.

A third way of forming special classes of readers is to group them by different kinds of abnormality. This will lead to special libraries such as hospital libraries, prison libraries, seafarers' libraries and libraries for the blind. The librarianship corresponding to the first three classes will have special features in circulation work and reference service. Librarianship for the blind will be special in every way. But it is doubtful if these are given much importance in *special librarianship*. Thus varying the readers does not lead us to *special librarianship*, as it is commonly understood.

3. "BOOKS"

The only other course is to make "books" the independent variable. We have already seen that varying them according to their subject does not lead to *special librarianship*.

Another way of varying "books" is to vary them by their physical characteristics. This will lead to special libraries like palm-leaf-manuscript libraries, paper-manuscript libraries, archival libraries, libraries of microfilm-books, etc. The technique of book-display and shelf- arrangement are bound to vary in these classes of special libraries. To that extent, *special librarianship* will arise. But usage does not recognize these kinds of librarianship as *special librarianship*. There is no other tangible or concrete characteristic by which we may vary the independent variable "books" so as to arrive at *special librarianship*.

We should therefore seek to vary "books" on the basis of some intangible characteristic of theirs, some more intangible and perhaps less recognized characteristic than their subject matter.

Here an analogy comes to my mind—the art of building-construction. In this art, it is easily recognized that the technique varies with the dimension of the building. The technique of constructing a toy-building with pieces of stick is very simple; that of putting up a cowshed is also simple. The technique of erecting an ordinary house is beyond the capacity of amateurs. Construction of a building comparable in dimensions to the legislative chamber of a country requires technique of a different sort. The technique of erecting sky-scrapers like the Empire State Building in New York is utterly different from all others in certain respects. This shows that technique may vary with the dimension involved. We may also state it in another way: Technique may vary with the unit of operation appropriate to a given context.

4. "EXTENSION"

One important and well-recognized dimension of the thought embodied in books and other forms of reading material is "Extension". The dimension of thought normally handled in a library may correspond to a whole book, or it may correspond to an article in a periodical. We may state this in terms of units as follows: The thought-unit of operation may be as large as the one embodied in a whole book or as small as the one embodied in an article in a periodical or a pamphlet.

The techniques which librarianship first forged were determined by the larger thought-unit embodied in books. The germ, which was ultimately to disturb the complacent continuation of these techniques, had its meagre beginnings in the eighteenth century in the form of the transactions and proceedings of learned bodies like the royal societies and academies of the different countries. These are now called periodicals. A periodical does not have the continuity of a book. It is really an aggregate of discrete articles embodying smaller thought-units.

Till the beginning of the present century, in almost all libraries, the thought- unit involved in classification, cataloging, circulation and reference service was generally the macroscopic one embodied in books. Even a multifocal book was deemed unifocal for classification and cataloging purposes. It was put in the larger class comprehending all the sub-classes forming the several foci. Its subject-heading, top, was chosen accordingly.

Periodical publications, which, are multifocal, were not circulated. Reference service had not even begun and there was, therefore, no organization to establish contact between readers and articles in periodicals or parts of books. Readers had to depend on their own wit in this matter. Even the bibliographical tools needed for the purpose had to be designed, constructed and published by the world of readers—the scientists and others.

The monumental Royal Society's *Index* is an instance in point. It was compiled by persons who were amateurs in the building of bibliography, pre-eminent though they were as experts in science. The significance of this *Index* was that it based itself on the smaller thought-unit embodied in articles of periodicals.

Surgeon John Shaw Billings of the United States Army, who was given the task of building up the Army Medical Library in 1864, was the first scientist- cum-librarian to change the thought-unit in library practice. The large number of pamphlets which he collected appealed to him to shorten the thought- unit in such a way that might be individualized. He yielded to this appeal and designed his famous *Index Catalogue* whose publication was sanctioned in 1879.

The term *Index* in its title emphasizes the smaller thought-unit brought into operation. This change in thought-unit introduced by Billings in library practice was several years ahead of its being generally recognized as necessary or valuable. Even today, many libraries persist in the use of the macroscopic thought-unit embodied as books and decline to change over to the microscopic thought-unit embodied as articles in periodicals and pamphlets. However, the movement initiated by Billings is steadily spreading.

The techniques of circulation, classification, cataloging and reference service have to be changed if the thought- unit is changed. The work of estimating the world of readers and the world of reading materials and matching right readers with right articles embodying small thought-units is much more exacting. To mark each article in the current periodicals for every probable reader, to devise and work a mechanism of circulation which will ensure each article reaching its reader and each reader getting his article while it is still in a nascent state, and to save the time of the reader by adding an annotation to each article, require techniques which cannot be envisaged if the whole book is considered to determine thought-unit. The changes needed in the techniques of reference service and circulation work also presuppose a change in the techniques of classification and cataloging.

In my opinion, it is the new techniques of classification, cataloging, circulation work and reference service, necessitated by the contraction of the thought-unit in use, that connote *special librarianship*.

5. "DOCUMENTATION"

Historically, it was the industrial organizations in more developed countries like the United States and Great Britain that first felt the need for *special librarianship* of this kind. This need became apparent to them in the first quarter of the present century. Being industrial institutions, they were able to provide the necessary finance to foster the growth of *special librarianship*. The fact that the library of an industrial organization naturally specialized in a single subject led to the use of the term special libraries in describing them; and this in its turn led to the elusive term *special librarianship*. It was given to the acute French, famous for their precision in expression, to brush aside this misleading term with wrong associations and call the new set of techniques *Documentation*—a term which emphasizes the change in thought-unit from the macroscopic embodiment in books to the microscopic embodiment in articles.

During the last two decades many other classes of libraries also have begun to do documentation service. Of late, even public libraries have begun to do so. This is leading to the re-organization of public library stock on what is called *departmental basis*. This really means "subject basis". A public library may have, for example, a department of music, a department of technology, a department of commerce and so on. These departments in public libraries no longer regard books as units. Their thought-unit is the microscopic one embodied in articles, pamphlets and prospectuses. The result is intensive documentation or *special librarianship*. I was amazed at the thoroughness with which all published musical literature was being documented by the Edinburgh public libraries. The documentation service in steel industries offered by the public library at Sheffield and in textile industries offered by the Manchester public libraries are well-known. The libraries of many of the Departments of the Governments like those of the United States and Great Britain are also doing documentation work. The Library of the Ministry of Foreign Affairs of Holland does documentation work on all the 400 periodicals it receives and the result is printed daily like a newspaper. The Library of Congress has been doing documentation work for years. The Library of the House of Commons, too, has recently begun it. I found intensive documentation work being done in the Department of Mineralogy at the Sorbonne, in the University of Copenhagen and in the Royal Institute of Technology of Stockholm.

6. PENETRATION OF SPECIAL LIBRARIANSHIP INTO GENERAL LIBRARIES

This penetration of special librarianship into general libraries is inevitable and is bound to extend. This was reflected, for example, by the appreciable number of librarians of general libraries, such as public and university libraries, attending the Leamington Conference of Aslib in September 1948. Though special libraries is still only a slogan to a few, many have begun to understand it correctly. In the earlier years, when the general libraries had not felt the need for the contraction of thought-unit, the general librarian and the special librarian could not see eye to eye. A gulf existed between them. They could not agree that they belonged to the same profession. The special librarian was even allergic to the word *librarian* and called himself by various other terms like *information officer, research officer* and documentalist. He preferred to be classed with the scientists and the technologists whom he served rather than with the librarians whose art it was that he practiced though with improved techniques determined by the new thought-unit of his operation.

However, now, that the general libraries have begun to see the need for a smaller thought-unit and to practice documentation, the gulf is being bridged. In conformity with the well-known characteristic of the English-speaking people, the American and the British librarians are retaining the same old label *special libraries* but are quietly changing its connotation. But in its travel across the high seas or the sky, this term appears to lose all its new aroma by the time it reaches Indian shores. It continues to be understood in the original sense recorded in the U.D.C. and causes all the confusion to which reference was made at the beginning. It would be well if the American and British librarians would make their new connotation better known to the world so that unwary librarians in undeveloped countries like India would not fall victims to the much too infectious, but now empty, slogan of *special libraries*, and generate a centrifugal force in their ranks even before they establish themselves as a profession.

In India hardly any library, whether it restricts itself to a single subject or not, has begun to do sustained documentation service. Perhaps two or three departmental libraries may appear to be exceptions. But even in these it is due to the enthusiasm of stray persons. The necessary staff is not provided and the work done is amateurish—very comparable to what was in vogue when the Royal Society's *Index* was prepared by amateurs instead of by trained and disciplined documentalists. And again the amount of circulation work and reference service done or demanded on the basis of the smaller thought-unit is negligibly small. This accounts for the absence of a Special Libraries Association in India.

7. INDIA'S APPROACH TO SPECIAL LIBRARIANSHIP

It is to be hoped that the opportunity which political independence has created for intensive and creative work in every region of the field of knowledge (whether it is fundamental or applied sciences, technology or industries, social sciences or humanities) will create a demand for actual service at the level of *special librarianship*. Until this demand is created and grows in volume and documentation work is established in an appreciable number of libraries (be they industrial, departmental, research, university or public libraries), India's approach to the subject can only be from the theoretical angle. While circulation-work and reference-service as conditioned by *special librarianship* do not lend themselves much to theoretical investigation, the effect of the contraction of thought-unit on the technique of classification and cataloging lends itself to it. Moreover, the libraries in some of the universities and research organizations receive quite a number of periodicals including abstracting ones. These furnish the necessary means for the empirical verification of the findings of theory. They also serve as a means to isolate unsolved problems in the techniques and to indicate profitable lines of investigation.

When Billings introduced the smaller thought-unit in library practice, the discipline of library classification had not been born. Nor had even the *Decimal Classification* come into existence. He could, therefore, change only the technique of cataloging. Later on classification established itself for handling the larger thought-unit embodied in books. In 1876, the first attempt was made to adapt this new discipline to the needs of the smaller thought-unit embodied as articles in periodicals and pamphlets. But in the West, the two techniques of cataloging and classification are being developed practically independent of each other.

But the work already done in India has shown that a holistic concept of librarianship should not deem the two techniques to be independent or inseparable. This concept is reflected in the chain procedure developed in 1938 to solve certain problems at the level of books. This chain procedure is now seen to have great potentiality at the level of documentation. Most of the advantages of the punched card system, but without some of its disadvantages, are secured by the chain procedure. The chief general principle behind it is that classification and cataloging should be taken as an inseparable whole. Each is best fitted for a certain type of service; neither should independently attempt to do it all. There should be a healthy symbiosis between the two. If this is accepted, there is a considerable simplification in both techniques. These findings will be found in the writer's *Philosophy of Library Classification* being published by Dr. Jean Anker of the University of Copenhagen.

The request from Dr. Donker Duyvis of the F.I.D. for a memorandum on classification led to the tracing of the faults of the U.D.C. to its rigid Dewey core. These findings are contained in *Classification and International Documentation* published as fascicule 4 of Volume XIV of the *Review of Documentation* of the F.I.D. which came out in May 1948.

The opportunity, which travel in Europe, Great Britain and America afforded to gain first-hand knowledge of documentation work and to discuss the problem with those actually engaged in it, led to some clarification. The result is given in the paper "Self-perpetuating Classification" published in the *Journal of Documentation* for March 1949. There will be work for some years for a large doubt much more efficient and international team of promising thinkers. If it is done, documentation service will be beyond doubt much more efficient and international co-operation in the matter will become easy.

★★★

IFLA - What it Should Be and Do?

S. R. Ranganathan
Professor of Library Science, University of Delhi

Abstract

Stresses the need for Asia, Eastern Europe, Africa, South America and Australasia being allowed positions of responsibility in the IFLA. Gives illustrative lists of the possible spheres of action of the IFLA. Suggests organisational devices to make IFLA a truly international and effective body.

EDITOR'S NOTE

IFLA-Communications have been created with the purpose to serve as a forum for the free exchange of ideas on the present and future work of our Federation. Considering the intense work now in progress in eastern countries for the development of libraries of all description, partly fostered by UNESCO, I thought it of actual interest to hear more on what these countries expect from IFLA and on how we could help them more effectively in their activities. Therefore I asked Dr. Ranganathan who is so familiar with library trends in that part of the world to give us his personal views, and he answered most obligingly by drafting a whole and comprehensive program - so comprehensive in fact that its complete realisation would lead IFLA to go hunting on FID's grounds. Nevertheless, as it stands, his paper contains certainly many useful suggestions, and his frank statement will, there is no doubt, help us to a better understanding of the present needs of civilisations older than our which are on the threshold of a powerful revival.

P.B.

Reprinted with permission from Libri 5(2), pp. 91-102, 1954.

Dr. Bourgeois, the President of the International Federation of Library Association, has invited me to express my views on the IFLA. I welcome this friendly invitation. Here is a frank statement of my views.

1. REPRESENTATIVE CHARACTER

1.1. Historical Background

The IFLA was founded slightly more than a generation ago. At that time, public library service was widespread only in West Europe and North America. Asia, East Europe, Africa, South America and Austral-asia were still in the resting period of their culture. Therefore, "international" then meant only Western European and Northern American. Occasionally nationals of other areas used to observe the deliberations of the meetings of the IFLA. Those in possession of the IFLA were usually as courteous and condescending to such occasional visitors, as benevolent rich men are to their poor relatives. This is continued as long as these other nationals are meek and do not ask for any share of anything concerning the IFLA.

1.2. Recent Happenings

But by the end of World War II, Asia, East Europe, Africa, South America and Australasia have shaken off their rest and recovered from the state of cultural exhaustion. It is no doubt too early now for all of them to enter into the phase of turbulent growth. But what the West achieved in library matters in a century, the newly awakened people are bound to achieve within one generation. The present occupants of the IFLA do not all realise this. Since 1948, I have attended several meetings of the IFLA. They have been all courtesy. But in their proposals and action, the old view that "international" in IFLA is exhausted by Western Europe and Northern America persists. It may be unconscious and even unmeant on their part. But to us outsiders, it is as clear as daylight in the tropics. On account of the scant response of USA to the wooing of Western Europe, "International" means virtually Western European. The rest of the world is "undeveloped". Even an explicit suggestion that those outside the ring should have their share of places in the inner bodies and the cabinet of the IFLA receives only a benign sign of disapproval. The comer of the eye suggests, "Don't be presumptuous".

1.3. First Need

The first need is to make the cabinet and the inner bodies of the International Federation truly international. This can be done by convention. This can be done if the old guards wake up to the change coming over the world at large. On the other hand, the newly awakened nations should not be so rash as to claim even now places on population basis. But it is not unreasonable to distribute the places among the old and the new national groups roughly on the basis of literate population.

1.4. Avoidance of Fission

The more awakened and "developed" nations resent the vested interests developed by Western Europe. Its attitude in the IFLA is not unlike that of the mediaeval land-lords who were too blind in the last century to the agrarian upsurge sweeping against them. Land was equalised by revolution. The awakened countries feel that equalisation of opportunity can be had only by forming another rival IFLA. The U.N. and its Specialised Agencies, which are all at bottom political, have the political acumen to avoid such fission. They throw open at least some "figure-head" offices as baits to keep the newly awakened countries complacent, though all the strings and vital posts are kept among those within the ring. As the IFLA has no political power, it has not developed even this much of political acumen. Avoidance of fission is necessary. It can be done within, the present constitution, by the adoption of suitable conventions.

1.5. Transitory Provision

As a first, though transitory, measure, the places in the cabinet of the IFLA should be distributed in the following proportion:-

West Europe and North America........................40%
Asia..20%
East Europe..10%
Africa...10%
South America..10%
Australasia..10%

These figures will have to be revised periodically, say once in ten years. The Executive Board should be expanded by the addition of five more members. These and the two vice-presidents should be so selected as to secure the above representation.

2. FUNCTIONAL BODIES

2.1. Cabinet

The function of the 10-member Cabinet of the IFLA should be largely of a co-ordinating and activising nature. It should endeavour to pool all the library information of the world. It should also try to establish rock-bottom standards with sufficient tolerance to allow of necessary local variation. It should be able to harness the best brains in the profession uninfluenced by political considerations and predatory careerists. It should thus find competent men on a truly international basis, to form ad hoc Specialised Bodies for definite programmes. Each programme should have a more or less definite time limit attached to it. The cabinet should do effective liaison work with governmental agencies such as UNESCO and WHO, and non-governmental agencies such as FID and ISO.

2.2. Functional Bodies

The following are some of the functional spheres for which ad hoc bodies may be needed:-

1. One or more for each of the library techniques such as:-
    1.1 Classification;
    1.2 Cataloguing;
    1.3 Documentation;
    1.4 Subject bibliography;
    1.5 National bibliography;
    1.6 Union catalogue.
2. One or more for each of the service fields such as:-
    2.1 City library service;
    2.2 Rural library service;
    2.3 School library service;
    2.4 University library service;
    2.5 Business library service, including commercial and industrial ones;
    2.6 Library service for abnormals such as hospital patients, the blind, inmates of prisons and sea-farers.
3. One or more for each of the subject fields such as:-
    3.1 Engineering;
    3.2 Agriculture;
    3.3 Medicine;
    3.4 Music and dance;
    3.5 Cinema;
    3.6 Other fine arts;
    3.7 Incunabula;
    3.8 Translations.

4. One or more for each of the organisational fields such as:-
    - 4.1 Library legislation;
    - 4.2 Library finance;
    - 4.3 Library building and equipment;
    - 4.4 Statistics;
    - 4.5 Inter-library loan.
5. One or more for liaison-work with other trades and interests such as:-
    - 5.1 Paper-makers;
    - 5.2 Printers;
    - 5.3 Binders;
    - 5.4 Publishers;
    - 5.5 Micro-filming and related matters;
    - 5.6 Machinery for documentary each;
    - 5.7 Pre-natal classification and cataloguing of books.
6. Regional Bodies for the study and co-ordination of library problems lending themselves for pursuit on a regional basis such as:-

    East Asia, South Asia, Scandinavia, Semitic, Germanic, South America, Latin and Slav regions.
7. One or more for each problem connected with library personnel such as:-
    - 7.1 Content of education in library science for each of the levels and fields of service mentioned in (2);
    - 7.2 Methods of teaching library science at different levels;
    - 7.3 Training of teachers of library science;
    - 7.4 Status and emoluments;
    - 7.5 Exchange of librarians;

7.6 Exchange of teachers of library science;

7.7 Promotion of research in library science.

2.3. Quantum of Pursuit

The above enumeration of spheres is only illustrative. It is not meant that all the spheres should be pursued simultaneously or at all times. Each sphere will have to be taken up as and when need arises and facilities of finance and personnel are forthcoming. Some spheres such as library statistics may call for permanent ad hoc bodies. For some subjects the pursuit may be of the surveying kind, for some of the research kind, for others of the evaluating kind, and for still others of the standardising kind. For the same subject, the pursuit may be of these different kinds at different times.

3. SECRETARIAT

3.1. General

The general secretariat of the IFLA should be located at the place of the President. He should have the power (by convention or by statute) to recommend to the general body the names of secretary and treasurer. He should also have the power to appoint the paid staff, subject to the budget-sanction. To make the flow of work continuous, the period of office should be five years at a time for the President.

3.2. For Specialised Spheres

Each ad hoc body should have a Rapporteur General appointed on the recommendation of the President, based on (1) competence as evidenced by past work and learned contributions, (2) leisure, local facilities and willingness to do the work and (3) a reasonable distribution of responsibility, for all the specialised spheres taken as a whole, among the different nations. The rest of the members of the ad hoc body be nominated in consultation with the Rapporteur-General. The country of the Rapporteur-General should be able to supplement, if necessary, the financial aid received by him for his assignment, from governmental or non-governmental international bodies. In some cases each of the countries contributing members to the ad hoc body may have to give similar financial aid. In a few cases, such as Statistics, it may be best to locate the secretariat in an international governmental body such as the UNESCO, the IFLA playing only an advisory role.

4. HANDS-OFF

The IFLA should discourage the formation of vested interestes of any sort - be it in library organisation or library technique. The so-called developed countries generally obstruct new ventures by newly awakening communities. They develop a kind of cataract in the mental eye. No alternative form of technique or organisation is either looked into or tolerated. This mental cataract is the greatest social danger to the dynamic efficiency of library service today. Japan, for example had made much progress in its libraries before World War II. But now it is obliged to swallow the American pill. Western Asia has much of outmoded stuff thrust down its throat, even before it has time to look round and choose. In India, the subtle poison of diplomacy is winning predatories to buy everything coming "on board the ship". Anything developed east of the Red Sea is resisted, unconsciously perhaps, by many of the old guards of the IFLA. This tendency of the past for the West to perpetuate itself into all times and in all climes is dangerous in all human affairs. It is particularly so in the library sphere which concerns mental interests, so well-known to be fleeting and non-compelling.

4.1. A Fortunate Feature

But a fortunate feature is that the younger generation of the library profession of the West has not developed any cataract of the mental eye. It is free from imperialism. It is open-minded and receptive. But in the present set-up the IFLA does not have the energising benefit of such younger librarians. That is why one has to stress that the IFLA should make a special effort to be on the alert to accept new ideas even though they come from the newly awakened nations. In particular, it must say to itself and to the West "Hands off from the East and the South! No covert coercion please!! The world, including the West, will stand to gain by allowing the newly awakening communities to make new experiments to venture into new paths and to forge something new."

5. GENERAL CONFERENCE

General international conferences are far too expensive in money and energy. One cannot think of a library conference of that kind to be held more often than once in five years. Usually it cannot do much. It can at best be used as a platform for inspiring, addresses by savants of high personality. Of course, it will have to receive and record the reports of the cabinet and of the ad hoc bodies. Social contact will be there no doubt. There may even be some useful intellectual impact and exchange of ideas, if the virile younger generation is allowed to attend.

5.1. Regional Conference

There may be more positive work to do in a regional conference, for there may be more homogeneity of interests.

5.2. Ad Hoc Bodies

The money available for travel - from whatever source it is called - will give the best return by providing for the Rapporteur-General of some of the ad hoc bodies to travel round to the other members of their respective bodies for intimate discussion and check-up.

6. INTERNATIONAL EXPERTS AND TRAVEL AID

The IFLA is not likely to have much finance. It will have to be merely a promoting body in this respect. In that capacity, it can exercise some wholesome influence on the award of travel-aid and exchange of personnel in such a way that the pursuit of specialised subjects mentioned in section (2) can be helped. At present international travel-aids and fellowship are often wasted on undirected blitztravel by immature youth picked up from "undeveloped countries". Individuals with a positive personality or unwilling to accept blindly the practices of the "developed" politically powerful countries, are avoided. Some of the "experts" descending from "developed" countries on the "undeveloped" ones often encourage sycophancy, do little, and say that doing much will lead to regurgitation among the "underdeveloped". On going back, at the end of their assignment, some of them orally report contemptuously in confidence and give in writing a report for propaganda, whitewashing everything with a benign superior air. Tactical exigency makes the financing body use all its publicity machinery to howl how successful the assignment had proved to be! This state of affairs blesses neither the one that gives nor the one that takes. IFLA can contribute to the world's library future only if it develops its own stature so as to rise above such power-born human foibles and work for rectitude in international library relation.

7. HOPE

If the angularities observable today are analysed here, it is not out of misanthropy or cynicism. I am full of optimism for the future of humanity. Library service has a great part to play in making the different cultural groups understand one another with real sympathy, learn to see the essence of all cultures to be common at bottom, and convince themselves without mutual fear that the differences are only in the ever-changing periphery unduly arresting attention at the moment. To become something of the physician of humanity, to play its role in the promotion of international peace based, not on fear of armaments but on love born of understanding and, for that purpose, to make possible effective, full and faultless international communication of all intellectual thought and spiritual experience coming from anywhere in the world, the IFLA should heal itself first, rise above all obstructive insularities and prejudices and make itself truly international. I have every hope that the IFLA will be so transformed by the coming generation of librarians.

★★★

Library Science and Scientific Method

S. R. Ranganathan

Abstract

Defines "Scientific method" and "Science" in terms of it. Shows the emergence of Library Science. Describes the new library techniques evolved during the last twenty five years including the production of new types of reading materials, the emergence of documentation, and depth classification, and chain procedure, use of machinery for impersonal library tasks, new imports of the Fifth Law and Librametry.

1. WHAT IS A SCIENCE?

"Is there a library science?" is a question raised quite often. Sir P.S. Sivaswamy Aiyar raised it in the Foreword to the Five laws of library science (1931). A reviewer of the Preface to library science, containing the inaugural lectures to the Department of Library Science formed by the University of Delhi in 1947, challenged the term Library Science, in the pages of Nature. Sri C. Rajagopalachari raised the question again in his speech from the chair at the Silver Jubilee Celebration of the Madras Library Association in April 1953.

In reality, the answer to this question turn on the answer to another question — "What is a science?" The note of scepticism in regard to Library Science is often traceable to some restricted definition of the term Science. Two such restrictions are common; and they can be shown to be false restrictions.

Reprinted with permission from Annals of Library Science, 4(1), pp. 103-138, 1957.

1.1. Subject of Study

One restriction assumed in the definition of a science relates to the subject of study. The course of studies and the nomenclature in vogue in universities at first restricted science to cover only the study of the physical world and its phenomena. In course of time, it has been extended to cover also the study of the world of living bodies and its phenomena. But there is a growing support to another view of science. In this view, the subject of study is not relevant in determining the claim of a domain in the universe of knowledge to be deemed a science. Karl Pearson had stated this view as follows: "The material of science is unlimited — every group of natural phenomena, every phase of social life, every stage of past or present development is material (for science). . . The material of science is co-extensive with the whole life. " The two following dictionary definitions of the term Science reflect this generalised view of its subject of study; (1) A system based or purporting to be based upon scientific principles; a method of arrangement, functioning, etc, reconciling practical or utili–tarian ends with scientific laws; e.g. Domestic Science; Animal Husbandry. (2) Accumulated and accepted knowledge which has been systematised and formulated with reference to the general truths and made available in work, life, or the search of truth. Again, the epigram of Jevons, "Science arises from the discovery of Identity amidst Diversity", severely ignores the subject of study. The following dictionary definition also does so; A Science is "A branch of study which is concerned either with a connected body of demonstrated truths or -with observed facts systematically classified and more or less collected by being brought under general laws and which includes trustworthy methods for the discovery of new truth within its own domain". The essential characteristic of a science is then not what it treats about, but what it achieves in respect of what it treats about — what Omar Khayyam longed to achieve:

> Ah Love! Could you and I with Him conspire To grasp this sorry Scheme of Things entire. Would not we shatter it to bits — and then Re-mould it nearer to the Heart's desire!

1.2. Method of Study

A second restriction often assumed in the definition of a science relates to the method of study. Birckbeck introduced, at the beginning of the ninteenth century, experimental demonstration in teaching the pure sciences. Since then, in due course, the nomenclature in vogue in universities tended to restrict science to cover only a domain of knowledge admitting of experimental study and needing a laboratory. It was easily seen to be an over-restriction, as it would exclude, from the right to be called a science, an ancient science like Astronomy; for, it uses observation only and not experimentation. To escape this danger, Jeans makes a different approach: "A science teaches us to know and an art to do; and all the more perfect , sciences lead to the creation of corresponding useful arts. Astronomy is the foundation of navigation". Genung's illustration is more to the point; "Rhetoric, here called an art, is sometimes defined as a science. Both designations are true. Science is systematised knowledge; if the laws and principles of discourse are exhibited in an ordered and inter–related system they appear in the character of a science. Art is knowledge made efficient by skill; if the rhetorical laws and principles are applied in the actual construction of discourse, they become the working rules of art". This view permits observation also as a basis for the formulation of laws in a science. On the analogy of Genung's illustration, there can be an Art of Librarian ship as well as a Library Science.

1.3. Mode of Development

The approach to the definition of Science through the subject of study or the method of study has given only negative results. A positive help can be got by an examination of the mode of development of a domain of knowledge. In this approach.

Science is the name given to a domain in the universe of knowledge, whose development is characterised by a method called Scientific Method. We should therefore begin with a description of scientific method.

2. SCIENTIFIC METHOD

2.1. Assumed Terms

In the description of scientific method, we shall use the following as assumed terms:

Know, Knower, Knowee, Knowledge;

Senses, Sensation or Perception, Observation, Experimentation;

Intellect, Association, Reasoning, Logic, Inductive Logic, Deductive Logic

Memory, Remembering, Recalling;

Emotion, Feeling;

Intuition or trans-intellectual, trans-sensory, trans-emotional, and trans-memory mode of directly knowing anything-in-itself. In the Ramayana, the seer Bharadvaja uses the term Tapas to denote the means of developing it.

2.2. Emergence of Knowledge

When knower and knowee are brought into relation, the knower knows the knowee; and knowledge emerges. Knowledge is expressed in language; and expressed knowledge is stored in memory to make recall and communication possible. The simplest mode of knowing is for the knower to perceive the knowee with the aid of one or other of the primary senses. This action maybe called primary perception. Little is known about primary perception; perhaps it is ordinarily experienced only by the newborn baby. Soon after birth, association of the results of two or more simultaneous primary perceptions would take place. Each new perception will also be instantaneously, spontaneously, and inexorably associated with what is already stored in memory. In due course, the mode of knowing goes beyond perception and association; it includes reasoning: and reasoning progressively gets more involved. Increasingly sharper and more powerful logic is used in the reasoning course of time, two classes of knowee come to be recognised — one outside the memory of the knower, and the other inside it. An external knowee may be called a Concrete Knowee or an Object. An internal knowee may be called an Abstract Knowee or a Concept. The former adds to concrete know–ledge; and the latter to abstract knowledge. Further, a concept, with an object as an external correlate may be called a Concrete Concept; and one without it an Abstract Concept. Concrete and Abstract are only relative terms; they have a meaning only when used together either explicitly or implicitly. We can think of a Scale of Abstraction or of the reverse of it, viz a Scale of Concreteness.

2.3. Universe of Knowledge

Language, record, and other means of communication across space and through time make it possible for mankind to cumulate one another's knowledge and add to it co-operatively either in a systematic or in a casual way. Universe of Knowledge is the sum-total, at the moment, of such cumulated knowledge. It is being continuously developed and added to. Different domains of the universe of knowledge are developed by different methods. Scientific method is one of the recognised methods of development.

2.4. Spiral of Scientific Method

Scientific method is characterised by a never ending spiral movement. It is schematically represented in the diagram on the next page. The cycle implied in the spiral will be followed in the clock-wise direction. For convenience of reference, the four cardinal points of the cycle are denoted by the terms Nadir, Ascendent, Zenith, and Descendent. The nadir marks the accumulation of facts, obtained by observation, experimentation, and other similar forms of experience. The ascendent marks the accumulation of inducted or empirical laws got out of the facts accumulated at the nadir, by inductive logic including normal equations and other aids from statistical calculus. The zenith marks the fundamental laws formulated with the aid of intuition of some degree or other so as to comprehend all the inducted or empirical laws, accumulated at the ascendent, as compelling implications. The descendent marks the accumulation of the deduced laws got from the fundamental laws at the zenith, with aid of deductive logic including general semantics and all kinds of mathematical calculuses.

The four cardinal points give rise to four quadrats in the cycle implied in the spiral. For convenience of reference, the quadrants will be numbered 1 to 4 respectively, as follows : Quadrant 1 is the one between descendent and nadir; Quadrant 2 is the one between nadir and ascendent; Quadrant 3 is the one between ascendent and zenith; and Quadrant 4 is the one between zenith and descendent. The following statement is taken to be intelligible in the light of what has been said already,

2.4.1. Quadrant 1

Quadrant 1 corresponds to the stage in the development of a domain of the universe of knowledge, conforming to scientific method, in which;

1. primary senses are used either in their native state or with the aid of instruments of various degrees of powerfulness;
2. observations are made of knowees, either with or without experimental interference and conditioning;
3. there is progression towards particularisation and regression from generalisation;
4. there is progression towards concreteness and regression from abstractness; and
5. facts are found and recorded.

2.4.2. Quadrant 2

Quadrant 2 corresponds to the stage in which

1. intellect is used either by itself or aided by machinery constructed to speed up the work of the intellect and to give relief to it to some measure.

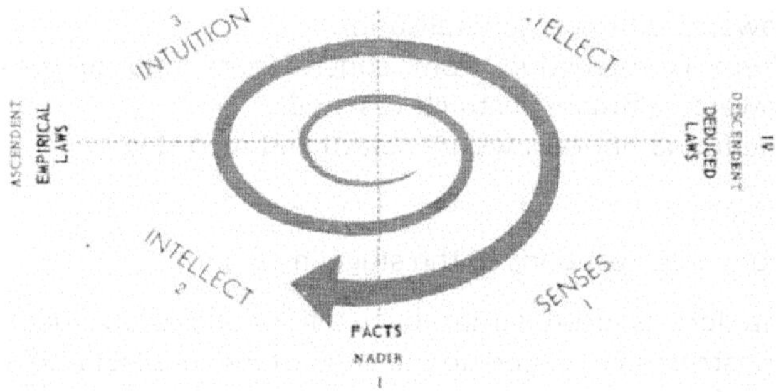

SPIRAL OF SCIENTIFIC METHOD

2. reasoning is made with the aid of inductive logic including normal equations and other statistical and other calculuses to boil down the numerous facts, accumulated at the nadir, to a small number of inducted or empirical laws - e.g. Kepler's Law of Equal Area in the motion of planets, boiled down from the facts recorded by Tycho Brahe - more easy to hold in memory than the multitude of the Facts themselves;
3. there is regression from particularisation and progression towards generalisation;
4. there is regression from concreteness and progression towards abstractness; and
5. inducted or empirical laws are formulated and recorded.

2.4.3. Quadrant 3

Quadrant 3 corresponds to the stage in which

1. intuition of some intensity or other is used unmediated by the primary senses or the intellect;

2. the inducted or empirical laws stand boiled down to a very small number of fundamental laws - e.g. Newton's Laws of motion to which many empirical laws such as the Keplar's Law stand reduced at one stroke - more easy to hold in memory than the more numerous empirical or inducted laws;
3. there is regression from particularisation and progression towards ultimate generalisation
4. there is regression from concreteness and progression. towards ultimate abstractness; and
5. the fundamental laws are seized and recorded.

2.4.4. Quadrant 4

Quadrant 4 corresponds to the stage in which

1. intellect is used either by itself or aided by machinery constructed to speed up the work of the intellect and to give relief to it in some measure;
2. reasoning is made with the aid of deductive logic including general semantics, and mathematical and other calculuses to work out all the compelling implications of the fundamental laws;
3. there is progression towards particularisation and regression from generalisation;
4. there is progression towards concreteness and regression from abstractness;
5. the deduced laws are derived and recorded:
6. the derived deduced laws include one and all of the inducted empirical laws; and
7. the number of deduced laws exceeds that of the empirical laws, if the fundamental laws had been seized with intuition of adequate intensity.

2.4.5. Entrance into the Next Cycle

The spiral of scientific method begins the next cycle thereafter, by re-entering quadrant. Two things happen at the stage of development corresponding to quadrant 1 in the new cycle: 1

Observations and experiments are made to verify empirically the validity of the new deduced laws; and 2 further observations and experiments are made continuously and this leads to accumulation of new empirical facts.

2.4.6. Helpfulness of the Fundamental Laws

So long as the deduced laws are verified empirically to be true and the new empirical facts are found to be in conformity to the implications of the fundamental laws, there is no further movement in the spiral; and the fundamental laws hold sway and continue to be deemed helpful. But, this seldom holds good for long. Disturbance arises sooner or later in almost all the domains in the universe of knowledge, as they are cultivated and developed.

2.4.7. Arduous Effect

As and when empirical facts and experience appear to contradict the fundamental laws, arduous effort is made to ensure absence of any kind of fallacy in the process of deduction, any kind of defect in the logic or the calculus used in the process, and any kind of fault in the experiment or observation or in the instruments used. When warranted, more powerful instru–ments of observation, more exacting experiments, and sharper calculuses for deduction are devised. Witness for example the invention of mass-spectroscopy which dissolved on apparent contradiction to Dalton's fundamental law about the atom, the devising of observations of stars during total solar eclipse, which dissolved an apparent contradiction to Einstein's fundamental law- of relativity, and the unceasing progress in the development of general semantics and the mathematical calculuses to make deductions penetrating and free from fallacies. Every effort should also be made to re-interpret the terms in the formulation of the fundamental laws with the aid of exegetics, so as to get out of them their fullest possible import, lying hidden until the necessary empirical experience draws attention to it.

2.4.8. Declaration of Crisis

Now and again, contradiction between the empirical facts of experience and the currently used fundamental laws persists, in spite of all the possible precautions to ensure absence of faults and fallacies in the building of the facts of experience and the inference of the implications of the fundamental laws, and in spite of every possible and proper use of exegetics. Then we have to recognise the existence of a new class of facts and declare the incidence of a crisis in the application of the scientific method.

2.4.9. Resolution of Crisis

Then, the new class of empirical facts are accumulated at the nadir; and a new cycle gets into full swing and carries the spiral of scientific method further. Work in quadrant 2 leads to a new set of empirical laws. Work in quadrant 3 leads to the seizing of a new set of fundamental laws. Work in quadrant 4 leads to a new set of deduced laws. Work in quadrant 1 is again started as before. This cycle is liable to be repeated without end in many a domain.

2.5. Definition of Science

Any domain in the universe of knowledge, irrespective of the subject and the method of study, which admits of the above-described spiral of scientific method in the course of its development is a science. In the natural science, including the physical and the biological sciences, the fundamental laws are called hypotheses. They furnish a descriptive formulation of the empirical facts of experience. In the social sciences, such as education, political science, economics, sociology, law and library science - which is also one of them - the fundamental laws are called normative principles. They furnish an interpretative explanation of the empirical facts of experience and of the techniques found necessary in experience.

The terms true and false apply only to facts and the empirical and deduced laws. They do not apply to hypotheses and normative principles. These can only be described as helpful or unhelpful, according as they fit in or not with the facts of empirical experience. Newton's laws did not fit in with certain new empirical facts found during the present century; and in this context, they ceased to be helpful hypothesis and gave place to the Einstein's laws of relativity. These two sets of laws belong to two different cycles in the spiral of scientific method. As it often happens, particularly if the laws are seized by a sufficiently intensive intuition, the Newtonian hypothesis is contained in the Einsteinian hypothesis. For, the former is got of the latter by taking the speed of light to be greater than any conceivable finite speed. Similarly, the old second law of library science viz. Books are for the Chosen Few - did not fit in with the library practices coming into vogue in community after community during the last century as a result of the onslaught of democracy. In this context, it ceased to be a helpful normative principle and gave place to the new second law – viz Books are for All. These two laws belong to two different cycles in the spiral of scientific method. It can also be seen that the former version of the second law is contained as a particular case in the latter version. Again the old normative principle of political science - viz King can make no mistake - did not fit in with the political practices coming into vogue in community after community during the last two centuries as a result of the onslaught of republic idea. In this context, it ceased to be a helpful normative principle and gave place to the new normative principle — Judiciary can make no mistake. As all the functions of the judiciary were vested in the king in the earlier days, the earlier normative principle was contained in the latter.

2.6. Delay in Recognising Social Sciences

2.6.1. Natural Sciences

Natural sciences were admitted as sciences, as tested by the use of scientific method in their development, much earlier than social sciences. This was because, in the case of natural sciences,

1. observation - corresponding to quadrant 1 of the cycle - can be impersonal and nearly objective, subject only to the errors of observation which could be corrected by the curve of errors and the calculus of observations designed more than a century ago by Gauss;
2. experiments - corresponding to quadrant 1 can be made without any let or hindrance in the case of physical sciences and with a minimum of mental revulsion even with the living bodies of the lower organisms; and
3. the mathematical calculuses, necessary and sufficient to make induction and deduction - corresponding to quadrants 2 and 4 - within the domain of the natural sciences, had been forged a few centuries earlier and there has been a continuous sharpening of them.

2.6.2. Social Sciences

On the other hand, in the case of social sciences, unfavourable factors prevail in all the three quadrants. Observation is vitiated by the observed entity being man himself with all the obstructions which his mind can cause. Experimentation is difficult if not impracticable and even impossible when man himself has to be the subject of experiment; even where it is attempted it takes several decades to collect adequate data, on account of the large span of each generation and of the low rate of multiplication - compare for example that bees multiply to a million within a year and that still lower organisms have a negligibly small span for each generation and their fecundity too is phenomenally high. Moreover, humane considerations prevent experimenting with the human species. Again, the statistical calculus necessary for work in quadrants 2 and 4 were either unknown or were found to be in a primitive state till about half a century ago. Karl Pear–son, who died only two decades ago, was a pioneer in forging the calculus and fitting it for really advanced work in quadrants 2 and 4. Statistical calculus, operational analysis, and other tools are being sharpened only to-day to a degree sufficient to make allowance for the vitiations, incidental to man and his society being the subject of study, As a result of the forging of such powerful tools, however, the development of many disciplines in the domain of social sciences is becoming progressively amenable to scientific method. Library science is one of them. The time has come to recognise the existence of library science as a science.

2.6.3. Other Disciplines

To appreciate the claim of some of the social sciences of to-day to the status of a science, it will be helpful to mention some other disciplines, whose development is not amenable to scientific method as outlined above. Theology is an obvious example. In this discipline, the zenith is occupied by unalterable autho–ritative principles, often taken to be revelation. Historically, even empirical experiences in the physical world, going contradictory to them, were denied validity: indeed, history is full of instances of treating the assertion of such empirical experiences as heresy and of the cruelty meted out to such heretics. Here, the left half of the cycle is thrown out of action; and there is thus no scientific spiral at all. Exegetics is put to the severest strain to reconcile the authoritative principles at the zenith and the contradicting facts at the nadir. One of the extreme devises used in this exegetics is known as Artha-Vada, which amounts to postulating the occurrence of meaningless words, phrases, sentences, and even paragraphs, to be unintelligible, and hence to-be-neglected, "noises" in the revealed texts occupying the zenith, Mimamsakas in Indian philosophy have provided outstanding examples of extreme forms of reconciliation of this kind. Christian theology also gives extreme, though earnest, attempts at such forced reconciliation of empirical facts and the Bible. E T Whittaker's Space and Spirit demonstrates this in a lucid way. Fine arts including literature form another domain in the universe of knowledge, which is not amenable to the scientific method described above. The development of these subjects do not present quadrants 1, 2, and 4. We can only recognise quadrant 3.

They are all products of intuition with little play of intellect. No cycle of scientific method is possible in that domain,

2.7. Emergence of Library Science

Unlike in theology and the fine arts, the development of library science is fully characterised by the spiral of scientific method. All the earlier chapters of the book Five laws of library science (1931) demonstrate it. They describe the typical library practices then current and corresponding to quadrant 1. They state facts of experience corresponding to the nadir. They also mention in a few places some empirical laws derived from the facts. The five fundamental laws seized in quadrant 3 form the normative principles corresponding to the zenith. Quadrant 4 is well provided for by showing the then library practices as compelling implications of these normative principles. In later sections, some indications will be given as to how new inferences are being made, and new library practices are explained or suggested by the same normative principles, and new interpretations of their terms are being given, in the light of the changes occurring in the boundary conditions imposed by society on library service. These factors indicate conformity of the development of library science to scientific method. This justifies deeming it a science.

2.8. Trivial Truism

Before dealing with these factors, a word should be said about the remark that the First Law - Books are for Use - is a trivial truism. The first law of most of the sciences is equally so. For example, Newton's first law of motion reads, "Everybody preserves in its state of rest unless it is compelled to change that state by impressed forces. " Is this not a truism? Perhaps the triviality of a first law is best illustrated by the first law of logic, commented upon as follows in the New foundations of logic (1947) by K R Popper:- "The most trivial and at the same time the simplest rule of inference is undoubtedly, "From the statement a, the statement a can be derived, " This rule is so trivial that many classical logicians have hesitated to admit it. They have felt that nothing could be gained by admitting it and that the dignity of the procedure of inference would be imperilled if this were called an inference. Since the rule is, obviously, not invalid we should have to admit it even if it were useless. But contrary to first impressions, it is far from being useless. It is even characteristic, altogether, of the triviality of the fundamental rules from which the edifice of logic arises. We should further more keep in mind that triviality of the basic assumptions is an advantage rather than a disadvantage, provided that what -we obtain at the end is adequate for our purpose. In spite of the triviality of these rules, the concept of derivability thus determined turns out to provide an exceedingly powerful instrument.

The implications of the first law have been profound, rich, and revolutionising, as worked out in the first chapter of the Five laws. We shall now state some of the library practices newly set up as implications of the other laws.

3. SECOND LAW AND NEW TYPES OF BOOKS AND NEW PRACTICES

Since 1931 many new library practices have come into vogue. These are all in conformity to the implications of the word "Every" in the enunciation of the second law. These implications suggest also some new practices, yet to be implemented. Stated in general terms , the second law regards every human being as a potential reader. Democracy should be allowed the fullest way in the interpretation of the second law.

3.1. Books for Children

"Every" includes children. They too are entitled to books. But adults' books are not suited to them. Children's books should cover the entire universe of knowledge in a special key, in a distinctive style of exposition, with a high proportion of illustrations, and with a physical get up of their own. Accordingly, a special class of children's authors and publishers have come into being in some of the countries. This is yet to happen in India. A scheme for it has been worked out in the School and college libraries (1942).

3.2. Books for the Abnormals

"Every" includes the blind and the cripple confined to bed. Books are now being transformed into sound records for the use of blind readers. Many of the public libraries of the U.S.A. are now engaged in their production with the aid of voluntary readers. The Library of Congress is taking a leading part in the organisation of their production, storage, and circulation. Ceiling books were seen by me for the first time in the Carnegie Library in Pittsburg. A ceiling book is a micro-film with projector equipment fit to be projected on to the ceiling by a cripple confined to bed, with the aid of any limb of his, such as a toe or a finger which is functioning.

3.3. Books for Artisans

"Every" includes artisans in the lowest quartile in the intellectual scale as well as the economic scale. To make them accept and benefit by library service, it is necessary to produce craft-centred sets of books. Each set will have a specific craft as the central biasing theme. The entire universe of knowledge will be covered by the books in the set, with one book on each class or region of knowledge, written from the angle of the craft in question. The need for such craft-centred sets of books was first sensed in Education for leisure (1946) and more fully expounded in a memorandum to the Government of India and in Social education literature (1952).

3.4. Books for Neo-Literates

"Every" includes neo-literates. Neoliterate adults will form an abnormal percentage of the Indian community for at least one more generation. There is need for a set of graded books for their use. The proportion of illustrations to letter-press will decrease from perhaps 10 to 1 in the lowest grade to perhaps to 10 in the highest grade. The details of this class of books will be found in Literature for neo-literates (1953),

3.5. Books for the Last Deciles

"Every" includes also the persons of lowest ability forming the last ten per cent in the intellectual scale. Even craft-centred books and the books of the lowest grade for neoliterates will not be suited to them. They need speaking-books. A speaking-book is a well- illustrated book written in a specially simple style, carrying in a pouch at its end sound- records of the letter-press in the body of the book. Thus, a sound-book will appeal to the reader in a triple way - through the ear, through the eyes, and through the phonetic symbols. The need for this class of books to satisfy the second law was first expounded in a talk given by me in the Chaucer House, London, before a meeting of the Library Association in 1950.

3.6. Books for the Men at the Bench

"Every" includes the foremen and the workmen at the bench in the factories. The current unbalancing between population pressure and natural and near-natural commodities of con–sumption calls for enormous productivity drive. Rate of production and avoidance and elimination of waste of evey kind ultimately depend on the foremen and the workmen at the bench. They have to be put in possession of the latest knowhow, from time to time. But they are usually of the lowest quartile in the intellectual scale and art reluctant to pick up ideas from the printed word alone. Their interest has first to be roused with the aid of audio-visual materials portraying the latest know-how. This has to be followed up by aggressive reference service to enable them to pick up the exact details from books specially written up to their standard, both in style and in the proportion and nature of illustrations. This class of materials and books are yet to be produced in most languages to the satisfaction of the second law.

3.7. Books for the Stray Specialist

"Every" includes the stray specialist in any subject, living all by himself in some part of the country far away from his peers. The second law would insist on his local library finding his books for him. But, it may not find any other reader for such a book for many years to come.

In view of this, the law of Parsimony would refuse to vote money for the purchase of that book. This dilemma has to be met by an organisational device. This is inter-library loan. This implies that all the book-resources in a country should be regarded as a single pool. This also implies a union catalogue. But this involves many problems still unsolved these problems are now engaging the attention of the IFLA. It is proposed to have a series of articles on this question in the Annals of library science.

4. THIRD LAW AND DOCUMENTATION

The greatest pressure on exegetics has perhaps been put by the third law - Every Book its Reader - in its attempt to yield all its implications in the context of the new boundary conditions set by the economic pressure developing in society to-day. Perhaps the most pressing developments in the library profession arise out of the march of library service into the economic sphere. World is becoming one in the economic sphere much faster than in the political sphere. The economic functions of library service are therefore pressing. One such function has been already referred to in section 26. The fact is this. For shelter, clothing, food, transport, and communication, natural and near-natural commodities have to be increasingly supplemented by artificial commodities, built out of extracts from raw materials quite unfit and even poisonous tor direct consumption, by their synthesis, and by other modes of processing. The building of artificial commodities for consumption has to be based on research. Their production on large scale and their prompt distribution to all the points of consumption on the surface of the earth call for a much higher order of management and transport than found sufficient hitherto.

This too has to be based on research. The urgency of these forms of research is such that research cannot be left any longer to the casual appearance of a man of genius, who pursues re–search spontaneously and inevitably to satisfy his own inner urge, unprompted by external necessity. Nor can we afford any delay in exploiting new inventions and discoveries for the economic service of mankind, though such delay had been quite common in the past. Compare for example the time-lag in the exploitation of the discovery of electricity and the rapidity with which the discoveries in nuclear physics are being exploited to-day. Research has therefore to be organised consciously and so as to proceed "in-series", rather than "in-parallel" as in the past.

4.1 Plough-Back in Research- in-Series

Research-in-series has many implications which force library service to move forward rapidly during its march into the economic sphere. In the first place, organised research has to draw its man-power even from intellectual strata far below that of genius. Secondly, a genius is a self-helper, not necessarily depending on organised library service. On the other hand, the persons now being pressed into research are in great need of being fed exactly and exhaustively by library service. This need is getting intensified every day by the very increase in the rate of output of new thought, caused by research-in-series all the world over. It is also intensified by the tremendous amount of cross-breeding and lamination taking place in the universe of knowledge, as a result of intensively organised research in many sectors of knowledge. Even in one and the same industrial house, wasteful, unintended, research- in-parallel sets in frequently, because of inefficiency in keeping every worker informed promptly of every new achievement of every other worker, which may be at least partly or remotely germane to the pursuit of many others. The heaps of unfed house reports on many research projects in one and the same enterprise - and even under one and the same roof - form a staggering monument of costly new thought left idle, without being ploughed back into the research-in-series which is in progress.

4.2. Generalisation of 'Book'

There is another factor in library service to be given attention in the economic sphere. Research-in-series will not be fully helped if library service confined itself to whole books and periodicals, as service-units. The unit of service should be an individual article in a periodical or a section and even a paragraph in a book. To use a jargon coined by me, the unit of library service cannot any longer be macro thought: it must be nascent micro thought in the research sphere. Efficient, prompt, pinpointed, exhaustive service of nascent micro thought to specialists, necessitated by the social pressure of to-day, has now come to be called Documentation Service. The reconciliation of this library practice with the third law and the other laws requires a generalisation of the connotation of the term book. It should hereafter be used in the sense of Document; this definition was attempted in the Headings and canons (1955), Even this stood out-moded in the light of the instrument-record of phenomena - unmediated by the human mind and untransformed into human thought - gaining in importance as document. This transformation of the content of the third law and the other laws by exegetical means and its repercussions on various library techniques have been discussed in detail in my Documentation in many lands: 4 Document, conventional and non-conventional published in the Annals of library science, 3, 1956, 22-32.

4.3. Effect of Generalisation on Classification

The effect of this generalisation of the term 'book' in the third law has been most pronounced on the discipline of library classification. The technique of classification was cultivated in the early years for mechanising arrangement of books on shelves. Superficial classification or classification of macro thought was sufficient for this purpose. Such a classification could afford to be enumerative from the very start.

But depth classification is necessary if the unit of service is micro thought. Depth classification has to be analytico-synthetic. In it, enumeration should be confined only to some seminal schedules and a few schedules of common isolates. Such a scheme is now being actively investigated by the profession. The techniques of phase, facet, and zone analysis, the concepts of fundamental categories and postulates for classification, and the separation of work in the idea and notational planes - largely initiated in India - are proving productive in this investigation. An international seminar is being convened in England in May 1957 to study the classificatory problems being precipitated by the shift in the connotation of the central term in the laws of library science.

5. FOURTH LAW AND NEW LIBRARY PRACTICES

The fourth law - Save the Time of the Reader - gives the corrollary "Save the Time of the Staff", in order to turn more hands on to reference service. This corrollary has as its implications many practices in library service. Some of these have already made a start, though they have to go a long way to give results to the full satisfaction of the fourth law.

5.1. Centralised Classification and Cataloguing

A fruitful practice gaining support is centralised classification and cataloguing of books. These two techniques are quite impersonal, in the sense that the class number of a book and its catalogue entries depend largely on the book itself and not upon the library using it. The slight extent to which they may have to be occasionally oriented to the unusual needs of readers of a particular class or of a particular locality is provided for by the Canon of Local Variation applicable to both the disciplines. In view of this, centralisation is possible in the technical preparation of books for service. It has been shown in the Headings and canons (1955) that centralisation will effect 79% saving in the manpower needed in the library system of a country to prepare the home-produced books for use.

The same book shows also that a similar 79% saving can be effected in respect of foreign books also, if each country practices centralisation and participates in the scheme set forth in that hook for international co-operation in the matter. The British National Bibliography is the best known demonstration of this implication of the fourth law. Though started only in 1950, it has already effected a considerable saving in the British libraries. Its recent organisation to print and supply catalogue cards within one day of the receipt of the order is a highwater mark of efficiency.

5.2. Pre-Natal Classification and Cataloguing

The fourth law has been always dissatisfied with the hold-up of books between their receipt in the library and their release for use, in order to classify and catalogue them. The pre-natal classification and cataloguing of books, the release of catalogue cards along with the release of the books themselves, the printing of the call numbers in the books at the time of printing of the preliminary pages, tooling them while casing the books and the associated routine for order work, described in the Headings and canons, will make it possible for a library to release a book within not more than a couple of days of its receipt. This is a practice that has not yet come into vogue anywhere. But during my visit to England in December 1956, Mr Wells, the editor of B N B, assured me that such pre-natal work was not as impracticable as it was thought to be when it was first expounded by me in August 1948 in an address at the Library of Congress. He does not anticipate any resistance from publishers in their offer of cooperation, when it could be started by him.

5.3. International and National Documentation

To save manpower and money, it has been found necessary to centralise documentation work even at the international level. But, in practice it leads to a time-lag of more than one year. This is a serious violation of the fourth law. Therefore, since World War II, the practice of restricted documentation work in each national centre is being tried. The periodicals scanned are restricted to those taken within the country. The subjects for which they are scanned are restricted to those in which work is being done within the country. These two restrictions bring down the quantity of work involved to a great extent, at least in the newly developing countries. The advance procurement of microcopies of the title pages of periodicals by airmail make it possible for the national documentation list to reach service-libraries almost simultaneously with the arrival of the periodicals concerned. A further step should be for the national documentation centre of each country to do pre-natal documentation of each of the articles originating within its territory and releasing the documentation list with abstracts. This suggestion of the fourth law may show a way also to make some saving in the money now being spent in the printing of the thousands of periodicals now current. This is a step in international and national economy and organisation, into which it is not proper to enter in the present context.

5.4. Mechanisation

Another way of saving staff-time will be to mechanise every item of impersonal work in a library. For example, the design of machinery for literature search has been in full swing since World War II. A combination of facet analysis in classification and machinery for search - beginning from punched cards and going to magnetic tape - will save the time of the reader directly also. So it will be with the electronic and other mechanical methods of charging and discharging work, Ralph Shaw has mechanised other kinds of library routine considerably with the aid of photography. This indicates the long vista of work to be done in response to the fourth law. But most of the work will fall within the province of technologists and managerial experts. The library profession can only state the requirements and indicate the spheres where mechanisation will prove useful and also harmless.

6. FIFTH LAW AND ITS DIVERSE IMPORTS

In 1931, the fifth law - Library is a growing organism - was interpreted only in one sense. Chapter 7 of the first edition of the Five laws brought out the implications of "Growth" only in the sense of "Child-Growth" - that is, growth involving steady increase in over-all size. But the term holds also another sense. It is "Adult- Growth" - that is growth by replacement of constituents without increase in over-all size.

The double import of the fifth law leads to an important principle in the organisation of a national library system. Two types of libraries are to be recognised, viz conserving library and service library. This distinction was seen and applied consciously for the first time only in the Library book selection (1953).

6.1. Conserving Library

In view of the continuous demand of a conserving library for additional building, shelves, and maintenance charges, economy would suggest a limit to the number of such libraries in a country. The National Central Library should be a conserving library; and it may prove sufficient in a country with a small area. Even in a country with a large area, their number need not exceed half a dozen. There can be no useful purpose except that of local prestige in maintaining two such libraries within sixty miles of each other as in Scotland. In a polyglot country like India, it will be necessary to have also a State Central Library in each constituent state for conserving copies of the publications produced within the state. A City or a District Central Library or any other service library such as a University Library be entrusted with conserving work except in the case of strictly local collections. When a country decides to have additional conserving national libraries - India has decided upon having three additional ones - it may be economical to have some or all of them in micro films. It may be further wise to have one of the microfilm collection located in a deep underground vault beyond the reach of nuclear vandalism such as that on Hiroshima,

The model library acts given in the Library development plan (1950) have provided for most of the above points; but, it needs amendment about the microfilm deposits; or perhaps such provisions may be made in the rules framed under the Acts.

6.2. Service Library

A service library will admit of a ceiling in regard to the number of volumes, the number of readers, and the strength of the staff, and therefore of the building and fittings. The annual accession and weeding out, because of wearing out by use or of getting outmoded, will ultimately balance each other. But, it will be the duty of each service library to notify the conserving library concerned of all the items to be weeded out, so that the latter may take action on the salvage and conservation of a few representative copies of each book. A similar procedure should also be carried out at the international level.

This implication of the second import of the fifth law shows that the Quincy Plan, mentioned in section 711 of the book Five laws, is not inconsistent with the fifth law, as it was assumed when only its first import was known.

6.3. Species Formation, a Third Import

A third import of the fifth law is phylogenesis, as distinct from ontogenesis. This third import emphasises and explains the formation of specialised libraries specialising in special functions. Till now specialisation on the basis of the classes of special readers has been observed. This has been elaborately dealt with in the Preface to library science. Certain functions may get elaborated, while others maybe dropped or thinned out in some species. The relative weight between conservation and service, found in conserving libraries and service libraries, is itself an instance. Among service libraries, the relative weight between macro documents and micro documents found in libraries for the- generalist and for the specialist is another instance in point. Examples of this kind can be multiplied. The perceptible difference in the ceiling for size between one class of service libraries and another is analogous to a similar phenomenon in different phylums in nature. This third import of the fifth law was focussed on the conscious level by Dr Martin Mollerot of the Bavarian State Library during an excursion arranged for the delegates of the IFLA Conference at Munich in September 1955.

6.4. A Fourth Import

Dr Mollerot brought up also a fourth import of the fifth law. It arises out of a fourth attribute of growth, seen in a social organism.

This is best seen in the human family, which divides into separate and yet closely related sub-families for convenience in existence. Analogously, monolithic libraries of the past will have to give place to separate and yet closely related libraries for facilitating efficiency of service, in the changing conditions of society and of the social pressure on library service. This idea needs further pursuit.

6.5. Farmington Plan

The Farmington Plan formulated in U S A about a decade ago is a step in the reconciliation of these three imports of the fifth law. It is a new experiment in the formation of a new species of libraries with a considerable service function and with conserving function midway between those of a National Central Library and a normal City or District Central Library,

Growth of Class Index Entries

To illustrate the incidence of the light of the fifth law even in the details concerning a library, mention maybe made of class index entries in a library catalogue. The gamma function rate at which they will grow, if entries are made for each of the possible permutations of the terms forming the headings and subheadings, was brought out for the first time in the Theory of library catalogue. This led to the invention of Chain Procedure to prevent such general entries almost occulting the substantive book entries in the catalogue. This has been more pointedly elaborated in the Classification, coding, and machinery for search (1950). The chain procedure has been applied on a large scale in the British National Bibliography, ever since it was started in 1950. Its editor has stated in his contribution to Library science in India (1953), "The alphabetic part of the British National Bibliography, like the systematic part, owes its success to the theories of Ranganathan on which it is built." The theory of chain procedure has been due to the warning of the fifth law.

7. LIBRAMETRY

Mathematical tools of various kind are now applicable to work out many of the implications of the normative principles of library science and in some cases to settle once for all some of the issues which have been filling the pages of the organs of library science with uninformed wasteful polemics. In my talk before the Aslib Conference of 1948 at Leamington Spa, the term Librametry was coined to denote the mathematical study of the problems in library science in the light of or as implications of the five laws.

8. FAMILY OF BOOKS

Librametry is still only in its infancy. However, a considerable systematic development of the implications of the five laws has been in progress in diverse branches of library practice with the aid of verbal dialectics. The potentiality of the five laws, viewed as the normative principles corresponding to the zenith in the current cycle implied in the spiral of scientific method, can be inferred from the family of about four dozen books which it has been possible to write covering the various branches of the subject. Their pages will show how they all stem from the five laws, which were expounded in the first volume of the family. No end can be seen to the number of other such books and papers, bringing out more of latent implications, in the light of the changing boundary conditions set to library service by the continuous as well as sudden changes in social values experienced by society from time to time. The existence of such prepotent, seminal, normative principles, and the possibility of such an endless chain of inferences from them leading to ever-becoming, ever-new library practices and techniques, form a sufficient justification for answering the question, "Is there a library science?", in the affirmative.

★★★

Library Grant to Indian Universities: Some Suggestions for the UGC

S. R. Ranganathan

Abstract

Examines the difficulties in the maximum utilization of the UGC (University Grants Commission) grant to Indian University Libraries. Suggests a time-table for spreading out the work-load of Book-Purchase-Chain throughout the year on a weekly basis.

Recommends the allocation of one-fifth of the grant on the additional staff needed to cover the book-purchase-chain completely commencing with book-selection and ending with the release of the books for the use of readers, after being properly classified, catalogued and processed in every other way.

Examines the basis of apportionment of library grants between the Union and State Governments, Recommends the use of per capita formula for determining the library grant.

Examines the need for an accelerated training of about 250 librarians to enable the universities to use the UGC grant effectively. Recommends the provision of full-timed teachers in the Schools of Library Science being conducted in some of the Universities,

Stresses the need for continuous research in library science as of utmost importance for forging new library techniques. Suggests that the UGC may strengthen the Chair in Library Science recently created in the University of Madras for developing it

Reprinted with permission from Annals of Library Science, 4(4), pp. 139-164, 1957.

as the All India Institute for Advanced Studies and Research in Library Science.

0. INTRODUCTION

The University Grants Commission (UGC) have been giving substantial grants to Indian Universities for building up their library collections. It is very gratifying to note that UGC has got a liberal policy towards the University Libraries. However, in the utilization of the grants there are some administrative difficulties. Maximum benefit is not obtained due to a failure to grasp the problem as a whole. The factors involved are analysed and suggestions are made to UGC.

1. TIME FACTOR

1.1. Introduction

There can be no doubt that the intention is that the library grant should be used to buy the largest number of books in actual or anticipated demand, and that the books should be promptly brought into active use by readers. The administrative elements covering the giving of the grant should be so defined that the timetable for the absorption of the grant does not militate against this primary purpose of the grant. To arrive at the right time-table and administrative elements, I begin with a picture of what all has to be done in a library to absorb the grant.

1.2. Weekly Rhythm

It is a matter of long-established experience that the work behind the screen in a library should proceed with a weekly rhythm. In particular, book-selection, book-purchase, book-reception, technical treatment of books, and their release for use by readers are best organised on a weekly basis. Our chief market for books are now in London and New York. On account of the prevailing exchange difficulties, even books in the European languages other than English have to be bought in these markets. This is likely to continue for one more generation. The national bibliographies and other book lists are now published on a weekly basis. And these are the primary source for book-selection. This fits with the weekly rhythm of work in libraries.

1.2.1. Book-Purchase Chain

The preliminary book-selection list initiated by the library in week 1 will get scrutinised by subject-specialists in week 2. Though antiquated and purposeless, each list has now to get the sanction of the Executive in many of the Universities. So long as this practice continues, the list started in week 1 will receive sanction of the Executive in week 3. The order will leave the library in week 4. It will reach London or New York as the case may be in week 5 if it goes direct and in week 6 if it goes via a local book-seller. For definiteness let us pursue the first alternative. The supply will reach the library in week 12 from London and in week 16 from New York. The books arriving in week 12 will be collated and passed on to the technical section for classification and cataloguing in week 13. They will be further prepared for use in the maintenance section in week 14. They will be released for use of the readers in week 15. Thus, a complete book- purchasechain will normally take I5 weeks - for completion. It must be remembered that book-selection will start every week in the year and books too will consequently arrive in the library every week in the year. Thus, every section will be kept continuously busy all through the year. This is necessary for efficient management.

1.3. Right Time-Table

To enable the first of the 52 instalments of payment in a year to be done in the very first week of the financial year - the first week of April - the book-selection of the corresponding book-purchase-chain should have begun at the beginning of the preceding December. The chain initiated by the book-selection

malpractice of getting advance bills without the supply and passing them on as make-believe vouchers for receiving the grant and formally satisfying the audit. Of course, this involves false certification by the librarian. There are cases when librarians had to leave their jobs for reasons of conscientious objection.

1.4.2. Chain Left Incomplete

Once the grant is drawn without supply, a pseudo-satisfaction of work bravely done makes one sit back for a while. A mood of exhaustion comes thereafter. With the result the book-purchase-chain is left incomplete without attention to the links corresponding to the classification, cataloguing, and release of the books for the use of readers. Bundles of new books being piled up for several months seems to have now become common in several libraries. There can be no more serious flouting of the Laws of Library Science than this. Another practice is to purchase several copies of the books locally available without consideration of what is really needed for the work in progress in the several departments of the University. This converts the allotment and absorption of grants to a mere ritual. It is a waste of public money.

1.5. The Remedy

The UGC should take steps to arrest these unfortunate results. The following are recommendations to the UGC on this matter:

1.5.1. The UGC should inform the universities about the probable amount of grant during a financial year not later than the preceding November. It should be possible to estimate the probable amount at least to 50% of the amount expected. This will be quite easy if the grant is allotted on a five year basis.

1.5.2. The UGC should transfer the annual grant to the University libraries at the very beginning of the financial year. If the annual grant is transferred in instalments, the first instalment should be transferred early in April.

1.5.3. If there is any insuperable difficulty in announcing the probable grant four months in advance of the financial year, the procedure should be to decide the amount of grant on the basis of the expenditure in the preceding year.

1.5.4. The university libraries should be allowed to hold over the unspent balance of the grants for expenditure during the next financial year. It should be possible for audit to pre–vent any abuse of this provision and see that the money is fully spent eventually for the purpose for which it was granted.

1.6. An Example from Experience

When the Madras Government sanctioned a non-recurring grant to the Madras University Library, in 1926, permission was sought and granted to spread the appropriation over a period of five years. This helped a wise and beneficial use of the money. The recurring annual grant of Rs 65,000 made in the same year was exempted from being surrendered to the extent not appropriated within the financial year. This arrangement enabled the library not only to keep on to the weekly rhythm of the book-purchase-chain without in anyway interfering with service to readers, but also to spend the money on really needed books and with every satisfaction to the audit. There was never any adverse audit remark during all the years. So also the UGC can devise the necessary safeguards through audit against any possible abuse that may arise in this elastic and long-drawn-out time-table.

2. PERSONNEL

2.1. Introduction

Most of the university libraries in India are understaffed. It is barely sufficient to handle a small annual in-take of books and periodicals, which the miserly library budget used to allow. Apart from the staff working behind the screen to purchase and prepare books for use, the Library provides a counter staff to look after the circulation, issue and return of books. Only a small full-timed staff of one or two is provided for direct service to readers in the selection of relevant reading materials. It is this staff that does the most vital work in a library. It is designated Reference Staff.

2.1.1. *Effect of Additional Grant*

Whenever a library gets an extra grant, it is now totally set apart for the purchase of books and periodicals. Whether this is the fault of the university authorities or is a consequence of the conditions attached to the grant is immaterial. The extra work to be done behind the screen to spend this sum results in the withdrawal of the reference staff from service to readers. This is the unfortunate immediate result of the grants now being made by the UGC. There is every ground to believe that this is not being brought to the notice of the UGC. This memorandum is therefore turned on the staff necessary to utilise the grants properly without prejudice to the service proper to readers.

2.2. Staff Formula

Between 1945 and 1955, several libraries in the country asked for advice on the strength of staff to be provided. This led me to construct a staff-formula giving the staff required in terms of the quantity of the various items of work to be done in a library. This formula has been tested in other countries also and found to give a reliable method of determining the strength of staff impersonally, uninfluenced by any prejudice or emotion. The full staff-formula has been published in my "Library development plan: Thirty-year programme for India with draft library bill for the Union and the constituent states. 1950, (Delhi University Publications, Library science series, 2)."

2.2.1. *Staff Formula for the Book-Purchase-Chain*

Here is an extract from that formula for the staff needed to complete a book-purchase-chain of work consisting of book-selection, book-ordering, book-reception, accessioning and payment of bills, classification, and cataloguing, and the physical preparation of books before release to the use of readers and absorption into the live collection of the library. It does not cover the maintenance staff, or the reference staff, or the circulation staff or the, supervisory Staff.

2.3. Application of Staff Formula

Let us now apply the above extract from the staff formula to a university library. In such a library, book-fund may have normally to be divided between books and periodicals in the ratio of 4:1. Thus, if the book-fund is Rs 1,00,000, books will absorb Rs 80,000. Today, the average cost of a book as well as the average subscriptions to periodicals may be taken to be each Rs 20. Thus, a book fund of Rs 1,00,000 is equivalent to an intake of 4,000 books and 1,000 periodical publications. Substituting the values of NA and NP in the formula, we get the following results for the staff required for absorbing a sum of Rs 1,00,000 granted for the purchase of reading material.

$$NA/6000 + NA/2000 + NP/500 = 4NA + 12NP/6000$$
$$= NA + 3NP/1500$$

Where

NA = Number of volumes accessioned in a year

NP = Number of periodicals publications taken

2.3.1. Allocation of Grant Between Staff and Reading Materials

We may take the average annual cost of one professionally qualified librarian including leave salary and provident fund, to be Rs 3,400. Then the amount to be set apart for the employment of the staff necessary to utilise a grant of Rs 1,00,000 is Rs 20,000 in round figures. Thus, to ensure that the grant given to a university library is spent usefully without prejudice to concurrent service to readers and with prompt release of the books purchased for use by readers, the following recommendation is made.

2.3.2. Recommendation to UGC

The UGC should allow a university library to spend one-fifth of its grant on the staff needed to complete the book-purchase-chain including book-selection, book order, book-reception and payment of bills, classification, cataloguing, and the physical preparation of book before the release for the use of readers and absorption into the live collection of the library.

2.4. The Present Plight

Perhaps, the universities themselves have failed to bring this need to the UGC. Perhaps the university libraries themselves felt snowed down by this sudden increase in the book-fund and the in-take of books and periodicals and had failed to rationalise the problem. Whatever, the cause, the present plight is far from happy. As already stated, the effect of the grant, without earmarking one-fifth of it for the extra staff needed to utilise it, is the withdrawal of the reference staff from service to readers. Another sad effect is that the only link in the book-purchase-chain that are completed usually are those of a haphazard book-selection, placing orders for books and passing the bills. These links are forcedly completed under the pressure of the financial and account rules attached to the grant. There is no pressure whatever from any quarter to enforce the completion of the chain by classification, cataloguing, and absorption of the book into the livestock of the library so as to become available for readers. Often, the bills are passed even before the books are received. When the books arrive later, they are left for a long, long time in bundles. Hardly anybody even notices it, the book-purchase-chain being thus left incomplete.

2.5. Appeal to UGC

What is the benefit of making grants to a library receiving grants under these conditions? The users of the library are unable to sense the wastage involved. In fact, they have been all along accustomed to a miserly provision of books and periodicals. When they are denied even the usual attention and service they are told that all the staff have been turned on the work of getting books. This induces in them the mood of compliance with the withdrawal of service. But, the public seldom has the memory to follow up such points and protest if the promised new books do not reach them. There may be perhaps a few powerful readers who lodge a protest. Then, in self-defence, a clever librarian picks out and releases just those books as are wanted by them and tides over the difficulty. This is a realistic picture of the situation. There is a getting away from the fact that to spend every extra sum of money on the purchase and service of books, there must be proportionate addition to staff. I plead with the UGC to recognise this hard fact and give effect to the recommendation given in section 2.3.2.

3. FINANCE

3.1. Introduction

Who should provide the funds for a university library? Is it the student population, or the State Government, or the Union Government? The answer cannot be the same in all countries. Nor can it be the same in any country at all times. It will vary with the prevailing tax-pattern of the country on the one hand, and on the social outlook on the value of university education and research on the other. Both of these factors change from country to country and from time to time.

3.2. Social Outlook on University Education and Research

With regard to the social outlook on the value of university education and research, there is a strong trend towards a consensus of opinion all the world over. This itself is the result of a trend towards a socialistic pattern of education to meet the growing pressure of democracy and population. In this trend, the view is that the value of university education and research is more dominant in respect of the community in general than in respect of the individual subject to them. This is examined in detail in chapter 1 of my "Library development plan: Thirty-year programme for India with draft library bills for the Union and the constituent states, 1950, (University of Delhi, Library science series, 2)". As a result of this trend, in some countries, the entire cost of university education in general and of university libraries in particular is met from public funds. In other countries, the students are obliged to pay fees. But, this is only a token affair. For, 90% of the cost of university education and the entire cost of university library are met from public funds. The Madras University Library approximated to this standard by about 1926. This was due to a pleasant accident which brought the Chief Minister of the State and the university librarian together on a platform. An annual grant of Rs 68,000 to the university library was a pleasant outcome of this accident. This grant was made statutory three years later. Since then, the annual grant to the library has been steadily increasing, with the increase in number of departments of study and research.

3.3. Effect of the Tax Pattern

The very fact that the Union Government has begun to give grant to the universities is the effect of a change in tax pattern. At present the Union Government collects the greatest part of revenue. This naturally depletes the tax that can be collected by the constituent states. In normal times, however, the Union Government cannot find use for all the money that it collects. It therefore gives back a good portion of it to the constituent states. Happily, one of the forms of giving back is that of a direct grant to the university. Even more happily, the UGC has found it proper to give back a substantial sum in the form of grants to university libraries.

3.4. Method of Proportion: A Wrong Precedent

I learn, however, that the UGC grant to a university library follows the Victorian pattern of grant-in-aid codes. In this pattern, the grant-in-aid to an educational body can only be in a fixed proportion to the money that the recipient provides it from its own funds. Now, a university library has no source of income of its own. Nor has a university any independent source from which it can pay the university Library. Therefore, the only other source, the income from which can be shown by a university lib–rary as its own, is the State Government. Thus, the quantum of the UGC grant to a university library is determined by what the State Government is prepared to give to that library. But, the university library is several removes from the State Government. The latter is too preoccupied with so many problems to sense the consequences of the starvation of the university library. Therefore, the party that has to put down its own quota first in-order to bring out an adequate grant from the UGC is in reality a third party that has the least chance to be sensitive to the deferred reserve of a poor library grant from the UGC. From the point of view of a university library, the State is certainly a third party who is not immediately or visibly affected by a reduction in the total grant going to a university library as a result of its own default. As the saying goes, it is only the road underneath the harrow that knows where the pin-point goes. Basing the UGC grant on the method of proportion defeats its own purpose. It is futile. It must be given up.

3.5. Per Capita Approach

A more realistic and equitable approach to the quantum of UGC grant to a university library is the Per Capita Approach. In the previous period, world experience showed that the annual appropriation for the book-fund of a university library corresponded to Rs. 15 per student and Rs. 200 per teacher or research fellow. Also, the annual expenditure of all other kinds, including the cost of the administrative staff and the reference staff for service, was roughly equal to the expenditure on books and periodicals, For example, the total annual budget for the library of a university with 10,000 students and 500 teachers and research fellows should be Rs, 500,000 of which Rs 250,000 would be spent on books and periodicals. Perhaps, these figures will have to be amended in view of the inflation since World War II.

3.6. Apportionment between the Union and State Governments

Thus, the financial needs of a university library can be determined objectively. That money should be given to the university library in order that the return on the money spent on the university as a whole may be adequate. Again, this money should be found only by the Governments of the Union and of the State. Between the UGC and the State Government, it must be decided in what proportion the library finance should be shared between themselves. This proportion will depend on taxing powers of the Union Government and the State Government, Perhaps, the State Government may pay one-fifth of the requirements of a university library and the UGC the remaining four-fifths for the time being. The capital expenditure of a university library also may have to be found similarly. But it nullifies the intention, based on social value, to provide each university library with adequate finance to serve the students, teachers and research fellows with all the needed literature, if the UGC would pay its share only if the Government pays its own share or vice versa. The following proposals are therefore recommended for consideration and adoption: -

3.6.1. The library grant to a university should be determined according to an agreed per capita formula.

3.6.2. The entire library finance of a university library should be provided by the UGC and the State Government.

3.6.3. The UGC and the State Government should determine from time to time the proportion in which their respective grants to a university library should be.

3.6.4. The UGC and the State Governments should have a gentleman's agreement that each will actually pay its own share of the library grant.

3.6.5. The UGC should not withdraw or lower its grant to a university library because the State Government fails in its obligation, and vice versa.

3.6.6. The library grant in any year should be based on the statistical data of the preceding year.

3.7. Functional Approach

The annual finance necessary for a university library can also be determined by the Functional Approach. This will take into account the number of faculties and the number and nature of the departments of study and research in the university. The result is not usually very different from that of the per capita approach. A detailed discussion of both these methods will be found in my "Library development plan for the Allahabad University, 1947." This book has been fully reproduced as an appendix in the Justice Mootham Report on the reorganisation of the Allahabad University published in 1954.

4. LIBRARY MANPOWER

4.1. Introduction

It is a good augury that the UGC has seriously taken up the development of university libraries, as an essential aid to advanced studies and research, so essential for industrial advancement and increasing social well-being in our country. But neither money alone nor books alone can bring about the desired results. These are necessary but not sufficient. Another necessary factor is the library manpower, to build a balanced collection of books and periodicals in the light of the actual and anticipated demand, to classify and catalogue them in a helpful way, and to give prompt, pinpointed and exhaustive documentation service to students in close correlation to their work in the respective faculties.

4.2. Inadequacy of the Present Library Manpower

The question of manpower has not yet received attention. All our 30 and odd university libraries taken together will require about 300 well-trained professionals and 60 leaders with personality and drive, apart from 300 semi-professionals and clerical staff. Against the 360 of the first two categories we do not now have even 100 persons. This amounts to near-famine in professionally qualified library manpower.

4.3. Special School for Accelerated Course

This inadequacy of library manpower leads to a serious leakage, which prevents the good intentions of the UGC being translated into effective action and service, which can reach and benefit the students and teachers in the universities in full measure. An appeal goes to the UGC that this leakage should be stopped as quickly as possible. One method of stopping the leakage is to provide for a special accelerated course in library science to train about 250 persons for university library work, within the next two or three years. It is best to make this accelerated course independent of the present normal courses in the universities.

4.4. Part-time Diversion of Present Manpower

There is another matter about the existing library manpower to which the attention of the UGC may be invited. Two or three of the top-men in the university libraries which give a course in library science are made to give part of their time to teaching in that school. This also leads to a haphazard way in absorbing the library grant. This system of making the library staff part timed teachers of library science is an inheritance from the past, I myself may be accused of having started this practice, in 1928. The continuance of this unfortunate practice is proving to be ruinous both to the efficiency of the university libraries and to the schools of library science. History must be read with care in this matter; the pioneering years of three decades ago found a scepticism and coldness in regard to the library, the library profession, and still more to training for librarians. In those difficult days, our society did throw forth, as any other society, in a phase of awakening would have done, a few pioneering librarians with exceptional missionary zeal, who did both the running of libraries and the teaching of library students with some success. But without heed to the psychology of pioneership, which can only last for a short duration, and perhaps prompted by a sense of prestige to some extent, during the last 15 years, university after university began to establish diploma courses in library science with part-time teachers. This corrupted the standard both of teaching and of library work little by little. As visiting lecturer and examiner in some of these universities, I have been sadly watching the progressive degeneracy. We now seem to be heading towards a crisis. I therefore urge on the UGC to examine this matter and provide for full-time teachers in the schools of library science so that the library staff can devote their full attention to the library work properly. This is necessary to stop the leakage in the absorption of the library grants.

4.5. Recommendations

At the same time, it is not wise or even possible to divert any of the all-too-small number of trained librarians to full-timed work as teachers of library science. Therefore, the programme for creating more librarians should be properly phased. The following recommendations are commended for consideration:

4.5.1. For a period of two or three years, the UGC should arrange for a temporary school of library science to produce in an accelerated manner about 250 post-graduate diploma holders in library science to supply manpower to the existing university libraries so that the benefit of the library grants may reach the students and teachers without leakage.

This school may also aim at providing for the training of about 30 more persons who can become full-time teachers of Library science in the existing library schools in the university.

4.5.2. The university in which the temporary school is located will have to be selected without interfering with the existing schools with part-time teachers

4.5.3. The UGC should include in its policy the gradual replacement of part-time teachers by full-time teachers in the diploma courses in library science being conducted in the universities.

5. RESEARCH IN LIBRARY SCIENCE

5.1. A New Social Phenomenon

The current renaissance in our country is naturally producing an effervescence of activities in the educational, industrial, and governmental spheres. These spheres hold the key to the development in every other sphere. Work in these three spheres has now reached huge dimensions. It has to face many unprecedented situations. It can no longer be based solely on the innate flair of a few exceptional top-men. On the other hand, it has to be based on continuous systematic research. Research is thus coupled today directly with the continuous flow of current work. Moreover, it has to be done by a team. This team has to include a number of persons removed somewhat from the position of the man of genius in the intellectual scale. Therefore, need has arisen to train in methods of research many persons low down in the first quartile of the intellectual scale. This is a new phenomenon in the world of today in general, and in New India in particular.

5.2. Greater Attention to Library Science

Research in the universities as well as in the industrial houses and the governmental establishments by a team of workers most of whom are neither self-centres of illumination nor self-helpers, has to be fed by efficient library service. In response to this new development, the UGC has begun to devote thought to the improvement of university libraries and to make grants to them. The industrial houses and the governmental establishments also have begun to devote thought to their own libraries and to provide large sums of money for them.

Another social necessity in a democracy is the establishment and maintenance of a nationwide public library system. This is also provided with a considerable sum of money. Thus, a large slice of public money is now being necessarily diverted to the libraries.

5.3. Instruments of Global Development

When so much money is turned on to libraries, special care should be taken to see that library service reaches the persons concerned not only without obstruction of any sort, but also in a more-aggressive and at the same time pleasant and acceptable manner. This means intimate personal service to top-management, persuasive service to the pedestrians making up the ranks and the file and the men at the bench, dissemination service to the general public, or provision of harmless, ele–vating, leisure-time occupation for everybody. This extended and universal use of the library as an instrument of global social development is a phenomenon taking shape only today. It needs the forging of new lines of organisation for the library system of the country as a whole and new library techniques for making library service to each and every reader efficient and pin-pointed.

5.4. Research in Library Science

The continuous development of the lines of library organisation and of the library techniques themselves has to be based on research of its own. In our own life time the problems of library service have entered the spiral of scientific method and have formed a fit field for systematic research. Indeed, a library science has emerged with its own normative principles. It is acknowledged all the world over that India has played a pioneering role in helping the emergence of library science. The Fundamental Laws of Library Science were formulated in India about 25 years ago. Practically, every branch of library science has been examined and continues to be examined in the light of the fundamental laws. The foundation for the Depth-Classification needed for efficient library service is being laid in India, in the light of the first self-perpetuating, analytico-synthetic scheme of classification called Colon Classification, which was itself created in India about thirty years ago. India is thus quite competent to cultivate the field of library science for its own benefit and incidentally for the benefit also of the world at large. From the point of view of the UGC, this field should be continually cultivated by research in order that all the past sums of money, spent on library systems in the country, can give an adequate return.

5.5. All India Institute of Library Science

No agency other than the UGC is likely to have the vision to sense the Long-range effects of the research and also have the courage to spend money on research projects of deferred return. As an insurance against the dissipation or non-fructification of its own grants to university libraries and the private and public provision of money for all other kinds of libraries, the UGC should exercise its farsight and provide for advanced studies and research in library science. Perhaps, for some years to come, one such institute will prove sufficient for the whole country.

5.6. Location of the Institute

Naturally, an institute of the kind should be located in one of our universities. That university should be chosen that has a tradition in the matter and also the nucleus for an advanced institute of that kind. One suggestion is the University of Madras, for, during the current year, an endowment has been made to that

University for the Sarada Ranganathan Chair of Library Science. The Laws of Library Science were formulated in that university. The Colon Classification was created there. The Chain Procedure for cataloguing, now being practised in many countries of the world was also discovered in that university. Thus, it has the necessary tradition and the nucleus for receiving the All India Institute for Advanced Studies and Research in Library Science.

5.7. Recommendations

The recommendations to the UGC is therefore as follows:

The UGC may strengthen the chair in library science in the University of Madras, by giving an annual grant for the maintenance of one reader, two lecturers, four research fellows, and a few students in the Master's Degree Course in Library Science.

It is estimated that an annual grant of Rs 50,000 may prove sufficient for the purpose. In view of the all-India nature of this project, it is in the fitness of things that this grant comes from the UGC in preference to the State Government.

★★★

Document, Documentation and Standardization

S. R. Ranganathan

Abstract

Examines the spheres of standardization, the resulting advantages, and the possibility of the extension to the repetitive elements in intellectual work. Sets forth the spiral of creation of thought, its expression for communications, its embodiment into a document, the organization and service of documents, the feedback into the human mind, and the repetition of this process *ad infinitum.* Mentions the role of the author, the publisher, the printer, the librarian, and the documentalist in this spiral movement. States the diverse problems in the different stages of the spiral, amenable to standardization and simplification.

Contractions Used

EC2	Documentation Sectional Committee of the Indian Standards Institution.
Standsimp	Standardization and Simplification

1. STANDARDIZATION AND SIMPLIFICATION

It is now generally accepted that standardization and simplification (standsimp) leads to economy in time, space effort, materials, man-power, and money. Here are examples of the

Reprinted with permission from Annals of Library Science, 4(4), pp. 165-186, 1957.

economy realised even about thirty years ago by the adoption of standsimp. We read on P 203 of the *Bulletin of the Taylor Society* (1924) that whereas 34 varieties and sizes of common brick were made, it was found possible to serve all purposes by one, whereas milk bottles were made in 49 sizes and types, it was found that nine sizes, all supplied with the single size of a cap would do. The saving by this standsimp is said to have been many millions of rupees.

1.1. Application to Materials

At first, it was material commodities to which standsimp was applied. This was but natural. The number of material commodities is so great and their use in daily life is so wide-spread that their standsimp has already made the greatest impact even on public mind.

1.2. Application to Services and Procedures

But the professional mind has begun to realise that stand-simp is of equal benefit even in regard to services and procedures of all kinds. Catering service, air-hostess service, filing of records, laboratory manipulation, and production technology are examples of fields of services and procedures, in which stand-simp has already begun to play a useful part.

1.3. Application to Intellectual Work

It is now being realised that there is a sector in intellectual work also for a profitable application of standsimp. It is true that intellectual work is individualistic in the extreme. It can be as varied as personality itself. To be more concrete, it is as individualistic as people's faces. But it must be remembered that intellectual work consists of a creative part as well as a pedestrian and repetitive part. It is the creative part that is truly individualistic. In this part any externally imposed stand-simp will prove fatal. This does not take away from the fact that truly creative work is characterized by economy of every kind; it is characterized by the Principle of Least Action, and simplification is intrinsic in it. 'Hands off', then, in the case of creative work of every kind. The ancient Indian sage Vatsyayana, has said that science and rules are by passed when creative force sets itself in action.

रस्र्स्वादे प्रवृते तु नैव शास्त्रं न च नय:

But the same Vatsyayana asserts that rules, regulations, external directives, standards and simplifications imposed from outside are of help in securing economy in the case of pedestrian and repetitive intellectual work.

शास्त्राएां विषय: तावत् यावत् मन्दरसा: नराः

1.4. No Freezing of Originality

One need not, therefore, be afraid of freezing of original thinking, if standsimp is applied to intellectual work of the latter kind. Even here, standsimp is tentative. The door for original thinking and for altering the standsimp is never closed either in the sphere of commodities, or of services, or of procedures, or of pedestrian or repetitive intellectual work.

1.5. Conservation of Mental Energy

Mental energy is as much in need of conservation by the adoption of standsimp, as manipulative energy and materials. Conservation of mental energy is equivalent to the conservation of the human resources. For, as stated in the Brhadaranyaka upanishad, the essence of man is mind.

मनोमय: प्रयं हि पुरुष

1.6. Ancient Standsimp in Intellectual Work

In a sense, all attempts from time immemorial at laying down definite processes in logic, exegetics, and mathematics are indicative of the application of standsimp to intellectual work. Nayyayikas of ancient India and the general-semanticists of today are equal in laying down standsimp to intellectual work.

Grammarians have always been pre-eminent in this matter. Panini's famous work on grammar, the Ashtadhyayi contains a masterpiece in the application of standsimp in the intellectual sphere — particularly in the sphere of terminology.

2. APPLICATION TO LIBRARIANSHIP

We shall then assume that standsimp is applicable, with due safeguards, to certain sectors of intellectual work, and proceed to examine the sector of librarianship amenable to standsimp. This will be facilitated by a preliminary examination of the functions of librarianship. Here is a helpful view of librarianship for this purpose.

2.1. Librarianship as Thought-Engineering

Librarianship is service. It is a social service, which is analogous to engineering service. In engineering, one form of energy is transformed into another. A latent or potential form of energy is activated. Librarianship plays a similar part in the transformation of thought-energy. Viewed from our angle, there is a perpetual spiral phenomenon in the creation and transformation of thought-energy.

2.2. Spiral in the Universe of Thought

The following diagram gives a schematic representation of the spiral phenomenon:

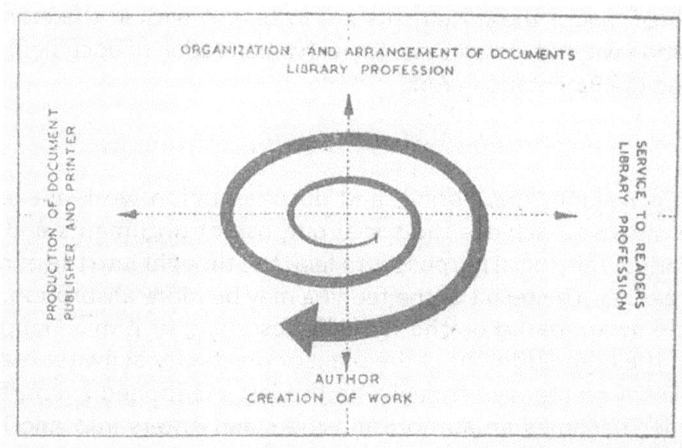

2.3. Author and Work

Author creates thought. To make it communicable, he expresses it in a language or in some other graphic medium. This is work.

2.4. Book-Trades and Document

The work is evanascent unless it is recorded in a material. The author's work may be either sound-recorded, or made into a conventional document, such as a book or a periodical publication. The latter form of record falls in the sphere of the book-trades. A work has to be transformed into a material document to preserve it through time and to transmit it across space, so as to be available for all without mutilation.

2.5. Library Profession and Documentation Work

The function of the library profession is to collect, store, and retrieve documents for use by readers. The storage of documents requires the techniques of classification, and cataloguing, if their retrieval, for a particular reader, is to be exhaustive, expeditious, and pinpointed, and if the documents are to be put back in the correct position without loss of time. Such an organization of documents is called Documentation Work.

2.6. Library Profession and Documentation Service

The collection, the storing, and documentation work are only the means to achieve the social purpose of documents and of libraries. This social purpose is to feed the thought into the minds of readers. The result of the feeding may be more absorption, or some action based on the thought absorbed; or it may happen that the bombardment of the brain of the reader activates it and makes it create new thought. In the last mentioned event, the reader becomes an author; and the spiral enters into another cycle.

2.7. Areas for Standardization

We may now explore the areas for standardization, in each of the four cardinal points in the spiral. Obviously for the reason set forth in section 13, the work of the author should not be standardized; for, it is creative. This is generally the case. There is however, an exception in the case of the authorial work which amounts only to compilation of reference books such as directories, administration reports, encyclopedias, bibliographies, and abstracting periodicals.

3. STANDARDIZATION OF COMPILER'S WORK

The work of compiling any of the materials mentioned in section 27 is amenable to standsimp. The ISI Documentation Sectional Committee (EC 2) has already established a standard for abstracting (IS : 795-1956 Canons for Making Abstracts). We have still to work out the standard for the lay-out of an abstracting periodical and perhaps, another standard will be required for the construction of the Classified Index of an abstracting periodical.

We have also to establish standards for various forms of reference books such as directories, annual reports, encyclopedias, and perhaps, even for office manuals. The library profession has to promote the standard for such reading materials, as the work of serving them to the readers falls to its share. Here it has to work in collaboration with the profession of the compilers concerned.

4. STANDARDIZATION IN THE PHYSICAL PRODUCTION OF DOCUMENT

Let us pass along the spiral in the clock-wise direction. The next cardinal point reached is that of the physical production of document. The parties employed in this area are the publishers, printers, book-binders, paper-makers, type-designers, and illustration-makers. But the fruition point of the work of all these parties is lying largely in the library. For, it is in the library that the thought, lying latent in the state of physical entity as book or periodical, is transformed into an active state so as to bombard and stimulate the thought of readers. It is the library profession that has the best opportunity to experience the efficacy or otherwise of the physical document. Its own success in finding Every Book Its Reader, in fulfilment of the Third Law of Library Science depends on the adoption of proper standards in book-production. Therefore, the library profession has to promote the establishment of standsimp in this area. Accordingly, EC2 began to interest itself in this subject as early as 1948.

4.1. Standard Established

The first topic taken up was the lay-out of learned periodicals. The Indian Standard of this topic is IS: 4-1949 Practice for Make-Up of Periodicals. The publishing and the printing trades on the one side and the library profession on the other have already published the following five standards concerning the preliminary pages of a book :

IS:	790-1956	General Structure of Preliminary Pages of a Book.
IS:	791-1956	Specification for Half-Title-Leaf of a Book.
IS:	792-1956	Specification for Title-Leaf of a Book.
IS:	793-1956	Specification for Author Statement in the
		Title Page of a Book.
IS:	794-1956	Practice for Table of Contents.

A paper in the Documentation Session of the Indian Standards Convention was presented on the Author Statement on the Title Leaf of a Book. It dealt with a new matter of great interest to the library profession and it sought the co-operation of publishers in implementing it in all books printed in the country. One of the papers was on the Make-Up of Periodicals.

4.2. Standards in Preparation

Rules for making Alphabetical Indexes and the Symbols of Proof Correction are two other topics, connected with the physical production of books, for which the draft standards are nearing the final stage. Separate papers have been written on these very topics.

4.3. Standards to Be Taken Up

There are still many standards to be taken up in the area of book production. Of these, the form of bibliographical references in books and periodicals has been engaging the attention of the International Organization for Standardization since the end of the World War II. EC2 would like to finalize it for India at an early date. There are also several materials and processes to be standardized. These concern the quality and size of paper, and particularly the reduction in the number of sizes, the nature of the illustrations and their number to be used in books of different standards and coverage, the binding materials, re-inforced library binding, publisher's casing, type-faces in relation to readability, and formats of books and periodicals. We do not have a sufficient variety of type-faces in Indian languages. Type-designers should be stimulated to pay attention to this problem. These and many other problems, standing in need of standsimp, are discussed in two books of Ranganathan : *Social Bibliography or Physical Bibliography for Librarians* (1952) and *Social Education Literature for Authors, Artists, Publishers, Teachers, Librarians, and Governments* (1952). As book production in the different languages of India has to make great strides in renascent India, all these problems should be taken up by EC2, and the book-trades and the National Book Trust should come forward to establish proper standards.

4.4. Non-Conventional Reading Materials

What has been stated so far concerns only the conventional printed books and periodicals. But a variety of non-conventional reading materials have now come into vogue. Micro-reproductions in cards, reels, and film strips is one of them. While the standardization of the processes belong to other technical committees, there are many questions such as: readability, size, and terminology in which EC2 should take active interest. It should also take interest in the standsimp of the reading apparatus necessary to read such non-conventional kinds of reading materials. Ceiling-books for the use of patients and the books for the blind should also receive attention in due course. Sound records of music are now coming very much in vogue. For some time, India should also produce sound-books for the benefit of the illiterate and the semi-literate. These records will have to be lent out like any other book. This raises the establishment of standsimp to eliminate scratches in the plates and also the establishment of standsimp for their receptacles when lent out. These standsimps will have to be stimulated by the library profession and in establishing them, EC2 should bring the library profession and the technicians concerned to work in collaboration.

5. STANDARDS FOR LIBRARY BUILDINGS, FITTINGS AND FURNITURE

Let us next move further up the spiral. It takes us to the cardinal point representing the storage and the technical treatment of documents. It also involves diverse procedures in library administration. This cardinal point cannotes among other things library buildings, fittings, and furniture of all kinds and sizes. EC2 has not yet turned its attention to the standsimp concerning them.

5.1. Cloud-Burst of Library Activity

And yet, we have now begun to bring a cloud-burst of library activities. A vast sum of money is being provided for the building and equipment of libraries. It is being provided by the University Grants Commission and by the Planning Commission. This sum has to be absorbed by the 32 university libraries, the score of libraries in the National Research Laboratories, and the libraries of many other research organizations in the pure and applied fields.

Hundreds of colleges and thousands of schools also are becoming library-minded and are receiving grants for their library buildings. There is again the large sum of Rs 1,75,00,000 provided in the Second Five Year Plan. An appreciable part of this sum will be turned on the library buildings, fittings, and furniture in hundreds of community centres. It has been announced that, within the next five years, each district will have a District Central Library.

5.2. Potential Wastage

This cloud-burst of library activity is most welcome. But we may fail to get even half-a-rupee return on each rupee spent on the buildings and their equipment, if each library has to drift along with its own trial-and-error method. Till about five years ago I had been consulted in my personal capacity in regard to the library buildings of about a dozen libraries. In my attempt to help them, I had evolved a few standards in consultation with a few friends in the architectural and furniture fields. This proved sufficient in those days, as progress was slow. This can no longer be sufficient. When so many different localities, authorities, and people engage themselves in putting up library buildings and equipping them, we will be providing for a great potential of wastage, unless ISI steps in to establish standsimp, and advise the University Grants Commission and the Planning Commission on the application of the resulting standards. EC2 should work in close collaboration with the architects, the building trade, and the furniture-makers in establishing the necessary standards as quickly as possible. Then only the community will get the money's worth on what they are asked to spend in library buildings, fittings, and furniture.

5.3. Sectors for Standards

Here is a list of some of the sectors calling for the establishment of standsimp;

1. Branch library building for a population of about 25,000.
2. City Central Library building for cities with a population of less than 2,00,000.
3. City Central Library building for bigger cities.
4. Rural Central Library building.
5. Travelling library van for rural library service.
6. Windows for stack-rooms in all kinds of libraries.
7. Unit book-racks.
8. Book trolleys.
9. Periodicals reading room tables. The standard design evolved by me is now spreading into foreign countries also
10. Other reading room tables and readers' chairs.
11. Library counter for issue work.
12. Stack-room lighting and reading room lighting.
13. Catalogue cabinet.

14. Tables for accession work, catalogue work and other specialised work.
15. Work table *cum* counter for periodical publications work.
16. Issue apparatus, including issue trays of different sizes.
17. Receptacles for different kinds of library stationery and other materials, on the basis of the quantum principle in issue,

6. STANDARDIZATION AND LIBRARY CATALOGUE

The sectors marked out for standsimp in sections 3, 4, and 5 are not wholly within the province of the library profession, though it is deeply interested in them. They fall in the penumbral region of the library profession's interest, where co-operation with other professions and trades is essential for the establishment of standsimp and for the execution of work in conformity with the approved standards. We shall now consider sectors for standsimp, lying almost solely within the umbral region of the interest and competence of the library profession. Library catalogue is one such sector.

6.1. Glossary of Cataloguing Terms

One of the items in the sector of catalogue engaging the attention of EC2 is the glossary of cataloguing terms. Till now work is being done only in the English language. But we are sure to have cataloguers, very soon, who will not know English. They will use perhaps one of the twelve Indian languages. Communication between cataloguers in different languages will be facilitated if EC2 could establish a standard glossary of cataloguing terms in each of the languages, in such a way that as far as possible cognate terms are used in the different languages. The need and the possibility of this has been shown in Ranganathan's Canons of Terminology, published in the *Abgila,* the organ of the Indian Library Association, in the years 1949-53, The fixing of such cognate terms has also been demonstrated in the

Anuvarga suchi-kalpa (1953) of Ranganathan. The draft standard on the subject in the English language has been prepared and is expected to be finalized next year.

6.2. Lay-Out of Library Catalogue Code

Another item on which EC2 is endeavoring to establish a standard is the lay-out of the library catalogue code. This is expected to be of value as catalogue codes will soon have to be established in each of the twelve Indian languages. At present, we have the *classified catalogue code* for the English language. *Anuvarga-suchi-kalpa* is its Hindi version Experience has shown that there are certain areas in catalogues which should be left to the care of the particular languages within the country. It is, therefore, necessary to frame catalogue codes in each of the Indian languages. This work will be facilitated and will be saved from centrifugal tendencies, by this standard which is now under preparation.

6.3. Standard for Alphabetization

In 1952, ISI established its standard for alphabetization. It has been published as IS: 382-1952 Practice for Alphabetical Arrangement. This is for the English language. It is time that similar standards are established for each of the Indian languages. This standard will be of value in making directories, such as telephone directories, voters' lists, and other alphabetically arranged documents.

6.4. Standard for Abbreviation of Names of Periodicals

The International Organization for Standardization (ISO) has for long been considering a standard for the abbreviation of titles of periodicals. At the Ascona Conference, held in 1950, it was decided that the international standard should not go beyond the establishment of the basic principles and leave it largely to the several linguistic groups to work out standard abbreviations for their respective periodicals. The basic principles have been studied in detail in Ranganathan's paper on 'Alphabetical arrangement - A survey of basic principles'. On the basis of this paper, EC2 established the Indian Standard on Abbreviations for Titles of Periodicals (IS: 18-1949). The time has come to establish a similar standard for the abbreviation of the titles of periodicals in the Indian languages.

6.5. Standard for Names in Headings of Catalogue Entries

Headings of catalogue entries can have names of persons, geographical entities, corporate bodies, subjects, sacred books, classics, periodical publications, and pedestrian books. The standardized form of rendering of personal names of Indian cultural groups, in headings of catalogue entries, was first explored by me as part of the Unesco project on the Rendering of Asian Names. This was in 1953. Since then, EC2 has also seized the subject. When the standard on this is completed, it will be of use in building not only library catalogues, but also voters' lists, telephone directories, and similar alphabetical works of reference. We all experience the chaos prevailing in voters' lists and to some extent even in telephone directories. We have next to take up the standards for the other seven, classes of names mentioned at the beginning of this section.

6.6. Transliteration

Cataloguing requires the transliteration of one script into another. EC2 is interested in the transliteration of Roman script into Indian script and vice versa. In this, it should work with linguists. Any standard established in this matter will be of use in several other spheres. Perhaps the library profession can play only a very minor part in this problem.

7. STANDARDIZATION AND LIBRARY CLASSIFICATION

The organization of documents in the stack-room and in receptacles is now made to depend quite often on a scheme of library classification. EC2 took up, a few years ago, the formulation of norms which should govern any scheme of classification.

7.1. Terminology in Classification

The International Federation for Documentation resolved at the World Congress of Librarians and Documentalists held in Brussels in September 1955 that a glossary of the classification terms of Ranganathan should be compiled. At the International Study Conference on Classification and Information Retrieval, held at Dorking in May 1957, also, several members expressed a wish that this should be done. This has been because most of the recent progress in the theory of classification has been attributed to India. Wyndham Hulme set this study in motion at the beginning of the present century. Two decades later, Berwick Sayers carried the work slightly forward. They were both English. Henry Evelyn Bliss, an American, made some contribution of his own during the thirties.

7.2. India's Contribution to Classification Theory

But a systematic scientific study of the theory of classification can be said to have begun only with my *Prolegomena to Library Classification* (1937). In 1947, shortly after my retirement from administrative work, Sir Maurice Gwyer, good friend of India and of library science, established the Master's Degree and the Doctor's Degree in Library Science in the University of Delhi, and invited me to organise the work. This created for me an opportunity to be a whole-hogger in research in various branches of library science. A succession of enthusiastic students made intensive investigation in the theory of classification possible. The course on the "Universe of knowledge: Its development and structure", instituted for the first time, gave much insight into the intricacies of the theory. This led to a series of fundamental results.

7.3. International Committee on General Theory of Classification

In 1948, the International Federation for Documentation invited me to contribute a paper on *Classification and International documentation* to its *Review of Documentation.* In 1950, it created the Committee FID/CA on the General Theory of Classification and entrusted it to my care. All these factors resulted in the creation of a vast body of thought on the depth classification, which is needed in documentation work. Naturally, this new discipline has created a vast technical terminology. The time has come for EC2 to work on the standsimp of this terminology.

7.4. Harbinger of Things to Come

At the twelfth meeting of the Standing Working Committee of the Engineering Division Council of ISI, the Council referred to EC2 the preparation of a classification scheme for machine tools, in collaboration with representatives of machine tool interests. This is a happy harbinger of things to come. It opens up a vast vista for work, for every industry need a depth classification. Because team work on a world basis is developing, each field in the universe of knowledge develops in a turbulently dynamic way. The literary output in each field is expanding beyond the capacity of the memory of any, however gifted. The use of the externalised memory that is, of documents has become imperative. The library profession has, therefore, to step in with a self-perpetuating scheme of depth classification with a great expectation of life; otherwise, there will be a waste of the research potential of the world. This can be done by intimate co-operation between the specialist in classification and the specialist in the field of knowledge concerned.

8. STANDARDIZATION IN LIBRARY ADMINISTRATION

There is ample scope for standsimp in the procedures and the materials involved in *library administration.* A first attempt was made in 1935 in Ranganathan's Library Administration. It has prescribed standard procedure for various routines, the three-card system for periodicals being an outstanding one. It has also given standards for forms, registers, and file arrangement. All these and other standards of a similar kind should be re-considered and re-established in the light of the requirements of today.

The fourth cardinal point — Documentation Service — is of an intensely intimate nature. It cannot, therefore, admit of standardization. This is the last lap in thought-engineering.

9. CONCLUSION

There is no end, however, to the areas in document-production and documentation work which will require standsimp. It is an ever-continuing process. When ISI was founded, ten years ago, its Director, Dr Lal C. Verman made the Documentation Sectional Committee the first Committee of the kind and invited me to become its Chairman. Little did we then realise the vastness of the work to be done. With the willing co-operation of the members and of the official representative, Shri Jainath Kaul, some good work has been done during the first ten years of our existence. I have every hope that the record of the first ten years will be beaten during the next ten years. We are thankful to ISI for providing this opportunity to the library profession to re-think and to think systematically many of its problems. May God grant this Committee a long future of useful work and service to Mother India.

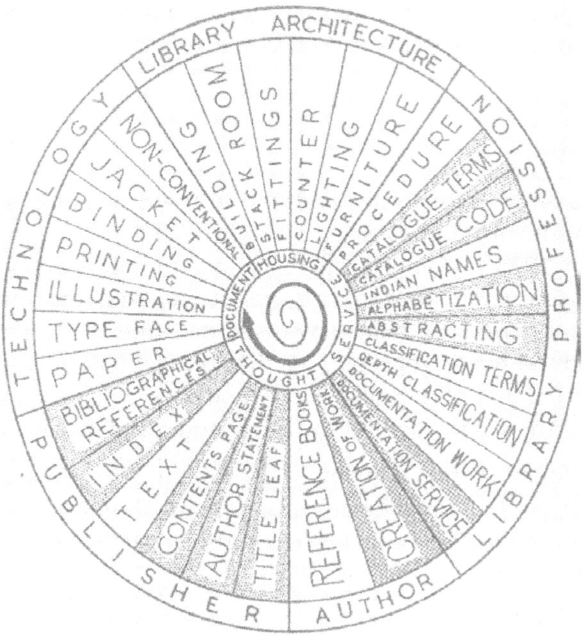

Subjects for which Indian Standards, have either been Published or are in the Process of Preparation
Areas not Amenable to Standardization

★★★

Library Development in India

S. R. Ranganathan

Abstract

Gives a picture of the fully developed library personality of India. At present, the school library system is under developed, college library system is not giving much service, but university libraries are developing fast. Development of public library system began in Madras and Andhra Pradesh from 1949. Though each district has its library system, implementing of the Library Act is being impeded. Bombay has made a new experiment. In the other States, library projects have begun to work in the Second Five Year Plan. Development of business libraries is just beginning. Systematic documentation service is being attempted by the INSDOC and the Libraries of the Ministries of Labour and Law.

0. SECTORS OF LIBRARY DEVELOPMENT

The library development of India will be reviewed in this paper in three broad sectors. These are:

1. Academic Library System, consisting of School, College and University Libraries;
2. Public Library System, consisting of District Library Systems, State Central Libraries and National Central Library; and
3. Business Library System, consisting of commercial Libraries, Industrial Libraries and Government Departmental Libraries.

This paper does not deal with other kinds of libraries, such as manuscript libraries, archival libraries, and libraries for the blind.

Reprinted with permission from Library Herald, 1(3), pp. 175-186, 1958.

0.1. Library Personality of India

In my *Library tour, 1948: Europe and America* (1949) giving an account of the impressions and reflections produced in me when I was a guest of the British Council. I concluded with a picture of the full library personality of India which, I wished, should be developed by 1960. This picture has been worked out in detail, on the basis of the census of 1941, in my *Library development plan: Thirty-year programme for India* (1950). The theoretical foundations of this development plan are applicable even today. The only matter in which the picture in that book should be brought up-to-date is in respect of the present political map of India and the present census figures. The full picture of the library personality of India present the following features:-

Academic Library System

Elementary and Middle School Libraries	200,000
High School Libraries	5,000
College Libraries	1,000
University Libraries	40

Public Library System

Delivery Stations in rural areas	300,000
Librachines or Book Mobiles	20,000
Branch Libraries in towns and divisions	5,000
City Central Libraries	200
District Central Libraries	600
State Central Libraries	15
National Central Library	1

Business Library System

Commercial Libraries	100
Industrial Libraries	100
Government Departmental Libraries	200

1. ACADEMIC LIBRARY SYSTEM

1.1. School Libraries

School libraries form the weakest group in the Academic Library System. Many schools do not have libraries at all. There is little book fund in most libraries. My suggestion is as follows: There should be a District School Library as a wing of the District Library in each district. The District School Library should pool together the book funds of all the schools in the district. This library should send collections of books to the different schools and keep them exchanged periodically. In addition to this, each school library should also be allowed to have a basic permanent collection of books, maps, and reference books. This will make the school book fund of India go the longest way. The school librarian will have only reference service to do. For this, a person trained as a teacher and as a librarian should have charge of a school library.

1.2. College Libraries

Most of the colleges have some books and a place where these books are stacked. Few colleges have reading rooms attached to their libraries. The University Grants Commission will have to rectify this defect. It will also have to help the colleges to build an adequate text book library and make it available for use for long hours on all the days say from 7 a. m. to 10 p. m. Perhaps, the ultimately economic course will be to help the colleges to put up library buildings according to the latest functional design.

1.3. University Libraries

In the Academic Library System, the university libraries were the first to develop. Active libraries were established by some of the universities about thirty years ago. In the Second Five Year Plan, the University Grants Commission is providing considerable finance to strengthen the stock of reading materials. Some rationalisation is necessary in the utilisation of the grant in the most profitable way. The Commission is also helping the universities to erect the library buildings. Library architecture is somewhat new to India. The Commission should, therefore, help in the functional design of university library buildings. Since 1950 the renaissance of the country is reflected in the development of a considerable research activity in most of the universities. Therefore, the endeavour of the University Grants Commission to help the development of university and college libraries is of great value.

2. PUBLIC LIBRARY SYSTEM

2.1. Service Libraries

The Public Library System was hardly thought of till about 30 years ago. The Madras Library Association, founded in 1928, actively promoted library consciousness among the people for about 20 years. The Andhra Pradesh Library Association and the Kerala Library Association also worked in the same direction. This led to the enactment of the first Public Library Act in India *viz* the Madras Public Libraries Act of 1948. This Act implied a new experiment in public library organization. It brings the cities as well as the rural areas of a district under a single District Library Authority. This was the result of certain difficulties in providing for library rates under the Act. However, this is incidentally an experiment worth pursuing. All the districts have now formed their Central Libraries. Many have also established branches. They are in the eve of reaching villages and hamlets through librachines. It has been found from experience that the proceeds from the library rate and the matching ground from the Government can provide satisfactory library service only for about one-third of a district. To cover the entire district, the library rate should be trebled. But the tax pattern in the country is now such that a local body cannot increase the rates. This is a serious situation to be considered. It occurs to me that the present tax-pattern indicates that:

1. The library rate should not be increased;
2. The grant from the state Government should be twice the proceeds of the library rate;
3. The combined proceeds of the library rate and the grant from the State Government should be used only for recurring expenditure on staff, purchase of current books, and up-keep; and
4. The grant from the central Government should meet all the capital expenditure for buildings, fittings, furniture; librachines, and initial stock of books.

The amount allotted for the development to the Public Library System in the second Five Year Plan is not being properly used. I feel that not even a quarter of the sum reaches the people in the form of real service. This implies a great wastage. A sum of nearly two crores of rupees is subjected to this wastage. I very much wish that the Planning commission examines this wastage, takes proper advice, and plugs all the leakages. Roughly speaking, the wastage is traceable to:

1. The distant Delhi having too much control and direction;
2. The handing over the administration of this new form of social service to a century old, rigid educational bureaucracy which has no library sense as it is shown by its failure all these hundred years to provide libraries in the thousands of schools under its control; and
3. The library fund being canalised through several agencies in an unco-ordinated way, with the result that one locality is sought to be provided with libraries independently by three or four agencies, whereas many localities go without any provision by any agency.

Moreover, whatever is being achieved will be short-lived, unless the library system is properly designed on the basis of comprehensive special library legislation, and the implementation of the Act is left to the competent and enthusiastic care of an independent Library Department in each state, which can be worked with single minded enthusiasm by well-trained and experienced members of the library profession. The book hunger of the people of renascent India is unmistakable. It is rapidly gaining in intensity to promote public opinion to spot out the present delays, callousness, and indifference and protest against the abuses current today in the library provision intended by the Library Act and by the Planning Commission. It will be wise to set the matters right, before the public is driven to the necessity of taking the matter into its own hands.

2.2. State Central Library

A State Central Library has been provided in Madras and Andhra Pradesh under the Library Act. In a few other States, it is functioning under some administrative measure. But no, where has the State Central Library been allowed hitherto to discharge all its necessary and legitimate functions. They are being strangled by the red tape being unwound ceaselessly by the Department of Education which does not have and cannot have a proper library sense. It is trivial administrative matters that loom large. They hold up every forward step. The larger social purpose of promoting library service to the public is prevented from being pursued. This cannot be rectified unless the State Librarian is a professional man of good personality, resourcefulness and drive, has direct access to the Government like any other head of department and is directly responsible to the Minister for Education in each state. If this is done, he will develop the copy-right collection along proper lines: he will bring out the periodical State Bibliography in the most up-to-date and helpful styles; he will be able to effect 79% economy by giving centralised classification and cataloguing service; he will establish a vigorous interlibrary loan so that books are not collecting dust in shelf of some libraries, while the same books are needed for use by serious readers in some other locality; he will be of real help to each District Library Authority to energise the development of the district library system; he will be a real and useful guide for the District Library Committee naturally made of the common man in a democracy like ours; and indeed he will hasten the day when the library personality of India will be fully dowered and enabled to become a source of entertainment, information and inspiration to all the people of India, so that our public affairs are run in a key of much higher efficiency than now.

2.3. National Central Library

As far back as 1948, the Special Committee on the formation of the National Central Library appointed by the Government of India approved a scheme for the establishment of the National Central Library. At its meeting held on 7 April 1948, this Committee had only one substantial item on the agenda. To quote from its minutes *"The functions of the National Central Library were taken up for discussion on the basis of Dr. Ranganathan's memorandum, etc"*. The second meeting was held on 14 May 1948. Then also the only substantial item in the agenda was *"Consideration of Dr. Ranganathan's Memorandum on Building, Contact Libraries and Union Library Legislation"*. We are now in 1958. Two general elections have come and gone. We are still to see that any substantial step is taken. In 1949 the Vice-Chancellor of Delhi University had a misgiving that the whole Memorandum and the Draft Union Library Bill might be lost amidst the archives of the Ministry of Education. He, therefore, had the memorandum and the draft bill printed in the *Library development plan: Thirty-year programme for India* (1950). As he feared, the memorandum appears to have been lost or at least withheld from the Planning Commission and from committees and the authorities of high level, concerned with the subject. It is hoped that these authorities will find access at least to the above mentioned book published by the Delhi University and take positive steps along right lines to establish and develop the National Central Library without further delay.

3. BUSINESS LIBRARY SYSTEM

In regard to the development of the Business Library System, the Ministry for Natural Resources and Scientific Research has taken positive action. The Textile Research Institutes have been helped to develop a good library service. The Indian National Scientific Documentation Centre (INSDOC) has been established to publish documentation lists. The *Insdoc list* has been coming out regularly twice a month since 1954. Steps are also being taken to publish periodically a documentation list of India's output in the scientific field. These documentation aids will in due course help in the avoidance of wastage in country's research-potential by un-intended and unwanted repetition of one and the same piece of investigation. They will also enthuse the promising men of the younger generation to devote themselves whole-heartedly to scientific research, both in the fundamental and in the applied fields.

Among the Government Departmental Libraries, mention may be made of the valiant work being done by the Library of the Ministry of Labour & Employment in bringing out a monthly documentation list of articles appearing in periodicals in the field of labour and allied problems. The Ministry of Law also has started similar documentation work. It is hoped that the library of every other Ministry in the Centre and in the departments and the secretariats in the various State Governments will come forward to help the administration and the development of the country by similar documentation service.

In October last, the Ministry of Commerce and Industry held a seminar on productivity Drive. That seminar gave top priority for developing documentation work and documentation service as a necessary aid to increase the productivity not only in the industrial sphere but also in the sphere of the governmental administration. May the finding of the seminar prove to be a true index of the things to come in the development of India's library personality.

4. LIBRARY POLITY

Library science has thus to help school education, college education, research and education in university, social education, industrial research, commercial interest and work in government department. To conserve the national resources in general and in the literary sphere in particular, there should be a department at state-level to co-ordinate all forms of service and to centralise many of the impersonal routine and technical operations in each State. At the head of this department, should be the State Librarian. He should be an experienced member of the library profession with vision, drive and personality. He should be able to maintain a high tone in the service rendered in each library of the State, by advice persuasion and inspiration. But unfortunately, a wrong tradition has been developing in this country during the last few years. Library organisation and department are set up as if social education were the only or the chief province of the library service in the State. In this matter the Union Ministry of Education has been systematically giving a wrong lead. The implementation of the Madras Library Act also put the development of library service on wrong rails. This has been most unfortunate. The Department of Education uses all kinds of specious arguments to protect what it feels to be a vested interest of its own.

5. AN APPEAL TO THE MINISTER

The above-mentioned trend is strangling the development of library service and making the setup of library service a ritual rather than a reality. Huge sums are now being wasted on jeeps and petty red-tape work by the persons appointed to run the library show. The members of the profession are shoved into the lower most ranks. No initiative is given to them to render reference service, to organise library extension work and to build up book collection in intimate relation to the needs of the clientele.

In other words the money voted for libraries does not reach the public in the form of actual library service even to the extent of 30 n. p. in the rupee. This situation should be corrected immediately. It is only Ministers that can take a whole view of situation. They should rise above the shackles and the misdirections showered on them by the bureaucracy. They should seek the help of enlightened and experienced librarians who are known to have a proper grasp of the way in which library service should be organised and safe to reach each citizen in the true measure of his needs.

★★★

Intellectual Problems and Equipment Consideration in the Design of New Systems

S. R. Ranganathan

Abstract

Describes the ideas forged by Dr. Ranganathan at the International Conference on Scientific Information held at Washington from 10-21 November 1958, which he attended as a Panel-Member of Area 5-Organisation of Information for Storage and Retrospective Search. Analyses six levels of writing for six levels of audience in terms of intellectual scale. Enumerates the field of documentation. Brings out the limitation and versatility of machinery in terms of various documents. Explains data-documents and knowledge-documents. States the approach of depth classification, the role of connecting symbols, and the exhaustive facet-analysis based on the concept of Round and Level. Evaluates postulational approach to classification and its implication on the notation of CC and UDC. Formulates a list of problems to be worked for future and suggests the establishment of a research team to work on those problems.

0. INTRODUCTION

My remarks have been prompted by two factors. These are: 1 A conflict in documentation implied in some of the papers, particularly in Area 1, the opening address on Sunday night, and the discussion during the last two days; and 2 the fourteen papers – 9 in Area 5 and 5 in other Areas – dealing directly or

Reprinted with permission from Library Herald, 2(3), pp. 199-214, 1959.

indirectly with the Facet Analysis and the Chain Procedure being developed in India for several years.

1. CONFLICT IN DOCUMENTATION

To see clearly the intellectual problems of Area 5, it is necessary to resolve this conflict. The conflict in documentation is the old, old conflict of Aristocracy *vs* Democracy. It is not here the aristocracy of birth, which is gone; nor is it the aristocracy of wealth, which has begun to go; it is not even the aristocracy of intellect, which will never die and which should never die.

1.1. Example

A friend of an Indian author of the seventh century said to him, "your recent work is too difficult for many." The response of the author was to add a new sentence at the very beginning of the preface. What was the new sentence? "Prayer goes to God that this work should not get into the hands of the dull many."

1.2. Short Paper in Epigrams

The scientific aristocrats to-day are worried over long papers. They would prefer short papers in epigrams. The fewer the epigrams, the better. According to an Indian tradition, maximum effectiveness in communication is reached at the limiting point where "the eloquence of silence" is the medium. If this ideal could be reached, the service of scientific information will be like snakes in Iceland. Perhaps such a communication may prevail in the world of men like gods, created by H.G. Wells. But will such a communication succeed in the field of science in the mundane intellectual world?

1.3. Repetition of Paper

Another trouble clogging the machine of storage and retrieval is the repetition of papers. The languages of the world are many.

There is, therefore, inevitable repetition in many languages. There does not appear to be much allergy to this kind of repetition, though my friend Prof. Kotani wished for a single world-language for all scientists. Our best wishes to that wish of Prof. Kotani.

1.4. Retelling in One Language

A more wide-spread, a version seems to be against the same idea being embodied in several documents in the same language. To ease the impending crisis caused by this factor in scientific information, it is suggested that there should be a ban on such retelling. But, it must be remembered that retelling in several organs is necessary, since, in many cases a single organ does not circulate it, to all. Apart from this, banning of retelling in varying styles and standards may not prove malefic, if all such re-telling stems from egotism. But it is not so. We have, therefore, to ask, "Are there valid reasons for such retelling?" The answer to this question will resolve this conflict. Here is one approach to valid reasons.

2. LEVELS OF AUDIENCE AND OF WRITING

We can recognise six levels of audience in terms of intellectual scale; and we, therefore, want the exposition of many of the ideas in six levels of writing.

2.1. Seminal Writing

There are men of creative genius-very few, of course. These are the few that generate really new ideas. These are self-centres of illumination. Their creation is spontaneous. Their writing is elusive. It scintillates. It has a message. The message is often found between lines and between words. Its implication has endless layers. Whatever mechanical abstracting may achieve some day, this class of writing will be beyond its reach. It is only a few top intellectuals that can profit from it. It belongs to level 1.

2.2. Research-Writing

Next in order come the top-scintiles among the intellectuals. They feel out by their laborious research layer after layer of the implications. Their work belongs to the fundamental sciences. They create new knowledge. For this, they need to feed on the knowledge created by their peers. If the peers are few and live near one another, they commune in person; whole-man-communes with the whole-man; and the benefit is full. But these conditions are not satisfied to-day when new life has burst forth in all sections of humanity - be it Asia, Africa, Europe, America, or Australia. If whole fruit is not available, we use its essence as a second best. If whole milk is not available, we use milk powder, as second best. So also, if whole man is not available, we have to use his writing as second best. And so, these top-intellectuals write. Their writings are too terse except to themselves. These belong to level 2.

2.3. Fact-Writing

Next in order come the next in the intellectual scale. They apply the knowledge evolved in levels 1 and 2. Few can stay long in level 1; not, even in level 2. They have to step down to level 3. They are many who belong essentially to level 3. Their application is turned on the production of new commodities, new services, and even new materials. Their writings abound in date, tables diagrams, and reports. These belong to level 3.

2.4. News-Writing

The population-pressure to-day is more than what can be supported by natural and near-natural commodities. These have to be supplemented by artificial commodities processed out of unconsumable raw-materials. This accounts for the enormous research activity to-day and the attempt to organise it. The research-potential of the world has to be commend. So, this research in parallel should be replaced by research-in-series. For this, every worker has to be promptly alerted in order to avoid unnecessary and unintended multiplication of effort on what is being newly achieved elsewhere. This calls for brief prior version of achievements. The cynic may attribute it to a vulgar race in priority. But it impiles a deep social purpose. This writing belongs to level 4.

2.5. Salesmanship-Writing

Then come the needs of common man. But new knowledge and new facts should be socialised. This is the insistence of democracy. For this wide dissemination, the essence of the writings of levels 1, 2, and 3 have to be dressed in attractive form and re-told. Gamot's books are examples. Prof. Hardy's inaugural address in Oxford on Wering's Problem is another example. Sir C. V. Raman often achieves great success even in this level. This writing belongs to level 5.

2.6. Elementary-Writing

Lastly come the needs of the teenagers in the physiological and in the psychological sense. Part of the matter of the other levels has again to be retold, in an elementary form. This belongs to level 6.

3. FIELD OF DOCUMENTATION

No whole librarian, who has his responsibility to persons in all levels, will agree to the stopping of documents in levels 4, 5, and 6. But the documentalist in the librarian will resolve the conflict in documentation by, restricting it to documents of levels 1, 2, and 3. This means selective storage.

3.1. Neglected Sector

This conference speaks of storage and retrieval. But little thought has been turned on the selection and rejection of documents at the stage of storing. Why? Is it because there is an overshadowing by the spirit of machine selection and rejection of documents? On the basis of the levels to which they belong, demand judgement. Machinery may externalise our memory.

They may recall what is stored. But they cannot exercise judgments of value, of style, of flair, a standard, or of any other intelligible quality of a document. Because the machine cannot do this it has mesmorised us from looking at this problem and facing it? Let us state explicitly that, this conference is on documents of levels 1, 2, and 3 only.

3.2. Wrong Delegation To Machine

At this stage, I wish to go back for a minute to all writings of level 1 and to most writing of level 2. The most frequently occurring word does not necessarily carry the focal idea. If Machine Abstraction works on the negative of this statement as a hypothesis, let us apply the telling phraseology. Let us not, delegate to the machine the work of abstracting documents of level 1 or perhaps even documents of level 2, where new seminal or fundamental knowledge is embodied, the abstracting should be the sole prerogative of the living man and not of a robber. This does not imply that we have nothing to get out of the machine.

4. DATA-DOCUMENTS

Documents of level 3 are not amenable to be handled by machinery. Here are the data. They are largely commutative and associative. Therefore, the problem of storage needs only a preliminary Facet-Analysis. It does not require Facet-Synthesis either in the level of class numbers or in that encoding or in that of input for storage. In other words, there is no need to arrange the facets consistently in a preferred sequence.

4.1. Versatility of Machinery

The machine can be more versatile than man in correlating different data. For example, it can bring out the names of entities which satisfy several data in co-existance. This service is essential in technology and in most, applied fields.

4.2. Data-Specialist

The wing of the library profession which picks out stones, and correlates data, is the wing of Data-Specialist. Reray and myself wrote in 1951 in detail about him in 1951 in the *Journal of documentation.* He has not only to store the data picked out from time to time but also to weed out from the store all out-moded data, as and when he finds more up-to-date ones to substitute in their place. This weeding out is a continuous work for the data-specialist. For data and facts are ephemeral and impermanent, whereas knowledge is more lasting and some may even be permanent.

5. KNOWLEDGE-DOCUMENTS

In a document, communicating knowledge, as distinct from data and facts, we reach a deeper level. We find a longer span of life. We find that classification alone does not reveal all its import. Class Number needs to be supplemented by an abstract. But the class number, the feature headings of the hierarchy of class derived by Chain Procedure from class number, and the abstract should work holistically. The abstract can then be brief and yet do its best. The printed volumes of *British National Bibliography* form a large-scale demonstration of the powerfulness of my Chain Procedure, not only in establishing feature-headings in the classified part of a documentation list, but also in providing headings for the subject index.

5.1. Non-Commutative

Again, in a knowledge-document, the facets are non-commutative and non-associative. The sequence of facets is determined by what is helpful for the majority of readers. This does not imply any blind resistance to the demand of a minority - who may be a permanent majority in a specialised library or a temporary majority during a short stretch of time in a general library. In the democracy of the library, the Second Law of Library Science is the custodian of the rights of minority-permanent or temporary. It finds classification in an impasse. It involves the aid of the catalogue built on the basis of the Chain Procedure or the grouping of books belonging to several class numbers under the vigilance of the Collection Number for a special class of readers. This control is called the Principle of Parallel Movement and is described in my *Library administration*, ed. 2 (1959), chap.6 We have to respect the denial of Commutative Law in order to avoid homonyms and synonyms in class numbers. These will produce noise and vitiate the efficiency of retrieval. The Laws of Library Science, therefore, tell the tools-Classification and Cataloguing, "Work in harmony. Don't compete with each other. Do what you can do best."

5.2. Connecting Symbols

The notational device to respect the denial of Commutative Law by knowledge-document is the use of connecting symbols. These too should be encoded and put into the machinery if machine-search is employed. Perhaps the machine can negotiate the connecting symbols directly or indirectly.

5.3. Depth Classification

It is not macro-thought embodied in whole books or whole periodicals that form the essence of service to workers in level 2. It is the minute micro-thought embodied in a few paragraphs of a book or in an article that is sought. Usually, such a micro-thought presents more facets than macro-thought. For example, "Agriculture of wheat" has only two facets - the basic facet "Agriculture" and the isolate facet "wheat". But "Leaf-varies of wheat and spraying of chemicals from aeroplane in the coastal areas of South England during the wet, summer months in the present decade" presents 14 facets-*viz.* Agriculture, Wheat, Leaf, Disease, Vinus, Cure, Chemicals, Spraying, Aeroplane, South England, Coast Districts, Present Decade, Wet and Summer. Arranging the facets in this sequence is found in practice to arrange the documents and their entries so as to be helpful for the browsing of readers and for economic retrieval. Depth Classification takes care of all the 14 facets and does not overlook any of them. This deep and exhaustive facet analysis has necessitated the introduction of the concepts of Rounds and Levels.

5.4. Documentalists

The wing of the library profession which analyses the thought of a document into all its relevant facets, determines the helpful sequence of the facets, assigns class numbers accordingly and prepares the documentation list - its classified part as well as its alphabetical part-depends on the co-extensiveness of the class number of each document and on the use of the Chain Procedure which in its turn demands that the Class Number should be expressive of all the relevant facets.

6. INTELLECTUAL PROBLEMS

We can now have a closer view of the intellectual problems forming the subject of Area 5. The analysis into relevant facets and the arrangement of the facets are intellectual problems. In my terminology, they belong to the idea plane - neither to the verbal plane nor to the notational plane. What the idea decides, the notation should implement. The notational system should have sufficient versatility to do so. The decision in the idea plane ad hoc for each document is tantalising. Nightmare is often the result. For the number of possible sequences of the facets, out of which one and only one is to be chosen consistently, is very large. It is 120 for 5 facets, 720 for 6 facets, several millions for 10 facets and so on. We know how steep the gamma function is. The probability for inconsistency is very great if we decide their sequence ad hoc in each case. Inconsistency will lead to chaos.

6.1. Work In India

It is here that work pursued in India during the last two decades has given some relief. Our British colleagues were the first to recognise its value. The first step was to separate out work in the idea, verbal, and notational planes. During the last two years, further relief has been obtained by basing the work in each of the planes on an independent set of postulates.

6.2. Postulational Approach

This postulation approach to classification not only gives considerable relief to the classifier. It also gives relief in teaching. With this approach practical depth classification is learnt by a freshman in about a month or two without any dose of the theory of classification. The theory, so much needed to meet unexpected contingencies and to improve the classification system, is learnt, later after considerable experience in practice is gained. Very much like learning to swim before learning theory of swimming. Indeed classification is like swimming in the deep expanse of the universe of knowledge.

6.3. Postulates

There is one set of 10 postulates on which analysis in the idea plane is based. There is another set of postulates in the idea plane on the basis of which the sequence of the facets is determined uniquely. These postulates are virtually common to all the existing schemes of classification. These are the Universal Decimal Classification and the Colon Classification. The notational system of UDC and CC are equally able to implement the results of the work in the idea plane, with the aid of a small set of postulates, which are different for the two.

6.4. CC and UDC

The CC notation is stouter than the UDC notation. It is also more expressive. This is due to CC being based on the facet idea from its very core whereas UDC has been allowed to put on only a veneer of facet idea on DC core which is rigid and monolithic. It has been frequently suggested by me that this fault of UDC can be and should be removed. The CC notation uses about 70 distinct primary digits. At the Dorking Conference, in 1957, Mr. Fairthorne assured me that the machine can negotiate so many digits.

7. WORK FOR THE FUTURE

It is possible to give a small list of the work to be done in the immediate future in respect of the intellectual problems envisaged in Area 5.

1. The second set of postulates in the idea plane, governing the sequence of facets should be increased so as to meet the situations in areas like organic chemistry and social sciences.
2. Postulates should be formulated for the verbal plane.
3. The Postulates are based on the united experience gained on floor duty and on conjectures on the normal way of thinking - especially and the second set of postulates dealing with the sequence of the facets. Foskett's paper endorses the helpfulness of these postulates. But, it is desirable to examine their helpfulness more extensively by empirical observation of readers' reaction. Perhaps they may also be examined a *priori* by psychologist - particularly by specialists in the psychology of thinking.

4. The level at which the breaking up of a composite idea into more fundamental constituent ideas should be investigated. This should be done jointly by psychologists and classifications.
5. It is being attempted to confine enumeration to a few schedules of seminal isolates; which are relatively stable and in terms of which all the dynamic and turbulent formations in the upper expressed layers can be formulated. This is at the very basis of the postulation approach to classification.
6. It is conjectual that all but the first facet of a basic subject can be looked after by six schedules of common isolates. Three of these schedules have been partially constructed. The schedules for second level space, the first and second levels of time have been published by me in the *Review of documentation*. The other three of these should be constructed.
7. One of them is the schedule of properties and values - geometrical, physical, chemical, biological properties; and ethical, aesthetic, educational, political, economic, social and legal values. It is conjectured that this schedule may include a few thousand isolates.
8. Another is the schedule of materials-raw materials, intermediate commodities of various removes and ultimate commodities - and services of various kind. It is conjectured that this schedule may include many, many thousands of isolates - say of the order of 10.
9. We have also to construct an exhaustive schedule of all kinds of action - physical, chemical, muscular, emotional, intellectual, and spiritual kinds of action.
10. It is also desirable to set up various models of abstract classifications, which have no meaning in their abstract form. They are like moulds. By pouring into them basic subjects and isolates, we make them meaningful, useful schemes. The greater the variety of abstract classifications we have in stock, the more prepared we will be to take up the challenge of the universe of knowledge at times of crisis, without a temporary break-down.

8. ORGANISATION

It is estimated that some of the items like those of constructed by schedules of common isolates, which are of a routine nature may require about 100 men-years. But we need not wait till the 100 men-years are completed to get results for application and use. On the other hand, we can draw from the results of investigation continuously after say one or two men-years of work have been put into the scheme. The scheme of work admits of being organised in that way. Even from the first year the benefits will begin to flow to make the selection, the storage, and the retrieval of knowledge and facts more expeditiously, more exhaustively and more pin-pointedly, than it is possible today.

May we hope that this Conference will lead to the establishment of a research-team on the intellectual problems of classification, on the construction of basic, seminal, and common isolates and on the psychological factors which lie behind this.

★★★

Revolutions in Library Science

S. R. Ranganathan

Abstract

Based on the address delivered by Dr. Ranganathan under the auspices of the Delhi Library Association on 21 August 1960 at the C P W D Hall, New Delhi. India shows great respect to the library profession. The first revolution in Library Science happened in USA. It led to new developments and collection of empirical data, the second revolution was based on these data; and it stems from the formulation of the Five Laws of Library Science. New modes of library service called by changes in society can be deduced from the Five Laws. The Spiral of Scientific Method has been formed in librarianship. Therefore we have now Library Science. This second revolution happened in India. We should look forward to a Third Revolution in the next, few decades.

1. RESPONSE TO LIBRARY SERVICE

Our society has been much more responsive than the societies in other countries to the usefulness of the library profession. It is a statement which I make deliberately. Many of our young librarians complain to me very often that no one cares for them. Probably the young men who get the first shock, attribute it to their belonging to the library profession and so they say that society is not sympathetic with them. In my own life, while comparing librarians in other countries, I have found that our people are on the whole more responsive to our profession than the public of other countries.

Reprinted with permission from Herald of Library Science, 3(4), pp. 237-248, 1961.

1.1. USA

Take for example the doyen of our profession, Melvil Dewey. He was so much criticised in his life time; he was so much misinterpreted in his life time; he was obliged to retire altogether from library work prematurely. He was criticised in many ways. He was criticised for having invented the classification system. You should read the criticism that appeared in the nineteenth century against the Decimal Classification.

They said, "This man wants to create a new mystery in this world. This man pretends to talk about what is not easy; he wants to create a market for himself." The society criticised him in this cynical way. But our society has not done like this. Take Bliss, for example, one of the most accredited thinkers in our profession. He wrote to me about 1935 or 1936, "You are a very lucky man; you have a society in your country which is so friendly with you". That is why you do this and you do that; you don't know my fate. I am opposed; I am hated; they hit me below the belt". He was twenty years older than me. We were often exchanging letters. When he wrote the above letter, I wrote him back, "Don't think that there is no commonness between us. Your reference that I am treated very well in my country is not correct. But I ignore all bad treatment". I began to give him the *Gita* advice. "Why don't you be detached ?" I wrote back in this way, as I did not then know that he was older than me. Otherwise I would not have written like this. He wrote to me back, "That is the advantage of having been born in India. We say that your country's people are miserable. You do not have proper food; you do not have shelter; but you keep learning to be happy. On the other hand everything is in plenty in this country, but we are not happy".

1.2. Germany

In 1955, when I was attending the General Library Conference in Berlin, my mind went back to twenties. I then had correspondence with Hoffman - the pioneer in People's Library Movement. So I inferred from faces of that audience that they could not appreciate my homage to him. And yet it was a Conference of the German librarians.

1.3. United Kingdom

You take the United Kingdom. Think of James Duff Brown. Hardly any librarian would have left his famous *Mannual of library economy* unread. He was much older than me. One of his contemporaries was Wyndham Hulme. I met him in 1948. He was then 92 years. I had the unique Joy of spending a day with him. He told me the story. He told me that Brown and he started thinking of library science, especially of the possibility of some young minds having enough opportunity in the development of librarianship. When they began to say, "We want to form an association to discuss our problems". It was so much ridiculed by their own people that they decided not to have a society with a name attached to it. Still the urge to pursue the subject was so great that they met once a week, and decided to call it Anonymous Society.

1.4. India

On the other hand, in our country whether government business people, or politicians, they are all much more in sympathy with the library profession. They seem to understand the value of our work much more in our own country. I have all along met with good understanding and good response. All these thoughts came to me when Sundaram asked me to speak and I decided to speak to you about two Revolutions in Library Science.

2. FIRST REVOLUTION

The first revolution occurred round about 1876. It occurred in the United States of America. The makers of that revolution consisted of two great names in our profession-Melvil Dewey and Charles Ammi Cutter. Till 1876, there had existed certainly collection of books. There had been scholars who actually used the books. But the librarian did not come into the picture. One of the scholars was asked to look after the library. But they were not named librarians. That was the position till 1876.

2.1. Dewey

Melvil Dewey, even when he was an under-graduate, according to the American tradition which is prevalent even today, wanted to keep earning and studying at the same time. In our country, we say from the fifth year onward until one gets a doctorate, one should be treated as a permanent and full-timed formal student. We should not do anything to earn even during our holidays. In the United States, you can go and attend classes two months in one year and can go on continuing for ten years and then get the Degree. It is not so in our country. Is there anyone who has seen a picture of Dewey? You can see it in the 14th edition of his book. You will see his face; what a determined face it is! He wanted to earn by doing library work even when he was a student. Even today, the American practice is to pay the student, to pay some cents, while doing that job, which Dewey did. When he discussed with the chief of his library the arranging of books according to subjects and said "Can we not number them by subjects and arrange them". When he said it, people ridiculed him. They asked him, "How will you put a new book ?" He said, "With the help of *decimal fraction notation*". When the first edition of *Decimal classification* was published, it was only 40 pages. He was ridiculed for its bulk. After some time this idea was recognised. But inspite of all this, he continued with his scheme. That is the First Revolution. That is only with regard to the arrangement of books. He was also the first man to think about open access; he was the first to attract people to visit library; Cutter was also there.

2.2. American Library Association

Dewey said the usual remarks, "Strength is in unity". His colleagues like Cutter and a few other people joined and formed the American Library Association (ALA). Dewey at 23 had the courage to say, "Ask library anything". I interpret it, "Ask librarian anything". I would ask you to call it a *mantra*. Call it a slogan. He coined that slogan. That started a series of approaches to the different aspects of library work which Dewey himself singled out. Quite a number of people joined him in thinking collectively and intensively. It went on for nearly half a century. What was their method of work? The revolution in plain words was to recognise the library as a social institution which had a definite purpose to serve. The words, "Ask library anything" means to give information to everyone in society. That was not the case before 1876. A librarian generally tried to give out some books but not information. We say good bye to books on passing the examination. Then we do not try to collect information; but we find them only to gossip instead.

2.3. Empirical Method

Dewey said that we should give information as much as possible. As a result everything in the library has had to be changed. About 20 or 30 years ago, librarians in America began to re-think the whole work of library and introduced many of the methods we are using. They devised these methods, as most pioneers will have to do, largely by empirical methods, by discoveries, by trial and error, by stepping up experience little by little. When sufficient experience was gained, one abstracts from the experience, some principles which contain the experience in a potential form. That is empirical method. Library science cannot be an exception in this method. It had to go through those empirical phases. Those Americans thereby increased the service, created new problems and new methods by trial and error, and created new principles. This process had been going on vigorously for about half-a-century. Most of this work was done in the United States.

2.3.1. United Kingdom and Sayers

It was only in the beginning of the present century that its impact was felt in United Kingdom. Even library service can be based on research and experience. That sense reached the librarians in Great Britain. For research, discovery, invention, it happened that few librarians in Great Britain were then university men. Organised universities said, "We are an exclusive class. How can you talk about research and discovery?" Those British librarians had to face this. Therefore, they dare not come out openly. British conservatism was there. They had to call the subject Librarianship. When the *Five Laws of library science* appeared in 1931, no scientist took notice of the term "Library Science". When my inaugural lectures at the Delhi University were published as *Preface to library science* (1948), the experience was different. For in that book, I said, "It gives us the highest joy, the joy of discovery, invention and research". Immediately there appeared a scientist with the remarks, "Do you have measuring instruments? Do you have a laboratory? Do you have test tubes? How can you call your subject a science ?" In spite of there being only a few sensitive souls, the British people have made a very great contribution. The name of one of them comes to my mind. It is Prof Sayers. He examined frequently what the Americans had done in an empirical manner. He described that classification was an artificial language. He continued his work. It made the revolution go forward. But no great step was taken to cause a new revolution.

2.3.1. USA and Library Resources Incorporated

When a subject is practised widely, depending on empirical methods, you have to spend a good deal of money. That is not forthcoming easily. No one puts forth money for this subject. But America has been an exception. Empirical tradition was kept alive in the United States and about five years ago an American firm put millions of dollars for library research and discovery. It created the "Library Resources Incorporated". This foundation has worked on my suggestion about "Pre-natal Cataloguing." The results came out a few months ago. The general impression produced is that it bristles with difficulties. That study has thrown a flood of light on some of the difficulties that have to be overcome. They have demonstrated what is possible and what is not possible. I am convinced that the matter, if pursued along right lines, will result in something useful. The American friends were able to carry forward the empirical research intensively much more than what could have been done elsewhere.

2.4. Limit to Empirical Method

Fifty years of empirical study and practice had collected sufficient data to carry on future work along new lines, to pursue library science along more productive, less costly lines, namely the lines admitting the method of education. Enough data had been collected by 1925. Many libraries had been established. In every subject when progress has been made along empirical lines, a stage is reached sooner or later when the number of empirical principles that we need to control the vast experience gained from day to day becomes too large for retention in one's memory.

Those who are trained in library science can bring out a nice piece of work on the subject. Scientific method has to take a whole view of the field of the universe of knowledge and the mode of the evolution of various subjects.

3. SECOND REVOLUTION

3.1. Spiral of Scientific Method

When that stage is reached, fundamental laws are formulated. Given the fundamental laws, you get certain results by deduction. Then you try to test them by experience. Occasionally, we arrive at new experiences contradicting the deductions from the fundamental laws. In scientific method it is called a crisis. Then a new interpretation is given to terms in the fundamental laws. If it is proving inadequate, a new set of fundamental laws is formulated. This is continued again and again. This is the *Spiral of scientific method.*

3.2. India's Contribution

The Second Revolution came in our subject nearly half a centuary after the first revolution. Our subject became a science as a result. Science should be based on fundamental laws. This happened to our subject about thirty years ago. Five Laws of Library Science were announced in the course of lectures in the University of Madras in 1928. It has led to theoretical research. The implications of the Five laws were not first easily seen. After the Second World War, the position has changed. The Five Laws have given a lead in the pursuit of library science. This is Second Revolution.

3.3. Response to Changes in Social Factors

It is up to you to carry forward this revolution. The essence of its message was arrived at about 30 years ago. Library science is essentially a social science; and social science cannot be static. It must go on changing. In other words, conditions obtaining in library service change from generation to generation. We can deduce from the Five Laws many new canons and principles to meet those changes. Society is changing rapidly. The Second World War brought about vast changes. A new outlook in political and economic approaches has been noticed. There is a global change in the society. New forms of library service have to be given. And library technique has to be changed accordingly to meet the demands of new service.

The great change that has come and which has convinced us now was not recognised widely even by librarians before the World War. Instead of calling the practitioners of the new service, librarians, they called them information retrievers, documentalists and so on. But those narrow minded librarians were oblivious of the incidence of the Second Revolution. But a few of us recognised the Second Revolution. We gave it a shape, a basis, and a meaning. We see as plainly as day light that the practitioners of the new service are only fulfilling the new demands of the Five Laws of library Science - the demands they make to meet the new needs of the changed society.

I wish librarians write such a history of library science. They can straightway go into the subject. History in this evolutionery and evaluating sense has appeared on every subject; but not yet in our subject.

4. THIRD REVOLUTION TO COME

Let us not imagine that this Second Revolution brought about by India in our own life-time is the last revolution in our subject. As society changes, we must also change the work in a library. After Fifty years from now, if you look back and see the present day library, you will notice that a Third Revolution has come in between. I wish India does not pass on the task of the Third Revolution to any other country. I wish India herself initiates the Third Revolution.

★★★

Documentation: A Vital Link in Communication (Documentations in many Lands 7)

S. R. Ranganathan
Delhi University Library, Delhi, India

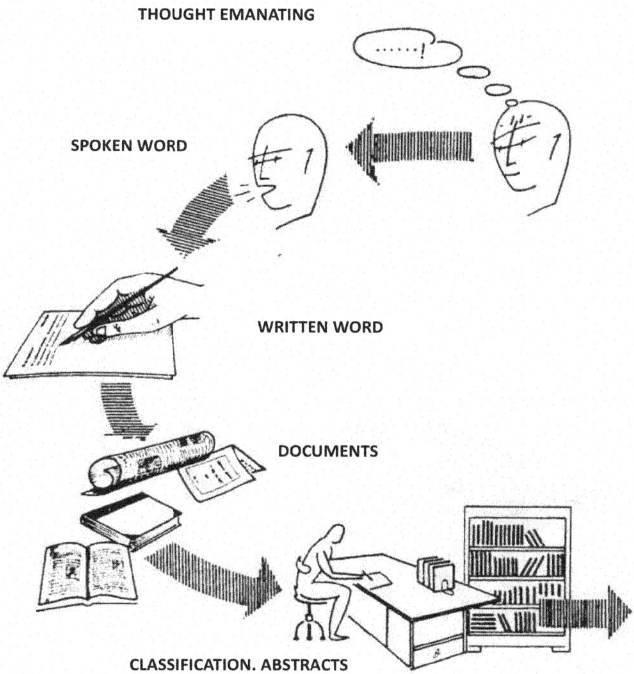

*Based on an exposition given in a Symposium on Defence Science Laboratories held at IRDE, Bangalore on 3 April 1962.

Reprinted with permission from Annals of Library Science, 9(4), pp. 287-294, 1962.

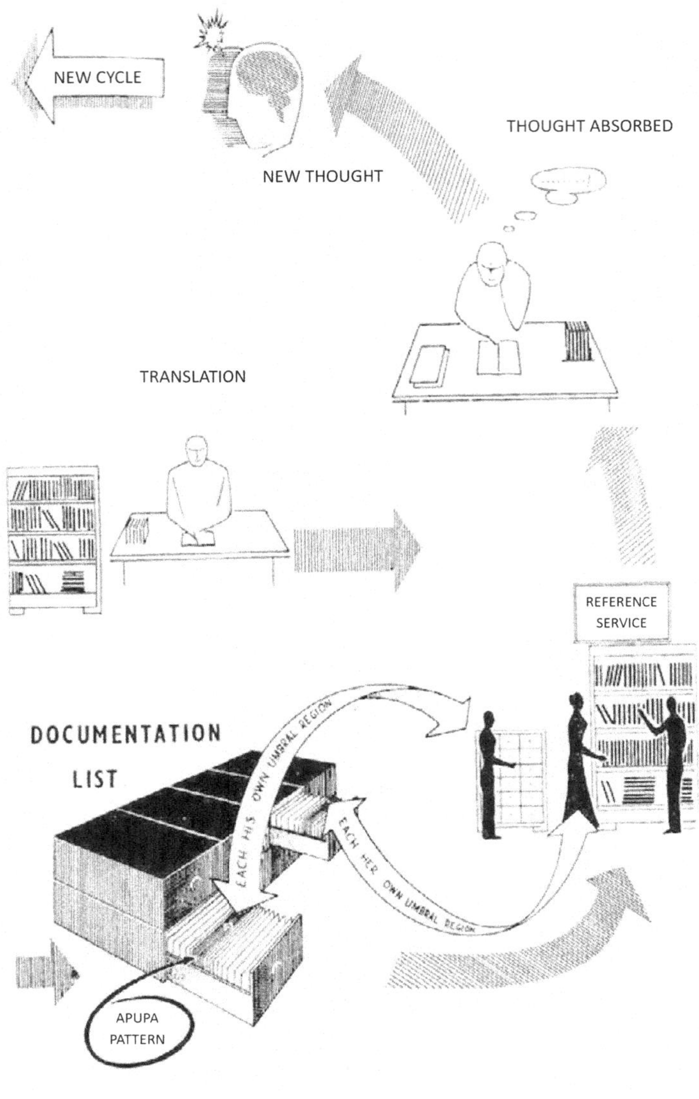
NEW CYCLE
NEW THOUGHT
THOUGHT ABSORBED
TRANSLATION
REFERENCE SERVICE
DOCUMENTATION
LIST
EACH HIS OWN UMBRAL REGION
EACH HER OWN UMBRAL REGION
APUPA PATTERN

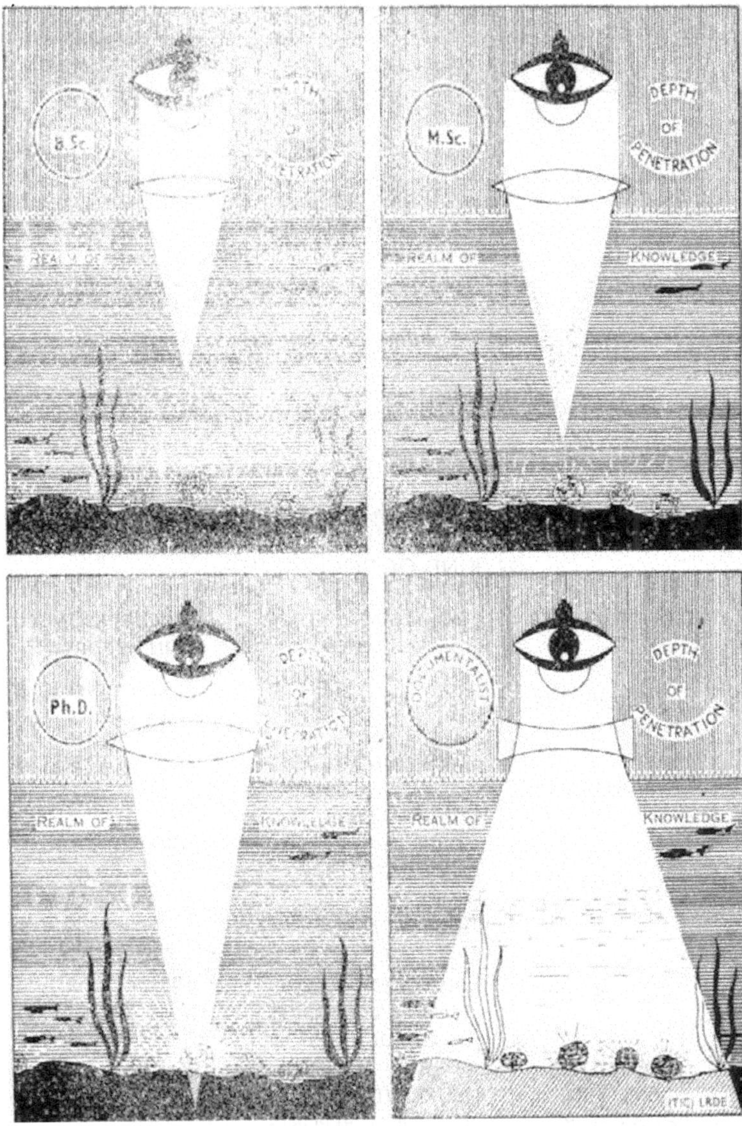
B.Sc.
M.Sc.
DEPTH OF PENETRATION
REALM OF
KNOWLEDGE
Ph.D.
REALM OF
KNOWLEDGE
DOCUMENTALIST
DEPTH OF PENETRATION
REALM OF
KNOWLEDGE
(TIC) LRDE

01 LEVELS OF SERVICE

LEVEL	CONSUMER	SERVICE PERSONNEL
SURFACE LEVEL	GENERAL READER	REFERENCE LIBRARIAN
MIDDLE LEVEL	TOP MANAGEMENT PRODUCTION ENGINEER	INFORMATION OFFICER
DEEP LEVEL	DEVELOPMENT FREE AND DIRECTED RESEARCH	DOCUMENTALIST

02 KIND OF DOCUMENTS

	KIND OF CONSUMER	DOMINANT KIND OF DOCUMENT	SERVICE PERSONNEL IN LIBRARY
1	GENERAL READER	BOOKS AND ARTICLES WRITTEN WITH FLAIR	REFERENCE LIBRARIAN
2	TOP-MANAGEMENT	BOOKS AND DIGESTS OF ARTICLES OF MANAGERIAL VALUE	INFORMATION OFFICER
3	SPECIALIST (1) (PRODUCTION)	CURRENT (APPLIED) ARTICLES DIGEST OF ARTICLES ON PRODUCTION ENGINEERING TRADE LISTS	
4	SPECIALIST (2) (DEVELOPMENT)	CURRENT ARTICLES TECHNICAL REPORTS TRADE LISTS	DOCUMENTALIST
5	SPECIALIST (3) DIRECTED RESEARCH FREE RESEARCH	CURRENT ARTICLES TECHNICAL REPORTS	

1 DOCUMENTALIST AND HIS REGION

1.1 Creation of thought	– Region of author – intellectual or intuitive
1.2 Expression of Thought	– Region of author – intellectual
1.3 Embodiment of Thought	– Region of Technician-Printer, Electronist etc.
1.4 Storage	– Region of Documentalist
1.5 Retrieval	– Region of Documentalist
1.6 Consumption	– Region of Specialist User

2 WHAT OF DOCUMENTATION

2.1 Service of documents with emphasis on nascent micro thought and specialist.	– (Law I of Library Science -Documents are for use)
2.2 Pin-pointed service	– (Law 2 – Every specialist his document)
2.3 Exhaustive service	– (Law 3 - Every document its specialist)
2.4 Expeditious service	– (Law 4 - Save the time of the specialist)
2.5 Inspite of the down-pour of micro documents and of the narrowing of the fields of research by specialists.	– (Law 5 - A library is a growing organism)

3 WHY OF DOCUMENTATION

3.1 Conservation of research potential

3.2 Canalisation of research in series instead of research in-parallel

3.3 Team-research as a follow-up of individual research by a person of exceptional intuition

3.4 Elimination of un - intended and unnecessary repetition of investigation

3.5 Social pressure in the form of Population Pressure and Defence Pressure.

4 HOW OF DOCUMENTATION WORK

4.1 Approximation 1	– Economy in browsing-Documentation list in anticipation
4.2 Approximation 2	– Economy in selection-Documentation list on demand
4.3 Approximation 3	– Economy in studying-Documentation list with abstracts and annotations
4.4 Approximation 4	– Economy in spotting out fallow regions in the universe of knowledge review type of documentation
4.5 Approximation 5	– Economy in crossing linguistic hurdle-Organisation of translation service and of translation bank.

5 WHERE OF DOCUMENTATION SERVICE

5.1 For Browsing	– Service in the periodicals reading room and in the stack room.
5.2 For selecting	– Service at the study-table of the specialist for nascent micro thought and in the stack room for books and old micro thought.
5.3 For studying	– Service at the study-table of the specialist.
5.4 Frequent us	– Supply of paper copy or micro-film copy for the personal file of the specialist.
5.5 Use of Translation	– Service at study-table or supply of copy for personal file as needed.

6 DOCUMENTATION BY WHOM

6.1 By specialist in subject field or

6.2 By specialist in documentation technique, or

6.3 By a two-faceted specialist with broad acquaintance with the highways and by-ways of subject-field and deep knowledge of documentation technique, or

6.4 By the gadget engineer and the hardware operator.

6.5 Translation by one with knowledge of the jargon of subject-field in both the languages.

7 DOCUMENTATION TECHNIQUE

7.1 For Document Storage	– Depth classification based on facet, zone, and phase analysis
7.2 For Document Retrieval	– Classified catalogue or machinery
7.3 For Document Replacement	– Call number
7.4 For highlighting fallow-spots in the universe of Knowledge	– Faceted or analytico-synthetic classification.
7.5 For finding out the needs of specialist enquirer	– Facet analysis of the enquiry.

8 DOCUMENTATION RESEARCH AND TRAINING

8.1 Training and routine research in the building of depth schedules in diverse subject fields.

8.2 Training and Fundamental research in depth classification.

8.3 Training and Fundamental research in chain procedure for subject headings.

8.4 Training and routine research in coding for machinery

8.5 Research in facet analysis of enquiries.

8.6 Research in general semantics and natural syntax.

9 DOCUMENTATION AREAS FOR STANDARDISATION

9.1 Organisation and presentation of article for learned periodical.

9.2 Presentation of the Proceedings of a Conference, Seminar, Colloquium.

9.3 Presentation of a book of reference and of a serial.

9.4 Presentation of administrative and progress reports.

9.5 Organisation of indexing, abstracting, and reviewing periodicals and serials.

9.6 Organisation of documentation centre-local, national and international.

★★★

Model Public Libraries Bill: an Evaluation Sponsored by the Union Ministry of Education

S. R. Ranganathan

Abstract

Examines the bill clause by clause. Indicates the undesirability of over-burdening Act with details. Shows that the bill does not show sufficient respect to the Viability Principle. Shows also that the organizational set-up can be less cumbersome than what the bill makes it.

1. INTRODUCTORY NOTE

In what follows, the clause number given at the top of each of the sections of this paper is the number of the clause in the Model Public Libraries Bill. Each section begins with the quotation of the clause of the bill evaluated. Then follows an evaluation of it.

2. CLAUSE 3 : LIBRARY FUNCTION OF THE GOVERNMENT

2.1. Clause 3(2)(a)

"3(2).— for carrying but the purposes of sub-section (1), the State Government may :

"(a) acquire for its public library system

(i) books published in the State;
(ii) books published in the regional language or languages;

Reprinted with permission from Library Science with a slant to Documentation, 1(1), pp.381-424, 1964.

(iii) books bearing on the State, its people and the regional language;
(iv) State Government publications;
(v) a representative collection of English books and books in other foreign languages;
(vi) a representative collection of books in Indian languages other than the regional languages for the use of linguistic minorities in the State."

2.1.1. Evaluation

1. This clause enumerates the classes of books that *may be acquired* by the State Government for establishing, maintaining, and developing an adequate library service in the State. Books will have to be selected and acquired for the different libraries in the State not by the Government but by the libraries themselves. Surely it could not be the intention of the Model Public Libraries Bill to take away this essential function from a library and vest it in the Government of the State. There is no justification for this clause. If it is retained, it will be harmful. It should be deleted.
2. Apart from this, the enumeration of the kinds of publications that may be acquired is unnecessary in the Act. Surely, a Library Act need not spell out the classes of books to be acquired by the library system. These are determined entirely by the measure of the local demand for them. On this ground also, clause 3(2)(a) should be deleted.
3. The retention of the clause will lead to some other difficulties. For, the enumeration of the classes of books made in the clause is not exhaustive. For example, while the acquisition of a representative collection of books in Indian languages, other than the regional languages, is mentioned, there is no provision for acquiring books in the English language or in Sanskrit published in any other State. For, category (i) imposes a restriction to "books published in the State". Again, it is difficult to see how it is proper for the Library Act to restrict

acquisition to "books bearing on the State, its people, and the regional language". Surely a library is a social institution for promoting universal understanding among the people of the world. It is therefore within the legitimate function of a library system to buy books bearing not only on the other Constituent States of India but also on any other country in the world. It should have been within the knowledge of the Drafting Committee that many of the countries are operating something on the lines of the Farmington Plan, according to which the library system of a country taken as a whole endeavours to have all worthwhile books published anywhere in the world and in any language of the world. The restriction imposed perhaps unintentionally by category (a) will be clipping the wings of development of the public library system so as to perform; its social function in full measure. For this reason also this category should be deleted.

2.2. Clause 3(2)(b)

"(b) offer in its-public library system an adequate book service and reference service to the people of the State."

2.2.1. Evaluation

1. According to this, the State Government may "offer in its public library system an adequate book service". Is it not a case of "shall offer"? How can there be a library without giving book service?
2. Secondly, the inclusion of "reference service" amounts to going into too great a detail in the Public Library Act. An Act should not do so. It is desirable to replace the words in (b) by

   "provide for a public library service in the State."

2.3. Clause 3(2)(c)

"(c) promote the use of books for the benefit of the people."

2.3.1. *Evaluation*

1. Among whom should the State Government promote the use of books? If the clause means "promote the use of books by the people", it should be stated clearly in that way. In other words, the phrase *"for the benefit of"* should be replaced by the word *"by"*.
2. Apart from this, the retention of the words "for the benefit of the people" would indirectly imply the exercise of censorship. The government has already sufficient power to censor undesirable books. But once the books have been passed by the censor, it is dangerous for anybody else be given legal powers to decide on what will be of benefit and what will not be of benefit to the people. The concept of "benefit" is determined by the social conditions prevailing in a community. Further, these social conditions are not static. As the social conditions change, the concept of "benefit" also will change. In these conditions to restrict the promotion of the use of books "for the benefit of the people" would throw an apple of discord. It will be open to any person to challenge the work done by, the library system for the promotion, of the use of books. On this ground also, the category (c) should be amended so as to read "promote the use of books, by the people."

2.4. Clause 3(2)(d)

"(d) establish and sponsor organisations and institutions with a view to promoting public interest and participation in the public library system;"

2.4.1. *Evaluation*

What is the kind of organisation or institution that the government can "establish . . . . . with a view to promoting public interest and participation in the public library system " ? It is only in a monolithic dictatorial system of government that the government will enter into such a work. In a democracy such as ours, these kinds of activities are best left to the care of voluntary organisations set up by the public, such as the Library Association. This category should be amended so as to read:

> "encourage the formation of and give aid to organisations promoting public interest in and acceptance of public library service".

2.5. Clause 3(2)(e)

> "(e) give adequate library service to all Government departments, and offices subordinate or attached to those departments;"

2.5.1. Evaluation

Does the government require legislative sanction "to give adequate library service to.... departments and offices"? Surely, the government is a business organisation. To secure its own efficiency, provision of library service for its employees is its inherent managerial right and duty not needing the sanction of legislation*.

This category should be deleted.

2.6. CLAUSE 3(2)(h)

> "(h) promote co-operation between the public libraries and cultural and educational institutions in the country;"

2.6.1. Evaluation

It is difficult to believe that the responsibility of promoting co-operation between the public libraries on the one hand and the cultural and educational institutions on the other should need provision in an Act of legislature. Normally, any library worth the name will co-operate in the manner suggested as a matter of course. For as a social institution, it is at once its inherent right and duty to do so. It is certainly superfluous to include this in a Library Act.

This category should be deleted.

2.7. CLAUSE 3(2)(i)

"(i) promote production and publication of useful literature;"

2.7.1. Evaluation

There is no doubt that the government should "promote production and publication of useful literature". But, the Library Act is not either the proper or the only legislation in which the government should take this power. The Universities Act, the Secondary Education Act, the Elementary Education Act, and any other Act bearing upon the promotion of the social well-being of the community will require for the fulfilment of their purpose the production and publication of books and periodicals and kindred reading materials. A government has always the inherent right, without the sanction of any legislation, to adopt any means for the production and publication of such reading materials and also vary their methods from time to time.

This category should be deleted.

2.8. Superfluity

1. If trivial details such as those in Clause 3(2) are mentioned in an Act, it will lead to the presumption that the details are exhaustive. Any other thing that a government may do on behalf of library service will appear to be foreign to the intentions of the Act.
2. Whenever details appear to be essential, they should be left to the Rules to be made under the Act. They should not be allowed to clutter the pages of the Act itself.

3. CLAUSE 4 : STATE LIBRARY AUTHORITY

3.1. Clause 4(I)(i)(e)

"4(1) The State Library Authority shall consist of

(i) the following ex-officio members:

(e) The chairmen of District Library Associations".

3.1.1. Evaluation

1. A State may have from 15 to 50 districts. This would mean swelling the size of the State Library Authority to a corresponding extent. The only function of the State Library Authority as laid down in cluase 4(2), is to advise the State Government in regard to development of library service in the State. It is presumed that district library association will be affiliated bodies or branches of the State Library Associations. The interest of this class of non-Governmental organisation can be sufficiently promoted by about two or three representatives of the State Library Association.
2. Such a slimming of the State Library Authority will make it a more compact and effective body than it would be otherwise. The cost of maintenance including travel expenses of the State Library Authority will be nearly reduced to about a half or a third of what it would be otherwise.
3. As it is proposed in the bill, the State Library Authority will be too unwieldy to be of much help. It will amount to making the top too heavy with too little of function. It is improper to swell bodies in such disproportionate way in the name of democracy.

3.2. Representation of Local Library Authority

It is desirable to add the following category in the cluase 4(l)(i).

(i) the chairman of the Local Library Authority of the capital city of the State.

(k) the chairman of the Local Library Authority of one city in the State, the cities being given representation by the Principle of Rotation.

(1) the chairman of the Local Library Authorities of two of the districts of the State, the districts being given representation by the Principle of Rotation.

Note:— If the number of districts exceeds twenty in a State, its Act may provide at the rate of one representative for each complete ten of the districts.

3.3. Clause 4(1)(ii)

> "(ii) a member of the State Legislative Assembly interested in library development to be nominated by the Speaker thereof;"

3.3.1. Evaluation

1. The provision of just one member to represent the State Legislature appears to be too meagre. It will be particularly so in a constituent state with two houses of legislature.
2. Nomination of the representative of the legislature by the Speaker does not appear to be happy. It should be thrown open to election by the Legislative Assembly or Legislative Council as the case may be.
3. It is suggested that clause 4(1)(ii) may be amended so as to read as follows:
   "(ii) (a) two members of the State Legislative Assembly elected from among themselves; and
   (b) one member of the State Legislative Council, if it exists, elected from among themselves."

4. CLAUSE 5 STANDING ADVISORY COMMITTEE

4.1. Clause 5(4)(i)

> "5(4)(i) to advise the State Library Directorate in all technical matters relating to library development and organization."

4.1.1. Evaluation

This Committee is, stipulated to be eight strong. Out of this, only two will belong to the profession of librarians. I wonder how this body is competent to advise the Director of Libraries on *technical matters*.

4.2. Clause 5(4)(ii)

"5(4) (ii) to make recommendations to the Authority on matters relating to the promotion and development of library service in the State."

4.2.1. Evaluation

According to Clause 4(2), the State Library Authority itself is only to advise government on these matters. What is the purpose served by providing a chain of advising bodies?

4.3. Fifth Wheel

The Standing Advisory Committee will be either a mere dummy or a delaying supernumerary. Coming in between the State Library Directorate below it and the State Library Authority above it, it has practically no positive function. As already stated, it is not competent to discharge one of the functions assigned to it. This kind of lengthening of the hierarchy of committees and authorities is not healthy. It will not contribute anything useful. By slimming down the State Library Authority as suggested in Sec C11 and the direct linking of the State Library Authority and the State Library Directorate will prove sufficient. It will also make for greater efficiency. It is therefore recommended that Clause 5 of the Bill be deleted.

5. STATE LIBRARY DIRECTORATE

5.1. Clauses 7(1) and 7(2)

"7(1) A State Library Directorate under the State Education Department shall constitute the Secretariat of the Authority."

"7(2) The Director of the State Library Directorate (hereinafter called the Director) shall be appointed by the Government and will have the rank of Joint/Deputy Director of Education."

5.1.1. Evaluation

Putting the State Library Directorate under the State Education Department is an anachronism. It will prove particularly harmful in the formative stage of the first one or two decades. The State Education Department is more than a century old. It has naturally become rigid in its outlook. Further, it is armed with Education Acts providing compulsory sections and positive sanctions at the disposal of the Director of Education. Therefore, unless he is exceptional in his human qualities, he cannot develop the attitude of persuasion and other non-coercive forms of public relation. The Library Act cannot have compulsory clauses. The Director of Libraries will have to work through persuasion. He must be daring enough to use all the legitimate methods of good public relation to make the people accept library service. His personality should not be corroded by the spirit of Bureaucracy. The Director of Libraries should have constant contact with the Minister for Education and the Education Secretariat. With the status of a Deputy Director of Education, he will be denied this opportunity. All this will stiffle the healthy development of library service in the State. The Department will suffer from inhibitions of all kinds. The working of the already existing Library Acts in the country under the control of the Director of Education has proved to the hilt the certainty of such mishaps occurring. Therefore, it is recommended.

1. That the words "under the State Education Department" be deleted from Clause 7(1); and
2. That the words "of Joint/Deputy Director of Education" be replaced by "and the privileges of the Head of a Department of the State."

5.2. Clause 7(4)(d) (iii)

"7(4) (d) (iii) he may absorb a subscription library into the public library system of the State;"

5.2.1. Evaluation

Surely, there should be a more elegant word than "absorb" to express the idea implied in this clause.

It may be amended to read as follows;

"He may sanction the taking over of a Subscription Library by the Local Library Authority of its area on such conditions as may be agreed upon between the Local Library Authority and the Subscription Library and approved by him."

6. CLAUSE 8 PUBLIC LIBRARY SYSTEM - THE SET-UP

6.1. Clause 8(B)

"8 The Public Library System in the State shall consist of:—

(B) the State Regional Libraries (only in bilingual States)."

6.1.1. Evaluation

Presumably this Bill was drafted just before 1960. Even at that time the only surviving bilingual State was Bombay. It too has since been bifurcated into two linguistic States. The following recommendation is therefore made:

Delete Clause 8(B).

6.2. Clause 8(C)

"C the District Library System, including Block, Anchal/ Panchayat/Rural and Subscription libraries."

6.2.1. Evaluation

The words, "including Block, Anchal/Panchayat/Rural and Subscription Libraries" should be deleted as they are redundant and are provided for elsewhere in the Bill, *viz* Clause 14(2).

7. CLAUSE 9 STATE CENTRAL LIBRARY

> "9 There shall be a State Central Library located in the State Capital."

7.1. Evaluation

This clause makes it obligatory that the State Central Library should be in the State Capital. What is the overwhelming reason that this should be made a statutory obligation? It is better to leave the location of the State Central Library to be decided by each State according to its particular conditions. In UP for example, it may be located in Allahabad, which is not the Capital of the State.

8. CLAUSE 10 BOOK STOCK OF THE STATE CENTRAL LIBRARY

8.1. Clause 10(1)

> "10(1) The stock of books in the State Central Library shall consist of books acquired through any legislation for the time being in force providing for compulsory acquisition of books published in the State, books acquired otherwise by purchase, exchange, gifts and bequest and its own publications."

8.1.1. Evaluation

This clause is partly redundant. For, some of the details mentioned in it are already included in the definition of 'Book' in Clause 2(1).

Clause 10 may be replaced by the following simple sentence;

> "The State Central Library shall acquire books, periodicals, and other kindred reading and kindred materials including tape-records, gramaphone records, and pictures."

9. CLAUSE 11 MODE OF BOOK ACQUISITION

9.1. Clause 11(1)

> "11(1) The Secretary, State Legislative Assembly, shall deliver to the State Librarian bound volumes of all debates and

proceedings of the Legislative Assembly and Legislative Council separately."

9.1.1. Evaluation

It is not quite necessary to provide in the Act itself for the donation of the debates and proceedings of the legislature to the State Central Library. It is better to leave such a detail to administrative action. Apart from this, it is not proper to throw on the Secretary of the Legislature the task of binding the volumes. Library binding has its own specification. The responsibility for binding should be vested only in the State Librarian.

9.2. Clause 11(3)

> "11(3) All books and other materials which have to be purchased by the State Librarian shall only be purchased on the advice of a Book-Selection Committee to be appointed by the Authority."

9.2.1. Evaluation

1. The provision, that, the State Librarian should purchase books only "on the advice of a Book Selection Committee to be appointed by the Authority" is an anachronism. This will also mean unbalanced selection without full relation to the needs of the clientele. The clause should really be amended to read as follows:-

> "The selection of books and all other reading materials for the State Central Library should be made by the State Librarian in accordance with the policy laid down by a Book Selection Committee to be appointed by the Authority and in consultation with an appropriate number of a panel of experts. The purchase should be made by the State Librarian. The Book Selection Committee shall review the books purchased, from time to time, in order to satisfy whether the policy is properly followed and to find out if there is any need for a change in policy."

2. It is doubtful whether Clause 11(3) is necessary at all even in this amended form. This is a detail which should be settled and, if necessary, revised from time to time by the Authority. It is bad to freeze the discretion of the Authority in this matter by the Act of legislature. Therefore, the recomrnendation is.

Delete Clause 11(3).

10. CLAUSE 12 DEPARTMENTS OF THE STATE CENTRAL LIBRARY

10.1. Clause 12(1)

> "12(1) The State Central Library shall have at least two departments, namely, the State Reference Library and the State Lending Library."

10.1.1. Distinction Without Difference

No purpose can be served by the legislation going into the details of the way in which the State Central Library should organize its stack room and its work. The overlapping in the distribution of functions between the wings proposed in the later subclauses by itself shows the unwisdom and impracticability of attempting such a distinction in the Act. For example, sub-clause (2)(j) asks the Reference Wing "to prepare and issue reports on the working of libraries, especially the public libraries in the State." But sub-clause (4) (b) asks the Lending Wing "to undertake supervision of all public libraries in the Capital". What is the purpose served by giving inspection to one Wing and reporting to another Wing? Again, sub-clause 2(g) asks the Reference Wing "to organise book exhibitions." And sub-cluase 4(c) asks the Lending Wing to arrange book exhibitions ". Clause 12(1) attempts to make a distinction without difference. It is recommended that

Clause 12(1) should be deleted.

10.2. Clause 12(2) (b)

"12(2)(b) to procure and maintain in a readily available manner all books, reports, especially the reports of the Houses of Parliament, the State Legislative Assembly and the State Legislative Council and Central and State Government reports together with their indexes as well as other reference materials needed for consultation;"

10.2.1. Evaluation

This is totally redundant. The level of pathos is reached when it spells out that the State Library should maintain "indexes" of Government reports.

10.3. Clause 12(2) (d)

"12(2)(d) to undertake bibliographical works, including special bibliographies for the use of scholars and research workers, and to prepare useful catalogues and bibliographies in the regional languages;"

10.3.1. Evaluation

The State Central Library is asked "to prepare useful catalogues... in the regional languages". In the first place, what is meant by "useful"? Is it possible to prepare useless catalogues? Secondly, does it mean that the State Central Library of any particular State should prepare catalogues in all the regional languages of the country ? Or, is the term "regional languages" a survival of the original draft made before the bifurcation of Bombay ? Again a State Central Library may have to prepare bibliographies of reading materials in any language whatever. It should, not be prevented by the Act from doing so.

The words "in the regional languages " at the end of the sub-cluase should be deleted.

10.4. Clause 12(2) (e)

"12(2)(e) to offer in co-operation with departmental and research libraries, book and bibliographical service to institutions, groups and individuals engaged in higher studies and research".

10.4.1. Evaluation

This sub-caluse makes the Reference Wing offer book and bibliographical service to institutions, groups, and individuals engaged in higher studies and research. To whom else can it give such a service? What is the purpose of spelling out this detail, which is the normal function of a library ?

10.5. Clause 12(2)(f)

"12(2)(f) to promote library-service for children;".

10.5.1. Evaluation

How can "promotion of library service for children" be regarded as a distinctive function of the Reference Wing of the State Central Library? Library- service to children should essentially be a matter for local libraries. The Director of Public Libraries should certainly promote it. But it cannot be the responsibility of the Reference Wing of the State Central Library.

Therefore Clause 12(2)(f) should be deleted.

10.6. Clause 12(3)

"12(3) The State Reference Library shall not lend books for use outside the premises of the Library."

10.6.1. Evaluation

let us read the above clause with the provision of "offer book and bibliographical service to institutions" found in Clause 12(2)(e). How can book service be given to institutions unless the books can be removed from the State Reference Library ?

10.7. Clause 12(4)(a)

"12(4) The function of the State Lending Library shall be

(a) to render home-lending service to residents of the State Capital."

10.7.1. Evaluation

It is certainly amazing and irrelevant to be put in an Act. Further, at the place of the State Central Library, there is bound to be a City Central Library and several City Branch Libraries. These local service libraries should share the resources of the State Central Library equally with the service libraries in the other cities and towns in the State and in the same way. In other words, the residents of the State Capital should draw their books only through their own local library. It is unnecessary to make the State Central Library rnaintain a circulation staff similar to that of local libraries and to duplicate the work of the public libraries. This would mean a waste, apart from other practical difficulties.

10.8. Clause 12(4) (c)

"12(4)(c) to Replenish from time to time the stocks of District Libraries;"

10.8.1. Evaluation

Does this mean outright transfer of the books ? If so, this is an extraordinary provision in an Act. Or, does it mean lending books to district libraries ?

10.9.1. Clause 12(4) (f)

"12(4)(f) to publicise its book-stock;"

10.9.1.1. Evaluation

To prescribe by an Act that a library should publicise its book stock is to reach the limit of triviality in any legislation.

The sub-clause 12(4)(f) should be deleted.

10.9.2. Clause 12(4)(g)

"12(4)(g) to publish library reports and literature,"

10.9.2.1. Evaluation

According to this, the Lending Wing should "publish library . . . lierature". This legal obligation on the part of the State Lending Library is unheard of. Nor can it be enforced.

10.9.3. Replacement of Clause 12

Clause 12 of the Model Public Libraries Bill should be deleted as it is. The departments of the State Central Library should be enumerated in an altogether different way such as copy-right department, department of library for the blind, bibliographical department, inter-library loan department, union catalogue department, and so on.

11. CLAUSE 13 STATE LIBRARIAN

11.1. Clause 13(3) (c)

"13(3)(c) The State Librarian shall advise the Authority on all technical matters."

11.1.1. Evaluation

According to this, the State Librarian has a duty to "advise the Authority on all technical matters Here, we must remember that Clause 5(4)(i) stipulates that the Standing Advisory Committee should advise the State Library Directorate in all technical matters. This is one of the results of listlessness of the maker of the Model Bill. Without any co-ordination, the Bill spells out details here, there, and everywhere in the Act — details which are not worth giving in a Statute.

11.2. 13(3)(e)

"13(3)(e) organise, conduct and supervise training courses for librarians of various categories."

11.2.1. Evaluation

If it is the duty of the State Librarian to "organize, conduct, and supervise training courses for librarians of various categories", do not universities have any part to play in this work ? Certainly they have. If so, no university giving a course for librarians will ever submit itself to supervision by the State Librarian. The Bill seems to be ignorant of either Library Science being a subject, of university standard or of our universties being autonomous statutory bodies.

12. CLAUSE 14 DISTRICT LIBRARY SYSTEM

12.1. Clause 14(1)

> "14(1) An integrated system, giving book-service to the residents of a district, especially in the rural area, shall constitute the District Library System."

12.1.1. Evaluation

It is totally unnecessary to insert the words "especially in the rural areas". In fact, the whole sub-clause serves no purpose. Clause 14(2) mentions the constituents of a District Library System. The very word 'system' means, that it is an integrated one. It is recommended that

> Clause 14(1) be deleted.

12.2. Clause 14(2)(2)

> "14(2)(2) Municipal/City/Town Library,"

12.2.1. Evaluation

1 It is reasonable and also usual to make the district library system responsible for library service to the rural parts and the towns in the districts with a population cluster below a stated figure such as 100,000. But the library System of a city with a population cluster of more than the stated

figure and that of the other areas in its district cannot go together with convenience. The vocation, the educational level, and even the literacy level of the people in a city will differ much from those in smaller towns and the rural areas. Accordingly the nature of the books and other reading and kindred materials needed by the readers will also be different, the kind of help to be given to them will also be different. Further, a city has usually better financial resources than the rest of its districts. In Madras, the City Library System was made part of the District Library System, virtually in order to rob Peter to pay Paul. The Education Minister himself wrote to me in 1948 that he had to take recourse to it as he could not at that time find a suitable basic tax in the rural areas on which a library surcharge could be levied. It is now 16 years since then that state of affairs existed in one State. Since then the tax pattern has changed enormously. The difficulty of finding a basis for library rate in non-city areas no longer exists in most of the States. Therefore, it is not necessary to imitate the outmoded provisions in the Madras Public Libraries Act of 1948 and merge the City Library System into the District Library System which is essentially rural in its character.

2 Further, it is not necessary to spell out the constituents of a District Library System in such details as are given in Clause 14(2). The nomenclature used for the different kinds of constituent libraries will not be permanent. It will change from time to time. It is desirable that an Act should use relatively more lasting terms to denote its intention. Clause 14(2) may therefore be amended so as to read as follows :

"14(2) A District Library, System shall consist of

1. District Central Library;
2. Town Branch Libraries;
3. Travelling Libraries to serve villages and hamlet ;

4. Book-Deposit Centres in villages and hamlet ; and
5. Such intra-district regional reservoir libraries as may become necessary from time to time for circulating reading materials to Town Branch Libraries and the Travelling Libraries, economically."

13. CLAUSE 15 FUNCTIONS OF A DISTRICT LIBRARY

13.1. Clause 15(1)(b)

"15(1) The functions of a District Library shall be as follows:

"(b) to give special reference service to the members of the Municipal Committee/Corporation of the town/city in which it is situated."

13.1.1. Evaluation

One is unable to understand the singling out of this class, of users of the library's collection. The members of the municipality are bound to get the reading materials needed for the discharge of their duties as members of the municipality, from the working library of the muncipality itself. If any service over and above what the municipality can give to them is necessary, no doubt will they seek the help of their local branch library of the District Library System. As City Fathers no doubt they will be given every consideration by the Branch Librarian. On the other hand, if they want service in their private capacity, they should naturally share whatever service the Branch Library can give to any resident of the town. Therefore, it is recommended that

Clause 15(l)(b) be deleted.

13.2. Clause 15(1)(e)

"15(1)(e) to feed Block Libraries with supply of suitable books."

13.2.1. Evaluation

It is not clear what the term "feed" implies. Does it mean outright transfer of books from time to time or only long-term loan ? Outright transfer will soon result in an unwieldy accumulation of unwanted and outmoded reading materials in the Block Libraries. The clause may be amended so as to read as follows:

> "to circulate books and other kindred reading materials to Block-Libraries."

14. CLAUSE 16 DISTRICT LIBRARY COMMITTEE

14.1. Clause 16(1)

> "16(1) There shall be a District Library Committee for each District Library System in the State which shall be constituted in accordance with such regulations as may be framed by the Authority."

14.1.1. Evaluation

This clause leaves the constitution, of a District Library Committee to regulations to be framed by the State Library Authority. It is strange that a Bill which mentions so many trivialities delegates this important constitutional problem to the care of subsidiary legislation instead of being provided for in the Statute itself.

14.2. 14.2.Clause 16(3)(b) & (1)

> "16(3) The functions of a District Library shall be as follows:
>
> "(b) to start branch libraries.
>
> "(1) to extend library-service in its area by setting up branch libraries, travelling libraries, deposit-centres and book-service by mail."

14.2.1. Evaluation

The starting and the setting up of Branch libraries is thus provided twice in this very clause. This is no doubt bad in drafting. Therefore it is recommended that

In Clause 16(3)(1) delete the words "branch libraries".

14.3. Clause 16(3)(d)

"16(3)(d) to employ in accordance with the regulations framed by the Authority, staff for the District Library;"

14.3.1. Evaluation

According to Clause 20(1), "The State Government shall create cadres for State Library employees similar to those of the employees of the State Education Department and lay down the qualifications and the other terms and conditions of service for those cadres." We should read Clause 16(3)(d) and Clause 20(1) together. If we do so, we see a certain conflict between the two clauses. While it is desirable that the Director of Libraries should informally consult the District Library Committee in respect of appointment and transfer of the staff of the District Library, it will lead to diarchy, full of friction, if the District Library Committee is empowered to employ its own staff. It would interfere with transfer of officers from one district to another. If such a transfer is denied, the substance of the benefit of having a library cadre for the State will be nullified. It is therefore recommended that

Clause 16(3)(d) be deleted.

14.4. Too Many Details

Clause 16(3) spells out far too many details - details which need not come into an Act, and details which are uneven in their potency. The sub-clauses of this section should be reduced to a few essential ones.

14.5. Clause 16(4)

"16(4) The District Library Committee shall meet as often as the Chairman thereof may decide to summon it, but preferably at least four times a year."

14.5.1. Evaluation

While Clause 16(1) leaves the very constitution of a District Library Committee out of the purview of the Act and relegates it to regulations to be framed by the State Library Authority, it implies far too much of unevenness when Clause 16(4) stipulates the minimum number of times the District Library Committee meets. Surely, either the constitution should be brought within the purview of the Act or the minimum number of meetings in a year should be left to the purview of regulations. It is preferable to bring both within the purview of the Act.

14.6. Clause 16(5)

This clause makes the District Library Committee a body corporate in the eyes of law. This fact reinforces the recommendation that the Act should take the responsibility to fix the constitution of a District Library Committee.

15. CLAUSE 17 CITY AND TOWN LIBRARY COMMITTEE

15.1. Clause 17(1)

"17(1) There shall be a City Library Committee for each city with a population of over a lakh, and a Town Library Committee for a Municipal town with a population not more than one lakh, constituted in accordance with such rules as may be framed by the District Library Committee concerned."

15.1.1. Evaluation

1. A town is invested with library powers. But it is not defined. Unless a minimum population is prescribed, a town will

not be a viable library unit. According to the present day experience, a population cluster with less than 1,00,000 population is not a viable library unit.

2. The formation of the Library Committee for a large town is too important a matter for it to be withdrawn from the purview of the Act. Strangely enough, it is withdrawn even from the purview of the State Library Authority. It is relegated to the purview of the District Library Committee concerned. This is not a happy situation. This is particularly bad since Clause 21(4) invests the City and Town Library Committees with financial powers to administer the Library Fund made of proceeds of cess and government grant.

15.2. Clause 17(2)

"17(2) The functions of a City or Town Library Committee shall, so, fair as may be, be the same as those of the District Library Committee within its jurisdiction."

15.2.1. Evaluation

1. The remarks in Sec Q11 get reinforced when read with clause 17(2) of the Bill. A City Library Committee is allowed to exercise powers and to discharge duties parallel to those of the District Library Committee.
2. The implication is that it can even administer its own library fund. In the establishment of branch libraries, conflict can arise between the will of the City Library. Authority and that of the District Library Authority concerned. The Act should avoid creating opportunity for conflicts so visible on the very surface.

16. CLAUSE 22 LIBRARY CESS

16.1. Clause 22(1)

"22(1) Every local body in a district shall levy in its area a library cess in the form of a surcharge on property-tax at such rate not being less than six naye paise nor more than . . ."

16.1.1. Evaluation

The sole basis for library cess is made the property tax. This is an anachronism in the new tax pattern prevailing in the country. There are now more elastic sources available such as octroi, profession tax, and basic revenue. It is not desirable to make the property-tax-payer carry the entire burden of the library cess;

16.2. Clause 22(2)

> "22(2) For the purposes of sub-section (1), property-tax on which the cess is to be levied shall, where it is not actually levied, be assumed to be levied at the rate of 20% of the rental value of the property ....."

16.2.1. Evaluation

This makes an extraordinary financial provision for a locality where no property tax is levied. It prescribes a cess on twenty per cent of the rental value of the property. This is surely a case of "the tail wagging the dog".

17. CLAUSE 21 PUBLIC LIBRARY SYSTEM FINANCE

17.1. Clauses 21(3)(1) & 21(4)(a)

> "21(3)(a) There shall be credited into a District Library Fund the amount transferred to it from the State Library Fund, the State contribution to the District Library Fund being in no case less than the total amount of library cess collected in the district."
>
> "21(4)(a) There shall be credited into a City, Town or Block Library Fund the amount raised as library cess within the limits of the City, Town or Block."

17.1.1. Evaluation

It is not obvious what part of the cess in a district will go to the District Library Committee, if each city, town or block will appropriate the cess collected in its area Perhaps none. The government is asked to give its grant to the District Library Fund, maintained by the District Library Committee. What is the destiny of this government grant? Is a city to depend entirely on its own library cess, unless the District Library Committee gives it a "special grant" ? The framing of the financial clauses is very bad and unrealistic.

17.2. Clause 21(1)

"21(1.) There shall be three types of library funds in the State:

(a) The State Library Fund.

(b) The District Library Fund.

(c) The City or Town or Block Library Fund."

17.2.1. Evaluation

1. the bad and the unrealistic quality of the financial clauses is traceable to a complete blindness to the Principle of Viability in respect of Library Fund and of the size of the minimum population, whose area alone can have a Library Fund of its own.
2. Surely, the State Library Fund is viable and it is also necessary.
3. A City Library Area is also viable and it should have a City Library Fund.
4. A District Library Area—consisting of the area of the district excluding the areas of the cities in it—is also viable and it is necessary to have a District Library Fund. Here it must be remembered that for purposes of viability of library organization and fund, a city is taken to be a population cluster of not less than 100,000 people.
5. A Town Library Fund will not be viable. It is not economical to provide a Town Library Fund. Let us take a typical town with a population of 25,000 as an example. Its house property tax may yield Rs 50,000 annually. A Library cess of six naye paise will yield an income of Rs 3,000 annually.

Even assuming that it gets an equal amount as a grant from government via the District Library Fund, its annual income will be only Rs 6,000. With this Rs 6,000, the town will have to buy the reading materials, pay the staff, maintain the library building, and incur binding and other contingent expenditure. The minimum staff that the library can have is one peon on Rs 80 p m and one librarian in the scale Rs 100-200, giving an average of Rs 150 p m. The annual salary of this minimum staff, including leave allowance, will be Rs 3,000 in round figures. The maintenance of the building or the house rent will require a minimum of Rs 700 per year. Binding and other contingent expenditure may require about Rs 300. Thus the balance available for buying reading materials will be only Rs 2,000. The Town Library will have to take some periodicals and perhaps some newspapers also. Allowing for this, the number of books that can be bought will be between 250 and 350. This is totally inadequate for a population of 25,000.

6. A Block Library Fund also will equally fail in viability in the present condition of the country. It may become viable after 20 or 30 years if the country develops normally.
7. In these circumstances, the district is the smallest viable unit for service to towns, villages, and hamlets.
8. As the provision in the Bill goes, the District Library Fund has only to receive the government grant and distribute it to the Town and Block Libraries after taking the necessary amount for its own expenses. All this is unnecessary.
9. On the other hand, if Town and Block Library Funds are not allowed, and the entire library cess of the district and the matching government grant are able to buy a sufficient number of books for circulation to the Town Branch Libraries and also to the villages and hamlets through Travelling Libraries. Instead of the books bought by a town from out of its own meagre library fund becoming a dead stock within a year or two, the entire stock of books in the district will

be kept ever in circulation and use. This way of pooling the resources of small non-viable areas into viable resources by a larger containing area is a recognised method of equalising and stepping up opportunities for development. In the sphere of Elementary and Secondary Education, the Union Ministry of Education is already taking steps to adopt this method. It is necessary and urgent in the sphere of library service,

10. Therefore, the following amendment is suggested to Clause 21.

    1. In sub-clause (1: delete sub-clause (c).
    2. Delete sub-clause (4).
    3. In sub-clause (3), insert at the proper place the words, "the amount raised as library cess within the library area of the district."

18. CLAUSE 23 POWER OF COMMITTEES TO BORROW

18.1. Clause 23(1)

"23(1) A Block or a Town Library Committee may borrow money.....with the approval of the District Library Committee."

18.1.1. Evaluation

a Block or a Town Library Committee is authorised to borrow with the approval of the District Library Committee alone. This is too big a financial matter to be exercised without the knowledge and approval of the Government.

18.2. Clause 23(2)

"23(2) A District or City Library Committee may borrow money ... with the approval of the Authority."

18.2.1 Evaluation

Even here, this important public finance matter cannot be made to depend, entirely on the approval of the State Library Authority. It must get the approval of the Finance Ministry of the Government. Public Loan requires both coordination and vigilance at the State Level in full measure and in some cases even of the Central Government in some measure.

19. CLAUSE 25 STATE LIBRARY ASSOCIATION: CO-OPERATING INSTITUTION

19.1. Clause 25(2)

> "25(2) The Director shall consult the State Library Association on all matters of importance relating to libraries and librarians in the State, and especially on all matters concerning library legislation, conditions of service of librarians, training of library workers and regulations concerning the book-trade."

19.1.1. Evaluation

1. it is a wholesome and desirable provision to make the Government Department and a non-governmental public body to work in unison.
2. However, it is not understood how a Library Act can give powers to the Director to make regulations concerning the book-trade. It is therefore recommended that,

In Clause 25(2), the words "regulations concerning the book-trade" be deleted.

20. CLAUSE 2 DEFINITIONS

20.1. Clause 2(1), (5)

> "2 In this Act, unless the context otherwise requites,
>
> (1) 'book' includes—
>
> (i) every volume, part of division of a volume, and pamphlet, in any language;

(ii) every sheet of music, map, chart or plan separately printed or lithographed;

(iii) newspapers, periodicals, and other such materials;

(5) 'reference service' means assistance from the library staff to the reader or user of the library to enable him to know, locate and consult books and other materials and to secure from such books and materials information relevant to his purpose."

20.1.1. Evaluation

It is not usual nor is it proper to include in the Definitions Clause of a Legislative Act definitions for terms such as 'Book Service' and particularly 'Reference Service'. Definition in an Act should not descend to this level of detail.

21. ERRORS OF OMISSION

21.1. National Economy

In a social service like library service, one of the essential functions of a State Library Directorate should be to promote the economic utilisation of the library fund and the library manpower of the State, by centralization of certain activities, co-ordination of certain kinds of work and responsibility, and such other methods as may become necessary. The Bill should include this explicitly in one of the clauses.

21.2. Relation to Registration of Books Act

The Press and Registration of Books Act came into force nearly a century ago. According to that Act, the Registrar of Books is in charge of the copyright collection. In some States, he is the Director of Public Instruction. In some others, he is the Translator to Government or some other officer. When a Public Libraries Act comes into force, the function of the Registrar is more fittingly exercised by the State Librarian. For this purpose, there should be a clause in the Public Libraries Bill indicating the amendments necessary to the Press and the Registration of Books Act in its application to the State concerned.

21.3. Local Development Plan

All the cities and districts will not be able to develop their library service abreast of one another or at the same rate. The pace and pattern of development may vary from area to area. It is not proper for the State Library Directorate to take the responsibility to work out the details of development for all areas. This is best done by local agencies - Local Library Authorities - with an intimate knowledge of local conditions. The function of the Directorate should be merely to see whether the plan proposed is reasonable and sufficient to carry out the intentions of the Act within a reasonable time and whether the financial implications are within practical limits. For this purpose, it is best to make each Local Library Authority to draft its own development plan. After it is finalised, gets the approval of the State Library Directorate, it must be made into a Local Library Order. This Order should form the blueprint and detailed drawings, so to speak, for the library development to conform to such modifications as maybe- come necessary in the light of its working.

21.4. Power to Appoint Committees

The District Library Authority and the City Library Authority should be empowered by the Act to appoint committees for advisory work or for the exercise of delegated powers. The clause empowering appointment of committees should prescribe what functions of the Local. Library Authority should not be delegated to a committee for example, passing the budget or the annual report.

21.5. Accounts and Audit

The Model Public Libraries Bill should provide clauses on the maintenance of accounts by the Local Library Authority, and getting them audited.

21.6. Utilisation of Existing Libraries

In many a State, it will be economical and appropriate to convert into the State Central Library an existing library, under the management of the government or of any other agency. A similar thing may also be possible in respect of the City and District Central Libraries. A Library Bill would have a clause making this possible. For, we are not beginning from scratch.

21.7. Co-operation

The Library Bill should also make provision for the collaboration of the State Central Library with the other libraries in the State and also with the State Central Libraries of the other States and with the National Central Library.

21.8. Supersession

By way of abundant caution, it is desirable that the Library Bill should provide for the superseding of a Local Library Authority for grave reasons for a definite period and for making arrangements, for the discharge of the powers and duties of the superseded authority.

22. ERRORS OF COMMISSION

22.1. Errors in Finance

The most grevious error in the Model Public Libraries Bill concerns the utilisation of the library cess raised in a district. It leads the cess collected within a town to be retained by the Town Library Committee and the cess collected in the rural areas (non-town areas) within a Block area to be retained by the Block Library Committee. This amounts virtually to the automisation of the proceeds of the library cess. This will mean dissipation of the all-too-small funds available for library service. In its turn, this will mean ever-poor libraries. We can examine it by an analogy. We usually impound the water available in a locality to increase its usefulness. Then only we can get the water-head necessary for the irrigation and power-generation. We can get little use from the self-same quantity of water if we spread it thin over a vast area with no depth and quantity anywhere. We shall only be dissipating it in that case. So it is with library fund, the lay-out suggested by the Model Public Libraries Bill makes dissipation inevitable. With the fund available in a district as a whole for public library service, we should build up a large "library lake" as the District Central Library or a City Central Library as the case may be. By drawing out from this "little library tanks" should be formed as branch libraries. The books in the "little library tanks" should be frequently sent back to the large "library lake" and fresh books brought therefrom. Further, there should also be "library irrigation channels" in the form of travelling libraries reaching all the hundreds of villages and hamlets.

22.2. Advisory Committees

This means that a Town Library Committee and a Block Library Committee should have no financial or accounts responsibility. This responsibility should be concentrated entirely in the hands of the District Central Library and the District Library Authority managing it. Each Town Library Committee should have only advisory powers concerning the kind of book service needed by the town and any deficiency in service. There should also be similar advisory library committees in villages to be vested by the travelling library. The Block Library Committee is probably unnecessary.

22.3. Doubling of High Offices

For some years to come, it is unnecessary and it will be too expensive to have two high-paid library officers as State Librarian and the other as Director of Libraries. The functions of both the officers can be merged into those of a single office. In the formative years, this is even essential. The Director of Libraries will not have opportunity to spend sufficient time every month in the holistic reader-cum-book setting to be found in the State Central Library. The absence of this experience will make him degenerate into a bureaucrat revelling in unwinding red-tape. There should be nothing more fatal than this to the flowering of the State Library System into a health-giving social institution bubbling with the spirit of service. The Director will also lose very soon all technical competence to foster library service among the people.

22.4. Trees Hiding the Wood

The Model Public Libraries Bill spells out far too many details. Legislative enactment should abstain from going to the details. The details are bound to require adjustment from time to time. Therefore, the modern practice is to leave the details to the rule making powers of the government, that is the administrative legislation. This principle should be particularly respected in the case of library service where everything is now in a state of flux. This important principle in the framing of an Act appears to have been much missed by the Model Public Libraries Bill. This reminds one of the trees hiding the wood.

22.5. Knowledge of Library Polity

The Model Public Libraries Bill does not embody much of sound and up-to-date knowledge of library organization in a country or a State. That such a Bill should have been produced after several months, if not years, of deliberation is amazing. It is unworthy of being taken as a model by the governments of the Constituent States. It is equally unworthy of being released as model and thereby making it acquire the hallow which the tradition in our country attaches to anything emanating from the Centre.

★★★

Evolution of Reference Service and Documentation Service

S. R. Ranganathan

Reported By M A Gopinath,

Documentation Research and Training Centre, Bangalore 3.

Abstract

This is a report of five lessons in DRTC, extending over 7 hours, given by Dr Ranganathan, during June 1964. Demonstrates the importance of making teaching library-centred and enthusing the students to discover for themselves instead of telling the final result. Examines the confusion in the idea plane arising out of the two-worded term of art 'Reference Service'. With reference to a century long time-grid traces the evolution of reference service from 1850 to the current period showing its intensification into 'Documentation Service' as it is now called.

Abbreviations used

P .. .. .. = All the Participants.
PI, P2 .. .. P8 = Participant 1, Participant 2, Participant 8.
T .. .. .. = Teacher.

0. INTRODUCTION

0.1. Harmonious Integration

T.— What is meant by Reference Service?

P2.— Helping the reader to have his reference.

P3.— Serving the reader at the time of his information needs

Reprinted with permission from Library Science with a slant to Documentation, 2(3), pp. 485-508, 1965.

P4.— Giving information to readers as and when they ask for it.

P5.— Guiding the reader in getting his information.

P6.— Personal service to reader in the library.

T.—The definition of P6 seems to be near the point. Here want to tell you an incident. I have many Marathi old students. They are all very enthusiastic. They have translated some of my books. They have formulated a standard terminology for library science in Marathi. In doing so, they happened to translate the two-worded term-of-art 'Reference Service'. They took the literal meaning of the two component words 'Reference' and 'Service'. They translated them into *'Sandarbha'* and *'Seva'*. Thus, the term-of-art 'Reference Service' was translated into *'Sandarbha Seva'* (= Exigency service).

You all know what a misleading term it is. When I came across this term, I was rudely shocked. I told my Marathi friends that their translation was wrong. They did not translate the idea denoted by the term-of-art 'Reference Service'. They asked me to suggest an appropriate term. After much thought I suggested the term *'Anulaya Seva'*. Do any of you know what *'Anulaya Seva'* signifies?

P's.—(Silence for a few minutes).

T.—Take the term *'Laya'*. What does it mean?

P5.— *'Laya'* means 'destruction' in Sanskrit.

P3.— *'Laya'* also means 'Rhythm' in 'Sanskrit',

T.— We come near our meaning if we take *'Laya'* to mean 'Rhythm'. Now, What is Rhythm?

P5.— (From the *Concise oxford dictionary,* Ed 4 (1959)) Rhythm means metrical movement determined by various relations of syllables.

P3.— (From the Dictionary). In musical composition 'Rhythm' concerns periodical accent and duration of notes.

P6.— (From the Dictionary). In Physics, rhythm means movement with regular succession of strong and weak elements.

P4.— (From the Dictionary). Rhythm also means 'Harmonious correlation of parts'.

T.— 'Rhythm' has so many meanings in different contexts. Here we have to pick out what is appropriate to our context.

It requires experience to do so. The meaning of Rhythm, given by P4, suits our context. We shall take Rhythm as the harmonious, correlation of parts. Each part integrates with all the others. And this produces Rhythm. Here *'Laya'* means 'Integration' – 'Becoming-at-one'. It means 'Getting merged'.

0.1.1. ANNOTATION 1

In the verbal plane there are many homonyms. To choose the meaning; appropriate to the context requires a considerable experience. If the teacher himself chooses the appropriate meaning and dictates it to the student it does not educate the student in the art of choosing the appropriate meaning. On the other hand the student will benefit, if and only if, he is exposed to all the possible meanings and is helped to eliminate the wrong ones and to arrive at the right one. How often such an experience should be given to a student is a matter of judgement. It is less harmful to err in excess rather than in deficit.

0.1.2. TERM-OF-ART

T.— Next comes *'Anulaya'*. What does the epithet 'Anu' mean?

P4.— We say *'Amisarana'* which means to follow up.

P5.—*'Anulayi'* means the follower.

T.— *'Anulaya'* actually means 'Harmonious integration'. *'Seva'* means 'service'. Thus *'Anulaya seva'* means 'Service-leading to harmonious integration'. This is a happy word. Is it not? The two-worded term-of-art 'Reference Service' really connotes 'Service leading to a harmonious integration of the reader and the book'. It is wrong to get its meaning by mechanically combining together the meanings of the component terms 'Reference' and 'Service'.

0.1.3. ANNOTATION 2

The concept of 'term-of-art' is an important one. The students should be given many opportunities to become familiar with this concept.

0.2. Origin of the Term

Can any one of you tell me how this term-of-art 'Reference Service' came into vogue?

P3.— Probably from the terra-of-art 'Reference book'.

T.— What is a 'Reference Book'?

P4.— A book which is used for reference.

P5.— A book giving specific information.

P3.— A fact-book.

P4.— A book not meant for continuous reading — such as a Dictionary, Encyclopaedia, and Directory.

T.— That is right. A reference book is one which is referred to or looked up for a specific piece of information— only for a short while. It is a book not normally read continuously. This term-of-art 'Reference Work' first appeared on the title of a book written by Wyers in 1930 (Wyer (James I). Reference work. 1930). From this, the term-of-art 'Reference Service' came into vogue.

0.3. Alternative Terms

T.— Can any one of you tell me what are the other terms in English used to denote the idea 'Reference Service'?

P4.— Information service.

P5.— Reader's Advisory Service.

T.— Information service, perhaps, connotes — at least meant for a long time — Ready Reference Service — that is reference service done in a few minutes. Reader's Advisory Service is a high-sounding term. It is offensive. It is offensive because it carries with it an air of superiority on the part of the librarian. Can you check up who actually coined this term?

P5.— (From Landau's *Encyclopaedia of Librarianship* Ed 2, (1961). The term "Reader's Advisory Service" and "Reader's Advise" probably originated in USA by the work of Miss Jennie M Flexner of New York Public Library in early 1930's. (Flexner (J M) and Edge (S A). Reader's Advisory Service. 1934).

T.— 'Today the term is almost vanishing. The term offends the dignity of the reader and it cannot last long. On the other hand term-of-art 'Reference Service' is free from such offence and it should be brought into vogue.

0.3.1. Annotation

If the only object of formal education was to fill the memory of the students, the teacher himself could have stated or dictated the name of the source. But in reality the purpose of formal education is to develop in the students capacity for self-education with the aid of sources. This alone will fit him for the journey of life. It is to secure this primary purpose of education that education has to be library-centred — not merely for students of library science but also, for students in any subject whatever.

0.4. Time-Grid

We shall now go into the genesis of the service connoted by the term of art 'Reference Service'. In tracing out the important stages in the evolution of Reference Service, it will be convenient to restrict ourselves to the evolution in a particular country. What country shall we choose?

P2.— India.

P3.— UK.

T.— Why do you prefer UK to India?

P3.— Because, in India, reference service is beginning only recently. In UK it began earlier. Further we have more of recorded library history about UK than about India.

T.— I agree. UK is used only as a 'Guniea pig'. The general tread of evolution is likely to be the same in most of the countries. Now that we have settled about the country, what year shall we take as the first epoch for our purpose?

P8.—1850 AD.

T.— Why ?

P7.—The First Library Act was passed in that year.

T.— This is good. Can you continue to look at the time: factor from the library angle ? What is the next important year?

P's.— (Silence for a few minutes).

T.— A convenient year is the year when the Library Association was formed and an eventful step was taken by Melvil Dewey by designing a scheme of library classification.

P2.— 1876.

T.— I agree. What is the next eventful year — a year which shocked the whole world, though not particularly significant from the library point of view?

P6.— 'The beginning of World War I — 1914.

T.— We have thus got two intervals of time 1850—1875 and 1876—1914. You know that 25 years is taken as a period for one generation. The interval 1876—1900 would have fitted with the idea of a generation. But we changed 1900 to 1914 as the end year of the second period on account of the world crisis of 1914. Let us recapture the generation idea and use the end of the third generation after 1850, in fixing the next interval. What then will be the next interval?

P4.— 1915-1925.

T.— On the basis of the analogy of what we have already done what will determine the end year of the Fourth interval of time?

PL.— World War II. The interval of time will be 1926-1939.

T.— The generation unit has been disturbed due to the reality of the world. Let us recapture the generation idea, as before, in fixing the end period of the Fifth interval.

P3.—1940-1950.

T.— *We* have next to take 1950 — 1975 as the probable sixth interval of time.

Please write on the Black-board the time-grid arrived at for our purpose. While doing so indicate by an arrow that our consideration of the first interval will also cover the entire past before 1850.

P7.—(Goes up to black-board and writes).

SN of the period	Interval in inclusive years	Name of the period
1	(1850-1875)	Aristocracy of learning
2	(1876-1914)	Universal education
3	(1915-1925)	Adult education
4	(1926-1939)	Spread of democracy
5	(1940-1950)	United Nations
6	(1950-1975)	Current

0.5. Controlling Factors

T.—Our object is to trace the evolution of reference and documentation service. This is certainly a service to humanity. What do we serve to humanity?

P1.— Books.

P2.— Information.

P3.— Knowledge.

P4.— Information and knowledge packed in a book.

T.— Is it necessarily the whole book?

P3.— It may even be an article or a part of a book,

T.— What is the generic term we have agreed to use to denote either?

P2.— Document.

T.— By what terms do we distinguish between the two kinds of documents?

P2.— Macro document and micro document.

T.— The two factors determining the stages of evolution of reference and documentation service are then:

1. Reading public — that is the extent of literacy and of scholarship; and
2. Documents — that is the number of books or macro documents and the number of articles or micro documents produced in a year.

0.6. Parameters

T.—The two main parameters in the study of evolution of reference and documentation service can then be taken as Literacy and Document. Each of the above parameters in reality is a bundle of more than one. Let us break it into the ultimate parameters. We shall then have the following:

1. Reader served;
    - 1.1 Number of ordinary literates or generalist readers;
    - 1.2 Number of scholars or specialist readers;
2. Document served;
    - 2.1 Number of scholarly books suited to specialist readers;
    - 2.2 Number of ordinary books suited to the average or generalist reader; and
    - 2.3 Number of micro documents.

0.7. Methodology

T.—Our method of tracing the evolution of reference service will be to examine the value of these parameters in the successive periods and to determine whether the combination of the incidence of these values would call for reference service or not, and if it does its scope.

(*Note.*—The table given in Sec 04 is the final one reached at the end of the discussion. In the class itself each item in the table was written in the black-board as and when it was decided upon.)

1. PERIOD 1 — (1850-1875): ARISTOCRACY OF SCHOLARSHIP

1.1. Parameter 1: Reader

T.— Can you mention an important legislation in UK during this period, which is relevant to the use of libraries by the public?

P's.— (Silence for a few minutes).

T.— What is the essential qualification which a person should have to be able to use a library and read the books in it?

P5.— Literacy.

T.— What is the means of acquiring literacy?

P6.— Education.

T.— Is it education at all levels? Does it include, for example, education at the university level or at the DRTC level?

P7.— Elementary education.

P8.— Now, I know. The important relevant legislation of the period is the First Elementary Education Act.

T.— Find out from the reference books the year of that Act.

P3.— (From the Encyclopaedia Britannica) *1870.*

T.— Let us examine the value of the various parameters during that period. To give accurate figures a knowledge of the statistics of that period is necessary. I hope you will pursue it sometime later. For the time being, we can work on a fairly reliable conjecture. Start with your conjecture about each of the parameters.

1.1.1. GENERALIST READER

P5.— Literacy might have been about 10 per cent.

T.— What do you expect about the number of generalist readers during that period?

P6.— Not many.

1.1.2. SPECIALIST READER OR SCHOLAR

T.—What about the number of scholars — that is specialist readers?

P4.—Extremely few.

T.—There is another factor to be reckoned with select scholars of that period using the libraries would have been mostly self-helpers.

1.2. Document

T.—Let us pass on to the next parameter—the documents.
Let us first make a conjecture about the average number of books published annually during that period. It is difficult for you to conjecture. I take it to be about 5,000 a year. You can get at the actual figure by looking up the volumes of the *English catalogue* of that period.

P5.—Would there have been so many books published during that period ?.

T.—So many will figure in the statistics. But books of good standard and lasting value might have been only less than 1,000. Further, there would not have been many books on the diverse arts and crafts needed by the common man. The worthwhile books would have been largley scholarly books in the fundamental disciplines.

The number of worthwhile books published in the earlier years would have been even smaller. Remember that 50% of the books get outmoded in 5 years; another 30% in 15 years; and the remaining 20% in 25 years. Taking all this information into consideration, calculate the maximum number of worthwhile books that would not have gone out of date in 1875. P3, begin with the books published between 1870 —1875.

P3.—5,000 worthwhile books would have been published in that period. Of these 2,500 would have gone out of date.

P5.—10,000 worthwhile books would have been published between 1860 —1870.

P7.—No. I would make it 8,000, because the annual output would have been slightly less in that period. Of these, 80% would have gone out of date by 1875. That is, only 1,600 books would not have gone out of date.

P6.—Similarly during the period 1850 —1860 about 6,000 worthwhile books might have been published. Only about 500 of these books might not have gone out of date.

T.—What would have been the cumulative total of the live worthwhile books in 1875?

P5.—About 4,600 books. In round figures 5,000.

T.—At the end of the first period—the period of Aristocracy of Scholarship—there would have been only about 5,000 live worthwhile books. The readers would have been largely self-helping scholars. What is the inference about the need for Reference Service?

P.—No need for Reference Service.

2. PERIOD 2 —(1876-1914): UNIVERSAL EDUCATION

T.—As you did in the case of Period 1, you should work out the values of the parameters and infer the chance for the emergence of Reference Service during the Period 2.

Finding of the class—The number of scholars would have increased. But most of them would have been self-helpers. The generalist reader would have increased considerably. The number of live worthwhile books in a library collection might have gone upto 20,000. More books of a recreative nature would have been available. Books on arts and crafts would have been few. Therefore, the generalist readers would have been seeking more of recreative books than of informative books. Need for Reference Service would not have arisen.

T.—You are nearly right. But ready reference books had begun to appear in these periods. I would ask you to scan through the ready reference books listed in my *Bibliography of bibliographies and reference books* (1941) and estimate the number of reference books originated during this period. Make also a subject analysis of them. This work was once done by your predecessors and presented in a symposium to the Indian Library Conference (1942) (Bombay). There would have been some need for the librarians to promote their use by readers. But this need would not have been sufficient to set apart a section of the library staff solely for Reference Service.

P4.—Will there not have been need to do Reference Service at least in the choice of recreative books?

T.—No doubt the chief new function of the public library in period 2 was to harness the leisure of the common man. It would have been helpful if Reference Service had developed in the selection of recreative materials. But as a matter of fact, it did not emerge. Reason might have been partly the fact that only the upper quartiles in the intellectual scale used the public library system. They could help themselves in the choice of their creative books suited to themselves. There was no drive on the part of the library profession to make all — particularly, the lower quartiles — accept library service.

3. PERIOD 3 — (1915-1925): ADULT EDUCATION

T.—All matters including library service were greatly affected by a political event of that period. What was it?

P2.— World War I of 1914 —1918.

T.— The post of a new Secretary of State was created during this period. Can you find out the jurisdiction of that Secretary of State. Find out also the year in which the post was created and the chief legislation that followed it.

P2.—(From the *Encyclopaedia Britannica)* Secretary of State for Education. The Encyclopaedia reads "In 1916, HAL Fisher became Minister of Education ".

PI.—In 1918, an Education Act was passed providing for Continuation Schools for the education of young persons from the ages of 14 to 18 years.

T.—The World War I was essentially a trench war. An army was scattered along trenches many miles long. Communication had to be through documents. But it was found that many soldiers could not read them though they had gone through compulsory education costing millions of pounds through years. This disclosed a colossal wastage of National Funds. "How could this relapse to illiteracy can be prevented? That was the question. The relapse to illiteracy can be prevented only by the exercise of literacy. Do you now see the new function to be taken up by the Public Library System?

P8.—Librarians should persuade people to come to the library and read.

T.—By reading library books, no doubt a literate will keep up his literacy. There is also an important educational by-product. What is it?

P4.—Further education.

T.—It is in this function of adult education — self education and adults — that the Public Library System took on itself during Period 3. Do you expect Reference Service to have emerged in this context?

P7.—Yes. The librarian should select suitable books for each adult and persuade him through satisfying personal service to come to the library frequently.

T.—This was the beginning of Reference Service. It was largely to the generalist reader. But the specialist reader still continued to be a self-helper.

Let us look at the second parameter—documents. Here you should examine the annual volume of the *English catalogue* for the period and verify the increasing number of books on diverse arts and crafts. The adult literate with no more than elementary education had to be helped in the selection of the right reading material to suit his vocational needs. Reference Service to the generalist reader began this way. As an aid to Reference Service, select bibliographies on diverse arts and crafts were necessary. Their preparation was a part of Reference Service. Very soon it was found economical to have such bibliographies prepared and published by a national organisation. The National Book Council came into being for this purpose. Find out when it was established and any other information on it from a suitable Reference Book.

P7.—(From the *Encyclopaedia of librarianship).* The National Book Council was established in 1924. Its name was changed to National Book League in 1944.

T.—The emergence of Reference Service to the generalist reader during Period 3 led the same period to the establishment of a national centre to prepare bibliographies as tools for Reference Service. This fact is worth noting. You will find a paralleled for it in Period 6 *(see* Sec 63).

4. PERIOD 4 — (1926–1939): SPREAD OF DEMOCRACY

T.—The period 1926 — 1939 was characterised by the spread of democracies in several countries of the West. In a democracy, Sovereignity is distributed over each citizen, though he delegates it periodically to a Government formed of elected representatives. Each citizen has a twofold responsibility in a democracy. He has to vote for a party with an acceptable policy in respect of every sphere of state of action and social need. Collectively the citizens have to be watchdogs between two elections to ensure that the government is proceeding along right lines. This requires knowledge on the part of every citizen — knowledge of current facts and knowledge of current ideas. Therefore, every citizen should be helped to get these. The agency to serve these should be an impartial one. It cannot be one of the political parties. The Public Library System is recognised to be the agency preeminently fitted for this purpose. In the discharge of this work the library should do aggressive Reference Service to every citizen, bringing to his notice all expressed and embodied facts and ideas of all political and economic, and sociological shades, in equal measure. For, ignorance and democracy would be a dangerous mixture. As a result, Reference Service to the generalist reader got itself established during Period 4—the period of the Spread of Democracy. But it had not become efficient enough in all the countries. World War II broke out in 1939. It was partly due to the insufficiency of Reference Service. Later, in 1955-56, when the Suez Canal trouble began, the averting of a war was at least partly due to the impartial and fuller Reference Service rendered by the Public Library System. I saw this is being done. It was almost guessed by some librarians that the fact of the citizens knowing the correct data from the library resources would go a long way in averting the war, though no librarian suggested this to readers by himself. This is out of respect due to the Canon of Reticence to be observed by the library profession.

{*Note.*—In the succeeding sections verbatim report is avoided in order to save space. The information directed to be gathered by the student is not explicitly indicated. Only the general conclusions are given. But it will not be difficult to expand it and to throw it in the form of verbatim report.}

5. PERIOD 5 — (1940-1950): UNITED NATIONS

T.—This period was characterised by an international crisis; in the political world—World War II. The war awakened the masses in several countries. People became aware of their responsibilities. New forms of governments were formed in many countries. The war also brought in a dangerous weapon — atom bomb — released by the invention of nuclear energy. The two bombs exploded in Japan in Hiroshima and Nagasaki clearly showed the harmful effects of this weapon. So a new kind of social force came into being by the co-operation of many top leaders of the world. To avert the dangers of a nuclear war a new organization was found. It is called United Nations. The main function of this organisation is to maintain the peace and security of the world and avert war. A charter was drawn by the principal members of the United Nations. Many countries like India became independent and formed their own governments with a democratic, set-up. Later they too became members of the United Nations and signed the charter. The war also reduced the natural resources in many countries. There was also an imbalance in wealth among countries of the world. Sportively, the industrially advanced countries came forward to help the other less fortunate countries. Thus amity among nations and promotion of peace was the main aim of this period. Many documents were exchanged between one country with another. Contact Libraries — the libraries maintained by a country in a foreign country in order to promote and cultivate cultural contacts and sympathetic correct cultural understanding among the people of all the countries of the world — came into vogue and formed a lively media of communication in a foreign country. This period was thus full of exchange of scholars, exchange of ideas, and exchange of industrial know-how and progress. Reference service in this period became more and more intensive and tended towards specialist users. Many new species of documents such as articles in periodicals, pamphlets, monographs etc came to prominence. The applied research instead of fundamental research came into prominence. The number of periodicals began to grow. Consequently the number of articles in a periodical—micro documents—also began to increase. By the end of the United Nations period it had grown to such an extent that intensive Reference Service to specialist readers became a necessity in many of the countries of the world.

6. PERIOD 6—(1950-1975): CURRENT PERIOD

Since 1950 the population pressure of the world is increasing enormously. This has made the natural and near natural commodities inadequate to maintain the population — almost to the point of their exhaustion. Hunger and disease are threatening to become imminent. The society has to meet this challenge. So the scientists are made to engage themselves in intensive research to produce artificial commodities — such as food, clothing, shelter, and transport from out of the directly non-consumable raw materials. This stimulates scientific research. The concept of 'Productivity' and of 'conservation of research potential' have emerged.

{*Note.*—The students worked out the necessary statistical data about population and economic products.)

6.1. Parameter 1: Reader

A world-wide team-research-in-relay has become a necessity. This team has to draw specialists, heavily even from the second quartile of intellectual scale. A majority of them are not self-helpers. Thus, the change in the first parameter—reader—has made intensive reference service as an absolute social necessity.

{*Note.*—The students worked out the necessary statistical data showing increase in research workers in India, UK and USA since World War II.)

6.2. Parameter 2: Document

This was characterised by the downpour of many macro as well as micro documents of research value. The very world-wide team-research-in-relay itself contributed to this. It is estimated that about 100 micro documents appear in print each day. The rate of increase of documents is beyond the capacity of self-help on the part of a specialist. Even if the few capable self-helpers relay only on their self-help more than half their time will have to be spent on literature search. To this extent productivity in research will go down. Thus for a specialist to say that he does not want any documentation service amounts to an anti-social attitude. Thus the change in second parameter— documents has made the aggressive, intensive reference service to specialist readers a distinctive feature of the current period.

(Note—The students worked out the necessary statistical data on the annual increase and rate of increase in documents in diverse subject fields.)

6.3. National Bibliographical and Documentation Centres

Many countries have begun to publish national bibliographies on weekly, monthly, quarterly and annual bases. So also they have begun to establish national documentation centres. These two institutions reduce to a considerable extent the load on the day-to-day work of reference and documentation service in local service libraries. This benefit will be at its best if the bibliography and the documentation list are of a classified variety based on a scheme such as the Colon Classification with adequate capacity for depth classification.

7. SUM-UP

Thus there was no chance for reference service to emerge during the nineteenth century, as the live books in that period was small in number and other readers being mostly self-helping scholars. During first half of the twentieth century the Literacy tended to become universal. Both to prevent relapse to Illiteracy and to put to literacy to social use, generalist readers had to be helped in the choice of their books. The annual increase in book production and production of books in diverse subjects including arts and crafts also made reference service necessity. In the present half of the twentieth century a social necessity has begun to launch a world-wide-team-research-in-relay. This has created a vast mass of specialists who are not self-helpers. These have to be fed with nascent micro-thought. Micro documents are increasing by leaps and bounds. Therefore, reference service has to be intensified with emphasis on specialist readers and on nascent micro documents. This new form of reference service is now called 'Documentation Service'. This is in addition to a widespread practice of reference service in the older form— service of macro document to generalist readers.

(Note.—In this evolution students were asked to trace out the part played by each of the Five Laws of Library Science)

★★★

Emergence of Library Science (Development of Library Science. 1)

S. R. Ranganathan
National Research Professor in Library Science, Documentation Research and Training Centre, Bangalore 3.

Abstract

Art and practice precede science. Library service is no exception to this. To understand the purpose of library service it is helpful to postulate that the personality of man consists of four sheaths,—vital (Physical), emotional, intellectual, and spiritual. Library service began with the satisfaction of intellectual wants alone and then extended to the satisfaction of emotional wants and then to vital wants. There was no library service when libraries were either unused collections or were small and used only by a few scholars. There was no library science when the scholar-librarian started reference service based largely on his flair. Flair proved insufficient and gave place to library techniques. There was very little chance for library science to be developed by the librarians of the nineteenth-century fiction-dominated libraries. Some *ad hoc* principles were evolved by Sayers in the early part of the present century. The present century has brought into operation the chain "Population pressure, economic want, development of technology, natural and social sciences, and intensification of library service". To satisfy the vital wants appreciable amount of team-relay-research is to be done. To conserve the research potential of the scientist, the production engineer and the manager, the documentalist is now recognised as a partner in their work. Since 1876, *ad hoc* library techniques of various kinds are being continuously improvised.

Reprinted with permission from Library Science with a slant to Documentation, 3(1), pp. 509-542, 1966.

The author observed the techniques during his visit to 120 libraries in the UK 1924–25. He experimented these techniques along with his own techniques in the Madras University Library. He modified the techniques in the light of the reaction of the readers and gained new empirical experiences. In 1928, the Laws of Library Science were formulated. Gradually all the possible implications of the Laws were inferred. Canons and Principles were deduced from the Laws to develop certain subdisciplines of library science. The concept of the Spiral of Scientific Method was evolved. Library science got established by admitting of the Spiral of Scientific Method in its development.

1. SEQUENCE OF EMERGENCE

Art and practice precede science. The art and practice of speaking began with the early man. It had to be practised through ages before the science of linguistics emerged. The art and practice of writing pieces of literature—poetry, drama, prose— began very early. But the science of prosody and rhetoric emerged only very much later. The practice of useful arts in an elemental form developed through several centuries before the physical sciences emerged. The art of healing was practised for long before biological sciences emerged. Economic and political life was lived for long before political science and the science of economics emerged. In fact, the emergence of the latter is quite recent. It has not yet established itself on an even keel. The emergence of the science of sociology is even more recent, though social practices have been in vogue for a long time. The library sphere is no exception to this sequence. The practice of library service had been in existence ever since books were produced in manuscript form. There is a legend about the kind of library service received by Sankara, the great philosopher—of the 6th century of the Christian era, according to the most conservative estimate. He wished to write a commentary on the Thousand Names of the Goddess manifesting as Lalitha. He asked for a copy of the manuscript of the thousand names of Lalitha. But the librarian brought him the manuscript of the Thousand Names of God manifesting as Vishnu. The librarian was sent back to get the right manuscript. Every time he came back with different manuscripts of the Thousand Names of Lalitha, Sankara was puzzled and looked at him. The librarian said. "A new lady reference librarian is in the stack room. She tells me that you should now really write a commentary on the Thousand Names of Vishnu". Sankara knew that there was no lady reference librarian. The mystic in him made him *see* at once Goddess Lalitha herself giving him that direction. The art and practice of library service had been continuing through centuries. But library science emerged only in our own lifetime. We shall begin with examining the emergence and progress of library service itself.

1.1. Postulate about Personality

At bottom, library service is service to a person-the individual. To understand the purpose of library service, it will be helpful to postulate a schematic view of the personality of man. In this view the personality of man consists of four sheaths-*Kosas* in our language. These are vital(or physical), emotional, intellectual, and spiritual sheaths. The following is a schematic diagram of the same.

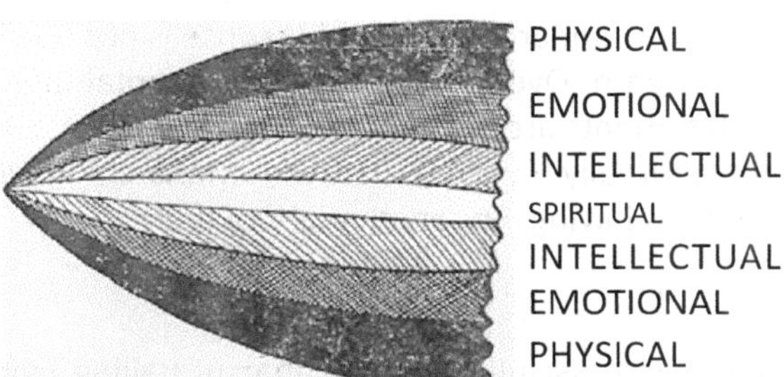

Fig 1. Sheaths of Personality

1.2. Human Wants

At bottom, library service is designed to satisfy human wants. The wants of the vital sheath are many and compelling. The wants of the emotional sheath come next in order. The wants of the intellectual sheath are fewer still and hardly compelling. The spiritual sheath is inert in most persons. In the few in whom it is activated, it feeds from its own inner resources; and its external wants are few.

1.3. Standard of Living

It is now common to relate human wants with standard of living. This term does not have a clear definition. But the general trend is to measure it in terms of the number of commodities and services used to satisfy the human wants. Their number is used as the basis for a measure of the standard of life. It is greatest in the case of vital wants. Very often, it is measured in terms of the quantity and quality of the food, clothing, and shelter in use and of the number of automobiles, telephones, and other similar material amenities. The measure of standard of life in respect of emotional wants is based on the talkie service, the radio service, and similar services, and on the number of the physical commodities on which these services are dependent, and of late, on the number of librarians too. In respect of intellectual want, the basis for the measure of standard of life is often the number of schools, colleges, universities, research institutions, laboratories, and libraries. The term 'Standard of life' in this sense is not applicable to the spiritual sheath. Overlooking this fundamental difference many wrong statements are often made. Some of them are even abusive. The spiritually evolved Ramana Maharshi might be hastily put down as having a poor standard of life!

1.4. Anecdote 1

A great admirer and disciple of the Maharshi hailing from the West met me about thirty years ago in the Madras University Library. I shall call him X, and denote myself as L.

X.— After living with the Maharshi for some years, I am getting disillusioned.

L.— So soon?

X.— After all, the belief that the rishis have few wants is not true. You have been telling me that our usual concept of standard of life is not applicable to spiritually awakened souls such as the Maharshi.

L.— I still hold that view.

X.— Probably you do not know that the Ashram of the Maharshi has put up hostels with furnished rooms. In the hostels there are radios. They have now a Manager with his staff. I think they will soon go in for a Staff Car.

L.— Is the Maharshi using them? Are they to satisfy his wants? Or, are they simply to provide the minimum of creature comforts to which his visitors are accustomed and without which they will be ill-at-ease-even in the immediate presence of Maharshi and in spite of his living example?

1.5. Field of Library Service

We shall then assume that the field of library service is confined to the satisfaction of intellectual, emotional, and vital wants. Library service began with the satisfaction of intellectual wants alone. It then got extended to the satisfaction of emotional wants. The supply of materials to satisfy emotional wants through library service depends on a prior satisfaction of intellectual wants. Lastly, library service got extended to the satisfaction of vital wants. The library does not itself supply the commodities and services needed to satisfy the vital wants. It merely helps the intellect in the production of the commodities and services needed. The above-mentioned direction of the extension of library service has been set by the chain, "population pressure, economic wants, development of technology, and library service". Till about two centuries ago, population pressure was comfortably low. Therefore vital wants and technology did not play much part in the development of library service. There was no global service pressure for it. On the other hand, the pressure for library service was largely created only by the intellectual and emotional urges in man. These urges were compelling only in a comparatively few people. Thus the field of library service was very much restricted.

2. LIBRARY SERVICE TO INTELLECTUALS

Till modern times, not even 10 percent of the people were literate. Not more than 10 percent of these-that is, not more than one centile of the population-were intellectuals. This than one centile of the population-were intellectual scale. Even of these few, perhaps most were not of a scholarly temperament. Indeed the persons of a nation drawing joy from Scholarly intellectual pursuit were very few. Further, for about a century or two after printing was invented, the number of books was very small. In this context, it was possible for each scholar to find out his book all by himself, from the library collection to which he was accustomed. Moreover, transport was not easy. Therefore, the scholar often used the same library collection. Again, scholars had been, as usual, poor and the number of library collections accessible to them was extremely small. There were no doubt library collections in royal palaces and in the house of rich courtiers. In most of these, the collections were often built as symbols of status. Indeed there are many anecdotes of poor scholars complaining of the rich courtiers hardly using their library collections and playing the "dog in the manger" against the intellectual thirst of scholars in poverty.

2.1. Anecdote 2

We have read about the story of a book market in Persia in the pre-printing days. Well-bound manuscripts were being auctioned. There was a keen bidding for one book. Ultimately there were only two bidders for it—a rich courtier in gaudy apparel and a poor scholar in rags.

Courtier. — My dear man, why do you go on raising the bid. Can we not come to an agreement?

Scholar. — This is a rare book. I had heard about it for long- But I could not get it till now.

Courtier. — Listen. Allow me to knock it down. Its binding is lich and lovely. It will fillingly fit and fittingly fill a gap in my library shelves. I want to fill up that gap before I receive the King in my palace.

Scholar. — But, then, I cannot get it for my use.

Courtier. — Do not be afraid of it. After the King's visit I shall give it away to you.

2.2. Anecdote 3

In India, having a beautiful and fully packed book-shelf in the drawing room has been regarded as a mark of nobility. Vatsyayana mentions it. It has been in vogue till recently. In my home district, there were two very rich people. Their literacy in English would enable them to sign their names and no more. However, both had a few cupboards of well-polished rosewood, filled with attractive books in English with richly tooled leather bindings. One of these two rich people lived in my home town. One of the boys in that family was my classmate. Therefore, I had the privilege of going into my classmate's house and admire the beautiful library. One day the classmate told me, "These books were all bought by my father, as the Collector of the District visited our home last year." About the other rich man of the District, he said, "He is richer than my father. Even the Governor of our Presidency visited his house. He, therefore, built for the occasion even a larger library of books with their spines tooled with gold even more lavishly than ours! "

2.3. Library Janitor

When libraries were either unused collections or were small and were used only by very few scholars, there could have been no need for a librarian in the modern sense. Only a janitor was necessary to keep the books clean and to safeguard them from pilferage. Indeed there was no 'Library Service' In this context library science could not have had any chance to-emerge.

2.4. Scholar Librarian

As time advanced more books were published. Further while the scholars were mortals, the books were immortals. Therefore, very soon the number of books in a library became considerably large—too large for a scholar to find his book without the aid of a catalogue. No doubt the catalogue might be a mere list of the most primitive kind. But even this required more than a janitor to prepare it. A scholar was, therefore, put in charge of the library. Some scholar librarians familiarised themselves with all the books in the library and acquired the flair to spot out a book answering the needs of a scholarly reader without the aid of any special techniques. This was the beginning of reference service. There are many anecdotes of such services being given by scholar librarians in the 18th and 19th centuries in a few libraries.

2.5. Anecdote 4

But in many other libraries even this incipient form of reference service was travestied. This brings to mind such a travesty even as late as 20 years ago in one of our libraries. I was invited by that library as a consultant to advise it on its reorganisation and staff requirements. One of the points stressed was that there should be a good reference staff to get the books fully and properly used. It was further stressed that the salary of the reference librarian should be high in order to attract men of ability and wide knowledge. The Chairman of the Managing

Council appreciated this recommendation. Then came the question of recruiting a reference librarian. Then arose the following incident.

Librarian.— I recommend my attendant to be appointed as the reference librarian.

Chairman.— Have you understood for what purpose the consultant has recommended the appointment of a reference librarian ?

Librarian.— Yes, Sir.

Chairman.— How can your attendant, who has not completed even his school course, do the kind of work which the consultant described ?

Librarian.— Sir, suppose a reader asks for the 40th volume of the *Nature*. My attendant can pick it out immediately (laughter). During lunch time, the Chairman told me, "Do you now understand why I insisted on your coming here instead of your writing to us on our requirements? When we meet after lunch, do not press for the salary scale of the librarian to be raised?"

2.6. Flair and not Science

But the scholar librarians of the last century were able to give helpful service to readers by their sheer knowledge of the books and as a result of their loving the work. Their success was based more on flair and a highly cultivated commonsense than library science. All honour to them. But as time advanced, and the number of books increased at a great rate and more readers sought service of the library, this dependence on more familiarity with books, flair, and commonsense was proving increasingly insufficient. Melvil Dewey was one of the first to sense this even when he was a boy. So did Charles Ammi Cutter. So also did librarians such as James Duff Brown and Wyndham Hume. Dewey developed special techniques and also formed the American Library Association to make the librarians think of well-planned library service with the aid of suitable techniques. Similarly did the three British librarians. They formed the Anonymous Club to discuss their techniques and practices and bring them as it were to the threshold of science. They had to call it Anonymous Club, because if they had mentioned their objective, they were afraid that the list of members would have had to face ridicule.

3. LIBRARY SERVICE FOR LEISURE TIME

By the middle of the Nineteenth Century, the Industrialisation of the countries in the West had given much leisure to the upper class. They had to use their leisure time. For, as it is well known, unoccupied leisure is a danger to the individual as well as the society.

One harmless method of using leisure time without dependence on other persons was found to be the reading of recreative books. Such books are usually read only once. They are then thrown away. Once a person was accustomed to getting entertained by books, he soon develops an addiction to it. To meet the demands thus created, a large quantity of fiction was produced. The persons found it too costly to buy all of them and also too wasteful to buy the novels which had to be thrown away in a short while. The Public Libraries used this opportunity to develop a collection of recreative and travel books and biographies, for leisure time use. The service from this collection did not, however, call for any improvement in the technique of service. Further, in the earlier years the staff of such libraries was largely recruited from teen-agers before they could enter a university. Therefore, there was very little chance for a library science to be developed by the librarians of such libraries. However, a few of them were men of exceptional ability. They developed and refined several library techniques in an ad hoc way. W C Berwick Sayers was one of the prominent among them. Work of these people also brought the *ad hoc* library techniques to the threshold of science.

4. INTENSIFICATION OF LIBRARY SERVICE

4.1. Population Pressure

During the present century, the population pressure has reached the saturation point. This has happened in most of the countries. But Canada, USA, Australia and some of the countries in South America perhaps continue to be the exceptions. In the other places—particularly in India—the population pressure has even crossed the point where the vital human wants— such as food, shelter, clothing, and transport—could not be met fully with the natural and, near-natural commodities produced in the traditional way. Agriculture has to be intensified with the aid of technology. So it is with fisheries. Even then the natural and the near-natural commodities will not be sufficient, to satisfy the vital human wants. Raw materials, which are not directly consumable, have to be transformed into consumable commodities. This transformation needs the use of technology of ever-increasing complexity. Further, due to the mischief of nature, the raw materials are concentrated only in certain spots on earth. Therefore, either the raw materials themselves or the intermediate commodities or the ultimate commodities ready for human use have to be transported through long distances. This requires the freight transport—be it land, ocean, or air—, to be increased enormously both in number, size, and speed. This again needs the use of technology of ever-increasing complexity. Large-scale production and commerce have also become a necessity. This has made Management itself transcend the capacity of the shrewd man with extraordinary flair. A Science of Management has become necessary. The overall political, economic, sociological, and legal consequences of large-scale production and commerce also require considerable continuous re-thinking and research.

The younger generation has to be prepared to do the necessary research and to put the results of research to social use. Further, education has to reach down to the lowest quartile in the intellectual scales. These needs transcend the capacity of the traditional methods of education, especially the method of examination-centred mass-lecture method. Need has thus arisen for considerable re-thinking and research in education. All these has brought into operation the chain:

> "Population pressure, economic wants, development of technology, natural and social sciences, and intensification of library service."

Library service has therefore to be intensified in order to meet the demands of technology and the natural and social sciences made necessary by the vital wants of humanity generated by increasing population pressure.

4.2. Team Research

The amount of overall research to be done to meet the vital wants of the teeming millions of humanity adequately is enormous. There has to be division of labour here. This division has to be based on the distinction between fundamental research and developmental research. Usually it is only a man of genius endowed with great intuition that can produce new seminal ideas. A few persons nearest to him in the intellectual scale will have to do the first stages of follow-up work in bringing the seminal ideas near to their application for social well-being. They will have to work out and uncover the implications of the seminal ideas capable of serving social needs. The term 'Fundamental Research' will be used to denote the research done up to this point. The successive later stages of research should be taken over by groups of men drawn from the farther positions in intellectual scale—positions of increasing removes from that of those engaged in fundamental research. In fact, we want a hierarchy of research workers to exploit the results of the fundamental research purposefully. The work of this hierarchy may be denoted by the term 'Developmental Research'. Those engaged in fundamental research and in developmental research should work as a team. This is the most economical organisation for Research. In this organisation, each person contributes to research in the measure of his own capacity. There is a pretty folk-story illustrating such team-work. A bridge had to be built across the sea dividing the mainland of India from the Island of Ceylon, to enable Rama's army to go across to Ceylon. This had to be done quickly. In this work a whole team consisting of the top-engineers down to the common soldiers worked together. The folk-story is that even squirrels look part in this team-work by dropping pebbles in the interstices between boulders. Rama appreciated this effort of the squirrels and gently rubbed on their back in token of his appreciation of their team spirit.

4.3. Relay Research

Team research alone is not sufficient. Several teams will be working on the same or similar projects in different parts of a country and in the world at large. The best result can be got only by each team carrying forward the work already done by another team. This is Relay Research.

4.4. Dissipation of Research Potential

Organised research by several teams working in relay will precipitate new ideas at a high rate. There is the danger of some of the nascent micro-thought created at one point in this team-relay-research being lost sight of at some other point. This would lead to the repetition of the same piece of work unknowingly or unintended. Cases are known of one and the same management having estimated the loss due to this repetition to run to hundreds and thousands of dollars. Some have even found such a repetition even within the team working under the same management and under the same roof. This amounts to dissipation of the all-too-small research potential available.

4.5. Conservation of Research Potential

It is necessary to prevent such a dissipation of research potential, if we can. In the earlier years of the present half-century, a few members of the research team itself was put in charge of the task of preventing loss due to unwanted repetition. It is only in recent years that it has been realised that it is equally wasteful to turn persons capable of research in a particular field on to the task of scanning the micro documents embodying nascent micro-thought and lying scattered among hundreds of periodicals. Moreover, a person with competence for research in a particular technological or scientific area cannot be expected to develop efficient methods of literature-search.

4.6. Documentation, A New Task for the Library Profession

It has now been found out that there should be a further division of labour in the overall attempt of humanity to find out efficient vital wants of the teeming millions. This division of labour has brought in the library profession as a supporting agency for the conduct of research. To emphasise this new role of the library profession, this task of feeding the research workers with nascent micro-thought, is denoted by the new term 'Documentation'; when engaged in documentation, the librarian is denoted by the new term ' Documentalist'. It is now recognised that the research workers in the positive fields of technology and sciences and the documentalists should be deemed as partners in research. It is only such a division of labour and such a cooperation that can conserve the research potential and get the best out of it for the benefit of humanity.

5. AD HOC IMPROVISATION OF TECHNIQUE

Since 1875 ad hoc techniques of various kinds are being continuously improvised. They are all based upon experience arising out of the difficulties actually met while rendering library service. I had the opportunity, in 1924, to observe many of the successive techniques developed ad hoc, in some library or other in the United Kingdom. This was observed in a visit to about 120 libraries. What was observed enriched empirical experience of diverse kinds. It was also possible to observe the further changes coming in the field of library service. This led to the feeling that the capacity of this series of ad hoc improvisations would soon be transcended. This feeling, released as it were, the trigger. The new feeling developed that the time had come to place the design of techniques on a scientific basis. It was further felt that such a scientific basis could enable new techniques being inferred as compelling deductions from the fundamental laws of library science—if only such laws could be formulated. With the aid of the fundamental laws, it was even felt that, as and when the boundary conditions laid by social needs changed, the new techniques necessary could be inferred readily. Even models of new techniques could be established so as to meet the demands of different kinds of changes in the social needs. These feelings were evidently pushed down to the deeper levels of science. There they were simmering for three years.

6. GENESIS OF LIBRARY SCIENCE

6.1. Empirical Stage

The rich experience, gathered while observing during 1924-25 the libraries in the West at different stages of development, was somewhat unique. Librarians in the West were all tied down to the libraries in which they were employed. They could not get an opportunity to visit different libraries in the country and make a comparative study of their varying practices. But for a visitor from

India, it was naturally possible to visit all the important libraries of a country within a few months with undivided attention and compare their varying library practices. This was a great advantage. The experience gained got soaked in the mind. During the next three years, the conscious mind was fully engaged in organising the Madras University Library from scratch. It was also engaged in experimenting with the library techniques picked up in the West and a few new techniques improvised in the course of the organisation of the university library. The students and the teachers of the university began to use the library in increasing numbers. They got interested in the new developments in the library. They were extremely participative. In the first place, this enabled the demonstration of the value of modern library techniques. Further, their participativeness permitted their being used as guinea-pigs, as it were, test the old and the new techniques, and modify them in the light of the reaction of the readers. This gave new empirical experiences which could be added to the experiences gained abroad. All these, empirical experiences went down into the trans-conscious level, as the conscious level itself was fully occupied with the reorganisation work and the experiments.

6.2. Haul up From the Trans-Conscious

In 1928, another unique opportunity came. The University of Madras and the South India Teachers' Union provided. this opportunity. About a thousand teachers were to meet in their Annual Conference in December 1928 in the Meenakshi College, Chidambaram—now Annamalai University, Annamalainagar, Chidambaram. It was arranged that the ideas of modern library service should be broadcast at the Conference. For this purpose the University of Madras asked me—then University Librarian in Madras—to deliver a course of Vacation Lectures at the Conference. This hauled up to the conscious level all the empirical experiences simmering at the trans-conscious level.

It led to the naming of the subject of the lectures as "Laws of Library Science". This naming was done in July 1928. This is a case of christening being before birth. What is it that was going to be born? This was then unknown. Therefore, the next few months were spent on cogitation.

6.3. First Formulation of the Laws

First came out a doublet. What are now known as Law 2 and Law 3 came out as a single Law. Then came the Fourth and the Fifth Laws. The First Law would not come out. There were only two weeks for the lectures to begin. The concentration and pain were enormous. About the end of the first week of December, the Professor for Mathematics—Edward B Ross, to whom I owe many things in my life—made his usual evening visit to the University Library. He walked into the Librarian's room.

Ross.—You seem to be very worried.

Ranganathan.—Not worry—but contemplation !

Ross.—You are too young to retire into contemplation! (He laughed).

Ranganathan.—In June last, I agreed to the University and the South India Teachers' Union to deliver a course of lectures this month on the Laws of Library Science. I had been trying to distil them out. I have succeeded in the formulation of some of the Laws. But they all look like corollaries. The Basic Law is still evading.

Then Ross and myself discussed the Laws that had come out. After a few minutes Ross started home. As usual I accompanied him to the porch. Ross got on his motor cycle. He was about to start the engine. Suddenly the familiar glow came in his eyes. The familiar twitching of the lips appeared. He said, "Books are for use". Is that not what you mean?" and rode away.

6.4. Four Laws of Library Science

Thus Professor Ross helped in completing the First Formulation of the Laws of Library Science. These were then formulated, as

1. Books are for use;
2. Every reader his or her book and every book its reader;
3. Save the time of the reader; and
4. Library is a growing organism.

Lantern slides were made of these laws. Several other slides were also made depicting the functioning of libraries. At Chidambaram, the Four Laws were expounded and their implications were drawn out one after another and illustrate with the slides. In the course of exposition, two reactions developed in me. In the Colon Classification already designed and brought into use in the Madras University Library, the digit '4' was mnemonic for 'Disease'. Therefore, there was a sentimental objection to have 'Four Laws'. Either one of them should be dropped or a fifth should be added. Five Laws were preferred as the digit '5' was mnemonic for 'Energy'. The next problem was "How to get it done?" Then came the intellectual reaction. The Second Law disobeyed the Principle of Unity. This solved the problem. The Second Law was broken into two distinct laws. This was the genesis of the Five Laws.

6.5. Five Laws of Library Science

Such was the genesis of the Five Laws of Library Science. They are

1. Books are for use;
2. Every reader his book;
3. Every book its reader;
4. Save the time of the reader; and
5. Library is a growing organism.

6.5.1. Corollary To Fourth Law

In the course of pulling out the implications of the Fourth Law, a corollary from it figured frequently. It is, "Save the time of the Staff".

6.5.2. Breaking up the Fifth Law

The Fifth Law was always giving trouble. It was because the full implications of the term 'Growing Organism' were not realised. The exposition at Chidambaram brought out the implications of 'Growth' only in the sense of 'Child-Growth'-that is,growth involving steady increase in overall-size. But the term has also another sense. It is 'Adult-Growth'—that is, growth by replacement of constituents without increase in overall-size. This double import of the 'Fifth Law' leads to the recognition of two types of libraries—Conserving or Storage Library, and Service Library.

6.5.3. Publication

The Five Laws formed the basis of teaching library science in the Library School established by the Madras Library Association in 1929 and taken over by the University of Madras in 1931. The students were all mature persons. They appreciated the a priori development of the library practices from the Five Laws. This was experienced in each of the three years. This experience led to the publication of the Five laws of library science in 1931.

7. RECOGNITION OF LIBRARY SCIENCE

7.1. Doubt Expressed by Scientists

The formulation of the Five Laws and the demonstration in the class room of the advantages of basing the teaching of the subject on these Fundamental Laws confirmed that the use of the term 'Library Science' was not altogether unwarranted.

In fact, the Five Laws had pushed into the Spiral of Scientific Method, what was originally called the art of librarianship and brought out a Library Science. The design of the Spiral of Scientific Method was provoked by the votaries of the Natural Sciences resenting the usurpation of the term 'Science' by the library profession. This charge led to an examination of what the term 'Science' connotes. This Spiral of Scientific Method has now given an objective definition of the term 'Science'. This definition indicates that the snake was not in the garden of librarians but in the garden of the votaries of the Natural Sciences. The next few sections describe the Spiral of Scientific Method and how Library Science got established as a result of the Art of Librarianship being pushed into the Spiral.

7.2. Spiral of Scientific Method

Scientific method is characterised by a never-ending spiral movement. It is schematically represented in fig. 2. The cycle implied in the spiral will be followed in the clock-wise direction. For convenience of reference, the four -cardinal points of the cycle are denoted by the terms Nadir, Ascendent, Zenith, and Descendent. The nadir marks the accumulation of facts, obtained by observation, experimentation and other forms of experience. The ascendent marks the accumulation of indicted or empirical laws got out of the facts accumulated at the nadir, by inductive logic including normal equations and other aids from statistical calculus. The zenith marks the fundamental laws formulated with the aid of intuition of some degree or other, so as to comprehend all the inducted or empirical laws accumulated at the ascendent as compelling implications. The descendent marks the accumulation of the deduced laws got from the fundamental laws at the zenith, with the aid of deductive logic including general semantics and all kinds of mathematical calculuses.

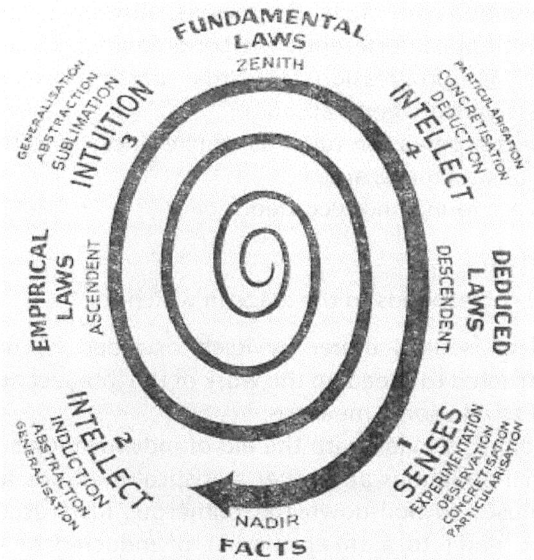

Fig 2. Spiral of Scientific Method

7.2.0. The Four Quadrants

The four cardinal points give rise to four quadrants in the cycle implied in the spiral. For convenience of reference, the quadrants will be numbered 1 to 4 respectively, as follows: quadrant 1 is the one between descendent and nadir; Quadrant 2 is the one between nadir and ascendent; Quadrant 3 is the one between ascendent and zenith; and Quadrant 4 is the one between zenith and descendent. The following statement is taken to be intelligible in the light of what has been said already:—

7.2.1. Quadrant 1

Quadrant 1 corresponds to the stage in the development of a domain of the universe of knowledge, conforming to scientific method, in which:.

1. Primary senses are used either in their native state or with the aid of instruments of various degrees of powerfulness;

2. Observations are made of knowees, either with or without experimental interference and conditioning;
3. There is progression towards particularisation, and regression from generalisation;
4. There is progression towards concreteness, and regression from abstractness; and
5. Facts are found and recorded.

7.2.2. Quadrant 2

Qudrant 2 corresponds to the stage in which:

1. Intellect is used either by itself or aided by machinery constructed to speed up the work of the intellect and to give relief to it in some measure;
2. Reasoning is made with the aid of inductive logic including normal equations and other statistical methods and other calculuses to boil down the numerous facts accumulated at the nadir to a small number of inducted or empirical laws—example, Kepler's Law of Equal Area, in the motion of planets, boiled down from the facts recorded by Tycho Brahe—more easy to hold in memory than the multitude of the facts themselves;
3. There is regression from particularisation, and progression towards generalisation ;
4. There is regression from concreteness, and progression towards abstractness; and
5. Inducted or empirical laws are formulated and recorded.

7.2.3. Quadrant 3

Quadrant 3 corresponds to the stage in which:

1. Intuition of some intensity or other is used unmediated by the primary senses or the intellect;
2. The inducted or empirical laws stand boiled down to a very small number of fundamental laws—example, Newton's Laws of Motion, to which many empirical laws such as the Kepler's Laws are reduced at one stroke—more easy to hold

in memory than the more numerous empirical or inducted laws;

3. There is regression from particularisation and progression towards ultimate generalisation;
4. There is regression from concreteness and progression towards ultimate abstractness; and
5. The fundamental laws are seized and recorded.

7.2.4. Quadrant 4

Quadrant 4 corresponds to the stage in which :

1. Intellect is used either by itself or aided by machinery constructed to speed up the work of the intellect and give relief to it in some measure;
2. Reasoning is made with the aid of deductive logic including general semantics, and mathematical and other calculuses to work out all the compelling implications of the fundamental laws;
3. There is progression towards particularisation, and regression from generalisation;
4. There is progression towards concreteness, and regression from abstractness; and
5. The deduced laws are derived and recorded;
6. The derived deduced laws include one and all of the inducted empirical laws; and
7. The number of deduced laws exceeds that of the empirical laws, if the fundamental laws had been seized with intuition of adequate intensity.

7.2.5. Entrance Into The Next Cycle

The Spiral of Scientific Method begins the next cycle thereafter, by re-entering quadrant 1. Two things happen at the stage of development corresponding to quadrant 1 in the new cycle;

1. Observations and experiments are made to verify empirically the validity of the new deduced laws; and

2. Further observations and experiments are made continuously and this leads to accumulation of new empirical facts.

7.3. Helpfulness of the Fundamental Laws

So long as the deduced laws are empirically verified to be true and the new empirical facts are found to be in conformity with the implications of the fundamental laws, there is no further movement in the spiral, and the fundamental laws hold sway and continue to be deemed helpful. But, this seldom holds good for long. Disturbance arises sooner or later in almost all the domains in the universe of knowledge, as they get cultivated and developed.

7.4. Arduous Effort

As and when empirical facts and experience appear to contradict the fundamental laws, arduous effort is made to ensure, absence of any kind of fallacy in the process of deduction, any kind of defect in the logic or the calculus used in the process, and any kind of fault in the experiment or observation or in the instruments used. When warranted, more powerful instruments of observation, more exacting experiments, and sharper calculuses for deduction, are devised. Witness, for example, the invention of mass-spectroscopy which dissolved an apparent contradiction to Dalton's fundamental law about the atom, the devising of observations of stars during total solar eclipse which dissolved an apparent contradiction to Einstein's fundamental law of relativity, and the unceasing progress in the development of general semantics, and the mathematical calculuses to make deductions penetrating and free from fallacies. Every effort should also be made to reinterpret the terms in the formulation of the fundamental laws with the aid of exegetics, so as to get out of them their fullest possible import, lying hidden until the necessary empirical experience draws attention to it.

7.5. Declaration of Crisis

Now and again, contradiction between the empirical facts of experience and the currently used fundamental laws persists, in spite of all the possible precautions to ensure absence of faults and fallacies in the building of the facts of experience and the inference of the implications of the fundamental laws, and in spite of every possible and proper use of exegetics. Then we have to recognise the existence of a new class of facts and declare the incidence of a crisis in the application of the scientific method.

7.6. Resolution of Crisis

Then, the new class of empirical facts are accumulated at the nadir; and a new cycle gets into full swing and carries the Spiral of Scientific Method further. Work in quadrant 2 leads to a new set of empirical laws. Work in quadrant 3 leads to the seizing of a new set of fundamental laws. Work in quadrant 4 leads to a new set of deduced laws. Work in quadrant 1 is again started as before. This cycle is liable to be repeated without end in many a domain.

7.7. Definition of Science

Any domain in the universe of knowledge, irrespective of the subject and the method of study, which admits of the above described spiral of scientific method in its development, is a science.

In the natural sciences, including the physical and the biological sciences, the fundamental laws are called hypotheses. They furnish a descriptive formulation of the empirical facts of experience. In the social sciences, such as education, political science, economics, sociology, law, and library science—which is also one of them—the fundamental laws are called normative principles. They furnish an interpretative explanation of the empirical fact of experience and of the techniques found necessary in experience. The terms 'true' and 'false' apply only to facts and the empirical and deduced laws. They do not apply to hypotheses and normative principles—that is, to fundamental laws. These can only be described as helpful or unhelpful, according to as they fit in or not with the facts of empirical experience. Newton's laws did not fit in with certain new empirical facts found during the present century; and in this context, they ceased to be helpful hypotheses and gave place to Einstein's laws of relativity. These two sets of laws belong to two different cycles in the spiral of scientific method. As it often happens, particularly if the laws are seized by a sufficiently intensive intuition, the Newtonian hypothesis is contained in the Einsteinian hypothesis. For, the former is got out of the latter by taking the speed of light to be greater than any conceivable finite speed. Similarly, the after old, second law of library science—viz, books are for the Chosen Few— did not fit in with the library practices coming into vogue in community after community during the last century as a result of the onslaught of democracy. In this context, it ceased to be a helpful normative principle and gave place to the new second law viz, Books are for All. These two laws belong to two different cycles in the Spiral of Scientific Method. It can also be seen that the former version of the second law is contained as a particular case in the later version. Again, the old normative principle of political science—viz, 'The king can do no wrong'- did not fit in with the political practices coming into vogue in community after community during the last two centuries as a result of the onslaught of republic-idea. In this context, it ceased to be a helpful normative principle and gave place to the new normative principle. The Judiciary can do no wrong. As all the functions of the judiciary were vested in the king in the earlier days, the earlier normative principle was contained in the latter.

8. NATURE OF FUNDAMENTAL LAWS

The term 'Fundamental Laws' is the generic one used to comprehend the 'Hypothesis' of the Natural Sciences and the 'Normative Principles' of the Social Sciences. The Hypotheses form a descriptive formulation. The Normative Principles are thus different from Hypothesis in its role. However, both admit of deduced laws different from the empirical laws from which they were intuited.

8.1. General Laws

In their application, occasionally conflict may arise between the indications of the different Normative Principles. Again the inference from them will have to be subjected to the boundary conditions set by the social factors from time to time. In the case of the Fundamental Laws of Library Science the boundary conditions concern the

1. Public finance available for library service;
2. Extent of literacy;
3. Extent of industrialisation ;
4. Scale of dominance of the vocations of the community served; and
5. Social pattern.
6. In the resolution of the conflict we usually invoke the aid of some of the following General Laws:
7. Laws of Interpretation;
8. Law of Impartiality;
9. Law of Symmetry;
10. Law of Parsimony; and
11. Principle of Local Variation.

8.2. Normative Principles for Sub-Disciplines

Just as we invoke the aid of General Laws as explained in See 67, it has been found helpful to formulate special and distinctive Normative Principles to develop certain sub-disciplines of library science. We call these distinctive normative principles 'Canons'. The Canons of any sub-discipline are at bottom implications of the Five Laws themselves and are consistent with them. Further, in developing a sub-discipline along the lines indicated by its canons, we generally require some other aids. These aids are called 'Principles'. The terms—Laws, Canons, and Principles—are introduced for convenience in order to distinguish their relative status. The canons and the principles applicable to the different sub-disciplines of library science will be illustrated in subsequent publications in this series. They will also trace the march of these subdivisions till today. Possible march of these sub-disciplines in future will also be discussed.

★★★

Reference Service through four Centuries

S. R. Ranganathan
National Research Professor in Library Science, and Honorary Professor, DRTC, Bangalore.

Abstract

Mentions reference service as the supreme and ultimate purpose of a library and indicates the emphasis on it by each of the five laws of library science. Shows the non-emergence of reference service in the centuries when the chief motive of a library was to build a good collection of books and not the promotion of their use, later on when only a few scholars used libraries, they relied only on self-reference service. Indicates the beginning of the provision of an occasional reference librarian or a panel of research consultants in the early nineteenth century. The emergence of ready reference service in the public library system coming into vogue after the middle of the nineteenth century is dealt with. The later emergence of long range reference service in generalist libraries for helping readers in the choice of books for the extension of their knowledge is described. Points out the latest development of reference service in the form of finding for specialist readers the nascent micro documents in the subject of specialisation, Finally, explains the work being done in DRTC in training documentalists and doing and guiding research in the highly sophisticated techniques of documentation and mention the intention of DRTC to provide for consultant service in documentation to industrial enterprises in the country.

Reprinted with permission from Library Herald, 9(2-3), pp. 543-554, 1966.

1. REFERENCE SERVICE AND FIVE LAWS OF LIBRARY SCIENCE

All the five laws of library science point to reference service as the supreme and ultimate function of a library. All its other activities, such as book-selection, acquisition of books, accessioning them, and classifying and cataloguing them are only the means to make reference service possible and effective. Reference is the act of getting the books of a library put into as wide a use as possible. This is the demand of the first law-Books are for use. Reference service is the pinpointed service of the books needed by the reader at the moment. This is the import of the second law-Every reader his book. Reference service insists that the librarian should not rest on his oars when there is even one book which complains of not getting its reader. This is the demand of third law-Every book its reader. One of the means of increasing the probability for the fulfilment of the third law is to bring to the notice of the reader an exhaustive list of the books in the library hearing on the subject of his interest at the moment. Time is of the very essence of reference service-both subjective and objective time. Pin-pointed and exhaustive service should be done as expeditiously as possible. No time of the reader should be wasted in this process. His time should be used only in helping him to formulate precisely his requirements-to state his subject of interest underlining each one of its facets and the exact focus will each of them. This is the demand of the fourth law - Save the time of the reader. If the number of books in a library is very small there would be no need perhaps to provide any reference service. It would be still more so if the collection in the library is fairly static. But the fifth law asserts that a library is growing organism. This means the collection will be normally evergrowing; it will be never static, so it is with readers too. Therefore the fifth law also makes reference service a necessity.

2. PERIOD OF COLLECTION AS CHIEF MOTIVE

The period of study covered by this paper begins with 1602 AD the year of foundation of the Bodleyan Library. The very first years of the Bodleyan Library show domination by the spirit of collection.

Bodley is said to have acquired even Chinese books though there was hardly any possible user for them at that time. No doubt, the few large libraries of those years did great service to make collection the dominant purpose. They collected books even as a museum would artifacts as the remains of culture. Perhaps there was also an idea that some days every book collected in the library would throw light on one aspect or another of history. To say this does not amount to saying that the books were not used. They were no doubt, used by a few scholars. But developing the use of the books appears to have been only a secondary purpose of the libraries at that time. In this context almost the entire thought should have been devoted to swell the collection, hardly recognising the need for reference service as defined in Section 1 of this paper.

3. SCHOLARLY LIBRARY AND SELF-REFERENCE SERVICE

There was another factor which did not make the institution of reference service necessary. The number of books published was small; the number of literates was also small; and the number of scholars keen to read books should have been only a fraction of the number of the literates. The subject-scatter of the books was very limited. In the early years of the period, a scholar knew most of the authors in his field. Even among the scholars, the antiquarians and the bibliophiles formed sizeable groups. A bibliophilic scholar often became the librarian or *vice versa.* Such a librarian knew most of the books in his library and if any scholar mentioned a topic, he could with the aid of his rich memory locate the relevant book. However, such a contact between the reader and the librarian was not frequent. I felt the impact of this early tradition when the National Library at Calcutta had to appoint a librarian shortly after independence Sir Maurice Gwayer, then the Vice Chancellor of the University of Delhi and well steeped in Oxford tradition, asked me to help an applicant on the ground of his wide scholarship. When the applicant met me, I found that he was a Professor of Sanskrit. I asked him why he wanted to change over. He said, "Much of time is lost in teaching! If I am appointed librarian of the National Library, I can spend all my time in studying, collating, describing, and evaluating the books in the library!" Often the motive of the bibliophile working as librarian was not so much the desire to disseminate widely and purposefully the ideas embodied in books as to fulfil his own satisfaction.

4. CASUAL REFERENCE SERVICE

Later in the nineteenth century, the number of books in the libraries had increased enormously. The number of scholars seeking the use of the library also increased. It was no longer possible for the scholar to be his own reference librarian. Nor was it possible for a scholar to depend upon some bibliophile in the library to bring out of his memory the titles likely to be of use to him. Therefore some of the big libraries began to set apart occasionally one member of the staff to help readers in the choice of their books. He acquired a good competence in the use of the catalogue of the library. He also spent time in dipping into the ideas contained in books - to the extent possible. The experience he gained in helping one scholar was often put to use in helping another scholar. In this way casual reference service began. Sometimes the reference problem would be too specialised for that one person. To meet the situation the Library of Congress is said to have had a panel of research consultants. These were retired scholars living in their own homes. When an occasional call came, they would go to the library and help the readers concerned.

5. PUBLIC LIBRARY AND READY REFERENCE SERVICE

When the public library system was established, the public were encouraged to look to the library for information about facts. The ready reference was instituted to supply such information. The librarian was hacked by a battery of ready reference books which came to be published from about the middle of the nineteenth century. In India, state-wide public library system has been estab–lished-now for twenty years-only in the constituent states of Madras and Andhra Pradesh. The Mysore State has just begun to implement its Public Libraries Act (1965). Even in the two former states, where public libraries have been functioning for nearly twenty years, an adequate supply of ready reference books is not available. Nor has ready reference service come very much into vogue. Probably the same is the condition in the few public libraries in the other states of India.

6. DEEPER REFERENCE SERVICE

The laws of library science will not be satisfied with ready reference service alone. They demand a deeper and more intimate form of reference service, which helps a reader to work his way through books to add to his knowledge and not merely to pick up a small piece of information needed at the moment. It is too early to expect this in the public libraries of our country today. I saw the supreme value of this form of our reference service when I started organising the Madras University Library in 1925. To distinguish it from ready reference service, I called it long range reference service. Long range reference service had to be backed by a good classified catalogue of the library with the profuse subject analyticals and also a large collection of published bibliographies. Apart from this, long range reference service depended essentially on a special section of library personnel. I called this section reference section. In a staff of 18, as many as five were assigned to the reference section. They soon acquired a good knowledge of facet analysis. This helped them to elicit from a reader in the quickest possible time an approximate formulation of his requirement at the moment. After getting the approximate formulation of the requirement, the reference librarian would use the method of trial and error to find out the exact books that would answer the purpose of the reader. He would also keep in intermittent touch with reader to make the books come closest to the needs of the reader. This enabled the reference librarians to acquire good knowledge of the varied psychology of readers - say superiority complex, inferiority complex, and traumatic complex. The reference librarian and myself used to meet frequently to discuss the problems arising from time to time. In these meetings I used to explain the psychological varieties of readers and the idiosyncrasies of books. My book *Reference service* (1943; 1961) is based on these experiences. Our knowledge of the ideas contained in the various books and of their standards grew like snow ball with every day's experience. It is not that every person selected was found fit to be continued in the reference section. For geniality is the foremost quality in a reference librarian if readers are to accept his service. By trial and errors we were able to get a stable corpse of the reference librarians of the right kind. They enjoyed meeting the readers and helping them. No reader entering the stack room was left to himself without being greeted and offered help by some reference librarian or other. During the last twenty years, I have been meeting here and there in India as well as outside India persons who had the benefit of reference service given by the Madras University Library. They always recall the service with appreciation and gratefulness. They mention in particular the names of C Sundaram and S Ramabhadran, who had been longest in the reference section, with great warmth and kindness. According to the five laws of library science, reference service of this kind should be established in every academic and public library, if the money that is tied up in the library in general and in the library books in particular is to give an adequate social dividend to the community.

7. SPECIALIST LIBRARY AND DOCUMENTATION SERVICE

After World War II, social forces have intensified reference service in specialist libraries. They have also made it obligatory. The essence of reference service in a specialist library differs from that in a generalist library. To emphasise this difference in essence, reference service in a specialist library is called documentation service. Documentation service is reference service with emphasis on specialist readers and on nascent micro ideas - mostly found in periodicals. To do documentation service there is need for the reference librarian to have not only a very intensified knowledge of the techniques of facet analysis and of reader psychology, but he should also himself specialise in the subject in which he is to do reference service. His specialisation in the subject is not like that of the specialist himself. His specialisation consists in knowing intimately the highways and byways in the special subject and the trend of happenings in the wave-front of knowledge in that subject. But even with this, the ordinary library catalogue and the published bibliographies of book will not prove sufficient tools for him. He should have at his elbow a bibliography of the current articles in the periodicals in the subject served. Such a bibliography is called a documentation list. It is not practicable for the same person to analyse the current numbers of all the periodicals and prepare a documentation list, and do documentation service to the specialist readers on the other hand. Nor would it be economical for each specialist library to prepare its own documentation list. Each nation requires such a list being prepared by a national documentation centre, for articles appearing in the periodicals currently taken in the country. After some months these lists can be replaced by an international documentation list-be it a bare list or a list with abstracts-making an exhaustive coverage of all the periodicals published in the world on the subject. However, for the periodicals in the interim period, before the national documentation list and/or the international documentation list arrives, the reference librarian himself should prepare a temporary documentation list for the most recent nascent micro subjects received in the library. Therefore, the reference librarian in a specialist library should be equally able in preparing a documentation list and in giving documentation service. To denote a person with such qualifications we use the term 'Documentalist'. When compared with the work of the reference librarian in a generalist library, the work of a documentalist is very sophisticated. It involves techniques of a much deeper kind. Moreover these techniques will be ever growing. Therefore, a documentalist needs special training not only in doing documentation service, not only in preparing documentation list, but also in doing his own tiny research-it will be mostly developmental research-in his own subject field in order to cope with the onslaught of the new micro subjects pouring into the library.

8. DOCUMENTATION RESEARCH AND TRAINING CENTRE (DRTC)

The DRTC conceived by Professor P C Mahalanobis was established in Bangalore in 1962 for two primary purposes. One is the training of the documentalist. As our country is getting fast industrialised and as the world conditions make it difficult and risky to depend solely or even largely as here to fore on the designs and the techniques of production imported from abroad, our industries should be home-based in every way. It goes without saying that we cannot continue the old designs and techniques of production which are fast getting out-moded. We must have our own designs and techniques of production and have them continuously improved. This requires, research at all levels-developmental applied, as well as pure. Both research of this kind and industrial production should be carried out with the least wastage of the human potential in a country. For this purpose, continuing research is necessary - developmental, applied, as well as pure-in the field of documentation. This is another primary objective of the DRTC. During the last five years its output has not been negligible. Among the end products we can count, nearly 120 schedules for the depth classification of the production of diverse commodities. There are also some secondary purposes to be served by the DRTC. One of them is to train persons in research in documentation. This activity has been taken up since 1966. Another activity intended is to take working documentalists into the DRTC for short periods of time and improve upon and design if necessary, the documentation and classification techniques suited to their parent bodies. This was also begun in 1966. For want of a sufficient number of competent teachers we are not able to carry out this purpose in a large measure. Another purpose is to provide consultant service on documentation to the industrial houses and research laboratories. This work cannot be taken up until we have a sufficient number of documentalists trained in research in documentation. Perhaps this stage may be reached by the beginning of the Fifth Plan period.

★★★

Documentation, Computer and Classification

(Non-conventional methods in document retrieval 4)
(Classification problems. 23)

S. R. Ranganathan
National Research Professor in Library Science and Honorary Professor, DRTC, Bangalore 3

Abstract

A computer can be of use in repetitive work in a library, wherever it is viable. But it cannot be used for classification for which judgement is necessary. The memory of a computer should be fed with classified main entries to enable it to produce for browsing a set of entries in classified sequence. The Freely-Faceted Classification is the most evolved scheme designed so far, for use in computer. Version 3 of CC is an example. Continuing concerted research is necessary in the fields of design of depth classification and of building of computer.

1. "LOTUS EATER" IN MAN

1.1. Native Inertia

The "Lotus Eater" in Man is inexorable. On the slightest pretext it makes man fall into a mood of inaction saying to himself, as it were, "Why should life all labour be, when there is a god or somebody else to do everything for us?". This mood begins first as complacence, then transitions into inaction, and finally lands man in indolence. Here the native inertia in man gains the upper hand. Any inner urge for an active life and work-satisfaction

Reprinted with permission from Library Science with a slant to Documentation, 4(3), pp. 597-644, 1967.

gets smothered. The danger of this is particularly severe and widespread in a profession just born; and the library profession is one such. Therefore, the library profession should keep itself on the alert against the "Lotus Eater". This is particularly necessary in India and the newly developing countries of today.

1.2. Self-Documenting Scholar

Till about a century ago, the librarian was often an approximation to an antiquarian in the book world and a descriptive and historical bibliographer. He did service fairly well to suit the needs of the few scholars in the Humanities, History, and their auxiliaries. Even to them, his chief service was due to his knowledge of the book as a whole and to his long-built memory which would enable him to bring several forgotten books to the notice of a scholar. But in regard to documentation work - that is, listing micro documents, particularly nascent ones - the scholars were self- documentalists. Time – as immediacy - did not exert much pressure on such scholars. Therefore, they did not find any need to delegate document-search, documentation work, and documentation service to the librarian. Library Committees - of say. University Libraries - were usually made of the Dons of the University. They would not even concede the possibility of a minute classification of reading materials or allow their arrangement in a classified sequence. For example, in 1925 I found the books in a Scotish University arranged in accession sequence. The librarian who was knowledgeable told me that the Chairman of the Library Committee would not allow him to classify the books and arrange them according to class numbers. A day later I called on a professor of the University, who was my professor's professor. He was a famous scholar.

Prof:- Why did you give up your teaching work and become a librarian ? What is there in librarianship to attract a man with brains ?

R.- Pinpointed service of documents to scholars and students is an important service. It would give a challenge even to the best of brains.

Prof.- Professors and students know what they want. They ask for it. What have you to do except to pull out the document asked for ?

R.- This assumption is not right. The librarian's duty is to bring to the notice of scholars and students documents not known to them - be they old or the latest ones published the other day. Their number is so great that no scholar or student will know all of them.

Prof.- What can the librarian do ?

R.- He classifies the documents minutely and arranges them according to the class numbers. In this arrangement, the documents follow one another in a helpful sequence, according to the degree of filiation of their subjects. When a scholar or a student mentions his subject, the librarian can show him on the shelves a subject-spectrum as it were. Browsing amidst the documents in the successive subjects appearing in the spectrum, helps the scholar or the student to find all the documents relevant to his search at the moment, in spite of his not having known many of them.

Prof.- How can such a classification be done? In what subject will you put Whittaker and Watson's *Modem Analysis* ?

R.- Classification and Cataloguing have together developed methods of dealing with such multi-focal books.

Prof.- How can a librarian classify books unerringly where even scholars fail ? The Royal Society started with an ambitious scheme of classification. It asked the specialist scholars themselves to classify. In spite of it, look at the absurd classification they have made. They classified, as Dynamics, the *Laws of motion* of Sylvester! As a mathematician, you know that Sylvester was an algebraist and that his paper was on the Theory of Indices!!

R.- This should have happened because the scholars who were engaged in classification did not know the first principle in classification.

Prof.- What is that principle?

R.- Never classify by the title. Dip into the document to determine its subject.

The conversation went on in this style for nearly an hour. The Professor slowly began to concede the helpfulness of classification in document-search and the advantage of leaving document arrangement and document-search in the hands of a specialised profession - the Library Profession.

Prof.- But why has not our librarian done anything of this kind ?

R.- He is an able man. He told me that he was prevented by the domineering self-willed Chairman of the Library Committee from disturbing the old arrangement by accession numbers.

Prof.- I may tell you at once that you are now talking to that very Chairman!

We had a hearty laughter and the Professor said that he would tell his librarian that he had full freedom to give the best of his profession to the scholars and the students in the University. In such a context the "Lotus Eater" in the librarian would easily assert itself and deprive him of any urge to develop documentation work and service and thereby become a partner in research. No need would be felt for any close classification of books - let alone the depth classification of articles in periodicals.

1.3. Service to the Generalist Reader

From the beginning of the present century, public libraries came to be established in increasing numbers for the service of the common man. These libraries created a new wing, as it were, of the library profession. Its main mission is to attract the common man to the library and give him "Whole Books" for recreation, inspiration, and information. The public librarian specialised in devising various methods of attracting the public to the library and of retaining their custom. He found that the "Finding for every reader his book, finding for every book its reader, and saving the objective as well as the subjective time of the reader" were facilitated by arranging the books on the shelves in a classified sequence in the measure of the degree of the filiation of their subjects. The DC served this purpose admirably well. But the generalist reader was seldom interested in the deeper layers of the new thought just being created in the diverse subjects. Therefore, there was no demand for classifying articles in periodicals. It is no wonder therefore that the "Lotus Eater" in the public librarian prevented him from refining the scheme for classification in use towards what we now call 'Depth Classification'.

1.4. Service to the Specialist Reader

But the specialists, engaged in industrial research, gradually felt the need for documentation work and service. For, their need was for nascent micro subjects just appearing in print as articles in periodicals. Moreover, immediate service without fumbling about was another need of theirs. The success or the failure of an industry would depend on these needs being met or not met. But neither the bibliophilic nor the public librarian seems to have sensed this for long. Therefore, the specialists were obliged to release a few from among themselves to do document-search. For some years, their specialist knowledge enabled their inner memory to absorb and store the titles of the nascent micro documents appearing in their respective subjects from time to time. *Little* was realised that the down-pour of micro documents would soon disable the inner memory from doing so. Therefore, hardly any serious attempt was made to develop an "externalised memory" with the aid of Depth Classification. The traditional subject heading was the at most limit to which the "Lotus Eater" in them would allow them to go whatever be the difficulties caused by it. Here is an example of the grip of the "Lotus Eater" on the specialist librarian. Some years ago, taking advantage of the hospitality given by the Rockefeller Foundation, I visited several industries and industrial libraries in USA in order to gain first hand knowledge of the problems involved in serving micro documents to specialists and in the design of the depth classification needed for documentation. A friend of mine introduced me, on the phone, to the specialist librarian of an *oil* enterprise. He mentioned me as Professor. He would not describe me either as Librarian or as Professor of Library Science. He said that I would know the reason later on.

SL (Specialist Librarian).- I am glad to have you with us, Professor. What can I do for you ?

R.- I want to study your documentation work.

SL.- I am ever so glad. I analyse every oil periodical and put in Subject Analytical Cards for every article.

R.- That is exactly what I want to see.

SL.- Here they are in this battery of cabinets.

R.- You have indeed put in a good amount of work on this. It should be very helpful to your research workers.

SL.- I improvise all the subject headings myself. I have no faith in the librarians trained over there in the University. They can only stamp books or talk 'theory' at best.

R.- Here is something interesting. Over there in the third tray, I found a certain article indexed under a subject heading. When I pull out this forty-ninth tray, I find an article on the same subject put under a different subject heading. Let me check up whether you have put it under the other heading also.. No you have not. Nor have you put that other article in this heading.

SL.- Yes. I see it. You should be quite thorough in your oil technology, Professor. No other Professor discovered this inconsistency nor did I. What enabled you to find out this error?

R.- Facet Analysis.

SL.- Facet Analysis! I have never heard of this in oil technology.

R.- No. You cannot. It is a technique in library science particularly in classification.

SL.- How did you find time Professor to be wasted on library science ?

R.- I am not a Professor of Oil Technology as you seem to have assumed. I am a Professor of Library Science.

Then the SL became very apologetic for his having used abusive terms so often in referring to the library profession. The "Lotus Eater" in him had not allowed him to step out a little and learn the techniques of classification; and what was worse, he even developed a contempt for it.

1.5. Post-war Demand for Depth Classification

After World War II the mounting population pressure has began to create a problem. To prevent havoc by the internal enemies such as starvation, squalor, and disease and to be prepared to meet war and aggression from outside, every country finds it necessary to maximise its industrial output and for this purpose to maximise its industrial and pure research. One of the steps necessary in maximising them is to introduce a division of labour in research and to mark off those with special aptitude for research from those with special aptitude for document-search. Another necessary step is to minimise the same research running in parallel in different wings of the same enterprise or in different enterprises in the same country, or even in different countries to the extent practicable. On the other hand research must be made to run in relay. Each team should take up its own research at the point where it was left by an earlier team, carry it forward, and hand it over to some other team for further pursuit. To secure this, documentation should be thorough. In other words, it should bring to the notice of every research worker or research team pin pointedly, exhaustively, and without any loss of time all the micro documents bearing on the subject of investigation. It is the nascent micro subject that is of vital importance. One of the known methods of securing this level of efficiency in documentation is to organise the documents or their entries in a strictly classified sequence with the aid of a scheme of depth classification, capable of giving co-extensive individualising class number to every subject, however narrow its extension and however deep its intension. This pressing social demand has led to a considerable amount of research in classification during the last twenty years. Two of the outstanding results that came out of his piece of research are Facet Analysis (based on certain 'Postulates and Principles) and Chain Procedure. The Facet Analysis helps in the work of a classificationist in designing a scheme for depth classification and in the work of a classifier using a Depth Scheme. The Chain Procedure helps in the construction of Subject Headings in a systematic and economical way for the Class Index Entries in the alphabetical part of a documentation list and in the construction of Feature Headings in the classified part of the list. The value of this Facet Analysis was emphasised in 1955 at the time of the International Congress of Libraries and Documentation Centres held in Brussels - even before it was refined with the aid of Postulates and Principles. One of the findings recorded at that Conference was that all future classification should be based on Facet Analysis, if it is to serve the purpose of depth classification. Thus the library profession has began to silence the "Lotus Eater" in it and see the wisdom of becoming a partner in research by doing document-search and by doing the research in Depth Classification needed for that purpose. The specifilists in the other subjects are also beginning to see the wisdom of withdrawing themselves from the field of classification and turning their whole thought to research in their respective subjects.

1.6. An Aside

In newly developing countries, the "Lotus Eater" seeks to linger on in the library profession with the old argument often repeated in the century before recovery, "Why should there be any research, any re-thinking in our country ? All that is needed is being done in the West". I have heard this argument quite often when the Indian Universities began to establish their Research Departments about forty years ago. Once I was pro–voked to ask, "If there is no need for research, why did you allow the establishment of Research Departments?" Spontaneous was the reply of the foreigners, "Just to provide places for a few educated Indians". But fortunately in respect of industrial research, the two unfortunate Border-Wars have given a shock therapy, as it were, in India. But in newly developing countries the old argument of the "Lotus Eater" is not easily withdrawn in many of the other subjects for research. It appears to linger on with obstinacy in respect of Library Science in general and of Classification in particular. The old gaurds still insist that anything useful in library classification can only be imported from abroad. This opinion is expressed *ex cathedra.* For the "Lotus Eater" in them prevents them from either seriously studying any indigenous attempt in the subject or applying the results of such an attempt. Perhaps this is due to their being too old and their mind having become too rigid. But, however, we should remind ourselves of Bernard Shaw's definition of a gentleman. The new generation of librarians in a newly developing country should take it as a matter of honour to their country to be a gentleman among nations. To be so, each country should give to the world at least as much as it takes from others in respect of research and design in Classification. If external threat and internal insufficiency make a country to take to research in other subjects and in industries, the moral obligation to be a gentleman among nations should make its own contribution by way of research in the library field. Hence the appeal goes to the library profession to exert itself in doing research; and to the older among them to value and support research within the country. The library profession of a country should also apply what is designed and discovered within it. Let not the young librarians allow themselves to be inhibited by the "Lotus Eater". Let not the young librarians eager to do research allow themselves to be discouraged in any manner. Let them not allow themselves to be threatened with the peril of their losing their places or jeopardizing their future, if they adopt any of the new techniques designed within their country. On the other hand, they should do everything to defy all such supports being given to the "Lotus Eater". They should find satisfaction and delight in the active pursuit of research in library science in general and in classification in particular, and in adopting the indigenous techniques, and in continuing to improve them from day to day, without of course shutting the doors against any of the newer and better ideas developed abroad.

1.7. "Lotus Eater" and the Prop From the Computer

At a time when the library profession in the world is accus–toming itself to its new function as documentalist and, for that purpose, to the cultivation of the field of classification, the "Lotus Eater" in it has picked up a new prop to reassert itself. This new prop has been furnished by the Electronic Age ushered into the world after World War II "The Computer is one of the versatile forms in which electronics can help mankind. We must accept the Computer. We must derive all the benefits it is capable of giving us. It can relieve us of much of repetitive routine work and thus it can release man to higher kinds of work - particularly creative work. Its versatility is being increasingly extended year by year. Naturally, the electronic engineers would like to permeate everywhere. They have tempted the "Lotus Eater" in the library profession with the very welcome words, "You need not hereafter slave at classification and cataloguing. Our Computer will do all that for you". The immediate result of such an assurance to the "Lotus Eater" was a cleavage in the library profession. Many said with relief, "No more bother". The Computer and the Programme Assistant will do all the necessary document-search. However, there is now a slow recovery from this naive faith in the Computer. There is willingness to examine the problem uninfluenced by the "Lotus Eater". Let us trace the stages through which the examination of the problem has been moving.

2. SCOPE FOR ELECTRONICS IN LIBRARY WORK

2.1. Viability and Scope

There are many items of work in the day-to-day management of a library which can very well be transferred from human hands to the Computer. Of course, this should be done only as and when it acquires economic viability. Economic viability would depend upon the work-load of each kind to be transferred to the care of the Computer and upon our capacity to make Computers ourselves without importing them from abroad at the cost of our all too poor foreign exchange capacity which is all needed for more urgent and vital purposes. Ultimately, it would depend on the stage of development of the country.

2.2. Hasty Mistakes

Whatever mistakes may be made in this respect in the first flush of amazement and wonder, the Laws of Economics will soon bring in wisdom. Avoidance of rash, precipitous, and unthinking change-over is particularly essential in a newly developing country with a vast population. The mistake of such a country in renting or purchasing Computers, at a cost too prohibitive for library purposes, should be avoided.

2.3. Cataloguing

A Computer requires a considerable capital investment. Therefore, it will not be economical at present for an individual library to resort to it in the work of cataloguing. To get an adequate return on the capital investment, it looks as if a Com–puter can be thought of only on a country-basis or even on inter-country-basis.

2.4. Classification

Apart from this, an important question is, "Can classificationists and classifiers abdicate their function and depend on the Computer to take their place in the chain of work involved in the rendering of library service to the satisfaction of all the Five Laws of Library Science?" They cannot because, classification involves judgement - judgement of the subject of the document in all its facets and arrays manifest in it. This cannot be done by the statistical analysis of the words in the document, which alone the machine can do.

2.5. Browsing, A Necessity

A Computer can inform a reader, almost instantaneously, the location of the book needed by him at the moment, if he mentions particulars, such as author and title. For, there is no judgement involved in this. But it is a matter of experience that the majority of readers do not and cannot always look for their document *via* the name of the author or the title. The most popular approach is the subject approach. Here, hardly any reader - particularly, a reader engaged in work in the wave-form of knowledge - can specify his subject in exact terms, with all its "individuating particularities" as William Blake would put it. He can identify it only when he sees spread out before him, in a more or less Apupa pattern, the subjects falling within his umbral and penumbral regions of interest. A homely parallel is the inability of a lady to specify the exact colour pattern and the other details which her new saree (the coloured silk cloth worn by Indian ladles) should have. It is seldom that her husband can give her satisfaction if he is guided merely by her verbal instructions. On the other hand, the moment the shop-keeper spreads out an assortment of coloured sarees before her, the lady is able to pick out her choice to her full satisfaction without any loss of time. So it is with a reader; the specific subject of interest is often ineffable. Therefore, browsing through a classified sequence of books or of catalogue entries is a necessity.

2.6. Current Live Books

Therefore, whatever be the case for computerising the old seldom-used books or their catalogue cards, the current live books - that is, books not yet outmoded in thought, say books pub–lished within the last fifty years - should be placed in stack-rooms and given open access; and their classified catalogue should be in the conventional form that can be directly read by the readers. The stack-room should be guided plentifully with tier-guides, gangway-guides, bay-guides, and shelf-guides. Each guide board or guide label should have a bilingual legend. It should carry the name of the subject in the favoured natural language of the library; this is obviously necessary. It should also carry the name of the subject in the classificatory language - that is, the class number of the subject - in order that the mind of the reader may be guided helpfully without getting irrigated by the absence of the familiar alphabetical sequence. Similarly, the classified part of the catalogue of the books of current value should have guide cards with similar bilingual legends. Further, close classifying is essential. To make close classifying keep step with the onward march of the Universe of Subjects, the classification system should be continuously refined and kept ever up-to-date. For this purpose, the service of the professional classificationist is essential. Continuous research in classification is also essential. Therefore, the library profession should not allow itself to be corrupted by the advent of the Computer and should not rest on its oars or desert the discipline of library classification.

2.7. Old Dead Books

In the case of the old dead books, the number of readers seeking them is likely to be small. But even they can get better help if browsing or scanning through a sequence of classified entries is made possible for them. Perhaps, the Computer is being fast sophisticated sufficiently to enable it to type out such a spectrum of classified entries in the Apupa pattern specific to the reader at the moment. But to do this, the memory of the Computer should be stored with minutely classified main entries of all the books and other documents. This again makes the old dead books also point to the same conclusion as the current live books do. The library profession cannot throw away the responsibility to learn the discipline of classification and to keep it continuously cultivated. To get the best result from the computer, classification may need enrichment of a new kind, which calls for special research.

2.8. Data Processing

Modern research is in vital need of correlation of data. A publication such as the *Tables annuelles de constantes* can only provide data. But they cannot correlate them. Nor is it possible for the librarian to do it. It is the province of the Data Specialists. They can use the Computer profitably. It is a fallacy to mistake this data-correlation work capable of being done by Computers to be the same as library service. This fallacy leads to statements such as "As data can be processed by Computer very rapidly, we now move literally into the age of patterned recognition out of the world of mere data classification". Let it be remembered that data-correlation is only a tiny part of the classification of subjects. Unlike the former, the latter requires judgement. The Computer cannot exercise judgement.

2.9. Inexorability of Classification

At present the Computer can do a good deal of the work in a library, not needing judgement. We can use it for that kind of work wherever the work-load is large enough to make the ser–vice by Computers cheaper, in the overall sense, than service by humans. But classification requires judgement. Therefore, it will have to be done by humans. It will have to be so until the Computer can have the faculty of judgement built into it. Further, the universe of subjects is ever-proliferating in unpredictable ways. Therefore, continuing developmental research in classification is necessary. Moreover, from time to time fundamental research too will become necessary in classification. Can the capacity to do research of these kinds be built into the Computer ? Perhaps not. In the meantime, the more thorough the classification used, the greater will be the possibility to feed the memory of the Computer, so as to have the least leakage and noise at the time of document-search. Further, the Computer cannot give its best service unless the "Programme Assistant" has a sound and sufficient knowledge of the latest practice in classification. Moreover, the Reference Librarian should be an adept in the method of facet analysis in order to facet-analyse the mind of the specialist enquirer and thereby lead him to the closest possible approximation to the full and detailed formulation of the subject interesting him at the moment of enquiry. Then only he can be helped to reach his exact Apupa region - be it in the stack-room or in the catalogue of documents - and choose his documents to the full satisfaction of the Laws of Library Science. Then only the Reference Librarian can help the Programme Assistant to give the right programme to the Computer. Thus, library classification is inexorable today and it may continue to be so. Let us therefore briefly trace the evolution of classification and have a look at the latest of its species.

3. SCHEMES FOR CLASSIFICATION

3.1. Five Species

The core of library classification is the classification of subjects. The following five species can be recognised among the schemes for classification of subjects developed till now:

1. Enumerative Scheme;
2. Almost-Enumerative Scheme;
3. Almost-Faceted Scheme;
4. Rigidity-Faceted Scheme - that is, a Scheme for Classification with Pre-determined Facets and Facet Sequence; and
5. Freely-Faceted Scheme - with the alternative name Analytico-Synthetic Classification Guided by Postulates and Principles and not subjected to a pre-determined facet formula.

3.2. Direction of Evolution

Generally speaking, the evolution of the species of schemes for classification has been in the sequence mentioned above. The Enumerative Species has been in vogue from the very beginning. The Almost-Enumerative Species was initiated by DC in 1876. Beginning with DC as core, the Almost-Faceted Species was brought into being by UDC in 1896. The Rigidly-Faceted Species was initiated by CC in 1933. Finally, the Freely-Faceted Species, the latest in the line of evolution, is being evolved out of CC itself since 1957. It reached a fairly advanced stage in 1963. It is now being widely applied by the Research Cell in the Documentation Research and Training Centre (Bangalore) in the design of depth schedules and in the depth classification of micro subjects going with a variety of basic subjects.

3.3. Cases of Regression

There have been some regression from the line of evolution. LC was designed as an Enumerative Scheme in 1904. The latest in this line of regression is the RIC developed in 1961. In this late year, it has been designed as a strictly Enumerative Scheme.

4. ENUMERATIVE AND ALMOST-ENUMERATIVE SCHEMES

4.1. Enumerative Scheme

An Enumerative Scheme for Classification consists essentially of a single schedule enumerating all the subjects - of the past, the present, and the anticipatable future. Such a schedule will have necessarily to be long. It will soon be overpowered by the emergence of subjects beyond the anticipated ones - over–powered in the sense, that it will be difficult to find for each new subject a class number that will individualise it and also imple–ment its filiatory position among the already existing subjects. Moreover, the class number of an enumerative scheme often consists of a succession of semantically rich digits, not separated into meaningful groups or facets as we call them. In this sense, its class number may be, said to be monolithic.

4.2. Practical Classification

To classify with an Enumerative Scheme we have successively to

1. Get a general feel of the subject of the document from its title, if it is expressive - that is, tell tale - and otherwise by a rapid perusal of its text;
2. Get the name of the subject formulated in the light of our general experience with the lay-out of the schedule of subjects in the classified part of the scheme for classification;
3. Locate the name of the subject in the index to the schedule;
4. Pick up its class number given in the index;

5. Turn to the section of the schedule containing that class number;
6. Verify whether that is the best number that can be found in the schedule to represent the subject; and in this way
7. Determine the class number by trial and error.

4.3. Necessity to Start with Index

Naturally the full schedule in an Enumerative Scheme will run to hundreds of pages. Even a schedule for the subjects going with a particular main subject will run to several pages. For example, even in such a broad and superficial scheme as RIC the schedule for the subjects going with Education runs through 20 pages. On the other hand, in a fairly close and deep scheme as LC the corresponding schedule runs through 178 pages.

In DC which comes intermediate between RIC and LC in its depth, the schedule runs through 30 pages, if we exclude historical and geographical treatment. The necessity to start with the index of the schedule in an Enumerative Scheme can thus be seen.

4.4. Rider's International Classification

RIC avowedly forces every subject into a Procrustean, bed of class numbers with three digits only. Even the schedule of geographical isolates is avoided with the following words:

"Wherever Geographical Subdivision seems by it to be called for, it sets out *as an integral part of its classification tables,* the exact amount and the exact kind of geographical subdivision which it deems necessary at that particular point". Its schedule runs to 922 pages. It enumerates about 18,000 subjects. The shortness of the schedule is secured by RIC at the peril of its being already overpowered even by the existing subjects. For it gives one and the same class number for several subjects. For example,

PPP Ships for all sorts of special purposes. Dredges.
Lighters. Floating docks and derricks. Light ships. Garbage disposal barges. Police and quarantine tenders. Fire boats, etc.

RAM Holders and containers.
Bottles. Beakers. Retorts. Flasks. Test-tubes. Supports for them. Laboratory glass manipulation. Bending. Cutting. Blowing.

XAK Phonology.
Comparative study of language sounds in all languages. Aspirates. Labials. Linguals. Palatals. Sibilants. Fricatives. Gutterals. Clicks. Sounds unique to one, or to a group of languages.

The provision of a single class number for many subjects is liable to produce "Chaos-in-Little" among the books carrying that single class number. While this is so in known subjects, one can imagine the extent of overpowering by the subjects emerging in the future. Therefore, the resilience of RIC is very limited. It is true that RIC is intended only for the classification of books embodying macro subject. It is far too inadequate even for this purpose.

4.5. Library of Congress Classification

In LC also common isolates, such as standard divisions and geographical isolates, have not been separated out into schedules of their own. It "tailors" even the geographical divisions according to the needs of the respective host subjects and builds their numbers into the monolithic class numbers differently in different subjects. As a result, its schedule runs to 29 volumes totalling about 7,200 pages. It enumerates about 300,000 subjects. What can be achieved to accommodate more subjects by a Faceted Decimal Fraction Notation, LC seeks to achieve by an Integer Notation with gaps - no doubt liberal - intended to accommodate newly emerging subjects. But subjects usually outwit our judge–

ment about the point where gaps are necessary in class numbers and about the size of the gap to be left. Therefore, LC also is likely to be overpowered by new subjects. The chance for this is increased as one and the same gap has to accommodate new subordinate classes as well as new co-ordinate classes. As a result its resilience too is limited though not as much as that of RIC. LC reinforces the resilience of its notational system by a profuse use of Alphabetical Device. Further, when a gap is chocked up, it adds a decimal fraction number to the integer number to represent new subjects claiming a place between two consecutive integer numbers. For example, in the schedule for the Main Class "L Education", excluding "LD Individual Institutions", 5 percent of the class numbers have such decimal fraction attachments. Here are three examples of chocked gaps propped up by decimal fraction attachment.

LB 1050	Reading (General)
LB1050.5	Remedial teaching
LB1051	Educational psychology (General works)
LB 1627	Entrance requirements
LB1627.7	Transfer credit
LB 1628	Curriculum (General)
LB3013	School management
LB3013.5	Visiting teachers. School social workers.
LB3013.6	School psychologists
LB3014	Special systems (Minor works)

4.6. Decimal Classification: Almost Enumerative

4.6.1. Basic Facet and One Additional Facet

Though essentially enumerative, from the very beginning DC had provided for one isolate facet in addition to the basic facet. That was the facet of, what is now called, Standard Subdivision. This was originally called Form Division. This earlier name was meaningful. It underlines the fact that the different class numbers derived by attaching a Form Division Number to the same host class number brings together all the documents giving particular forms of treatment of the host subject. The part of a class number representing the Standard Division is an isolate facet of it. The table of Standard Divisions is really a schedule of the isolates capable of forming such an isolate facet in subjects. This can be seen from the following statement of the Editor of DC Ed 17:

"3-37 STANDARD SUBDIVISIONS Having analyzed thru all the steps of the ladder the number chosen for the book in hand, and decided that it is the correct and most specific number, you are now ready to consider what further specification is desirable, *i.e.,* whether any of the standard subdivisions are applicable. If your book deals with technique and apparatus of the subject, you may add 028; if it consists of a collection of articles on the subject, you may add 08.

The connecting digit for an isolate facet of standards of Division is most often '0' (Zero). In a few exceptional cases, '00' '000' are prescribed. The schedule of isolates that can form Standard Subdivision Facets is given in pages 1255 to 1262 of DC Ed 17."

4.7. Basic Facet and Two Additional Facets

DC Ed 17 has provided for two facets in addition to the basic facet. One of them is the facet of Standard Subdivision already described in the preceding section. The second is the Geographical Facet. The geographical isolate number is called Area Notation. The Area Table gives the schedule of the isolates capable of forming a geographical facet. This can be seen from the following statement of the Editor of DC Ed 17:

"3.353 *Area notation* When a given heading has particular geographic significance and there are numerous books dealing with the subject in a given continent, country, locality, or other area, provision is made to expand the number for that heading by area. For example, under 331.29 Historical and geographical treatment of wages, you will find the instruction, "Add area notations 1-9 to 331.29". This means that a book on wages in Japan is to be placed in 331.295 2, that is, 331.29 plus the number 52 for Japan from the area table on page 1263. Wages in Tokyo would fall in 331.295 213 5, wages in rural regions in general in 331.291734."

The connecting digit for an Area Facet is '2' when it is so indi–cated in the schedule of basic subjects and otherwise '09'. The schedule of isolates that can form Geographical Facets is given in pages 1263 to 1503 of DC ED 17.

4.8. Synthesis Without Connecting Digit

DC has been all along providing also for what may be mistaken for an isolate facet. It has no connecting digit. A number taken from some schedule is directly attached to the host class number. This is indicated by the clever *"divide like"* note scattered all through the scheme. Ed 17 gives a summary list of these in pages 1505 to 1514 under the heading of "Synthesis of Notation". The following example is given in Section 3.353 2 of the Editor's Introduction. It relates to the following "divide like" note

256.16 Scraments. Divide like 265.1 - 265.7. Where

265 Other rites

265.1 Baptism

265.12 Infant baptism

265.2 Confirmation

265.7 Anointing of the sick

265.92 Consecrations and dedications

The host class number is said to belong to "Primary Sequence". The number in "divide like" is said to belong to "Secondary Sequence".

The example in the Introduction reads as follows:-

1	265.1-265.7	Full span of secondary sequence
2	265.12	Number in this span for "infant baptism".
3	(265.) 12	Cancel all repeating digits of secondary sequence.
4	(234.16) 12	Substitute repeating digits of primary sequence.
5	234.161 2	Described number

Strictly speaking, this is not a case of Facet Device, but that of Subject Device of a modified kind. But some mistake it for Facet Device. There is no doubt that this "divide like" device saves a considerable amount of schedule length. It is good that the Editor of Ed 17 has seen in this what I call "Synthesis in the Notational Plane" after the completion of the "Analysis in the Idea Plane".

4.9. Almost Enumerative Classification

The two schedules for common isolate facets occupy only 8 pages and 24 pages respectively. The Standard Division Isolates are about 100 in number; and the Geographical Isolates are about 6,000 in number. The schedule of Main Divisions equivalent to Basic Subjects, to which the common isolates can be attached, occupy about 1,100 pages; and they are about 20,000. Thus, though most of the subjects are enumerated in a single schedule, two short schedules of Common Isolates are provided. For this reason, DC is described as "Almost Enumerative" instead of as "Enumerative".

5. UDC: ALMOST-FACETED

5.1. Common Isolate Facets

UDC provides for the representation of four species of Common Isolate Facets in the class numbers of the subjects presenting them. The term 'Isolate' is denoted by the term 'Auxiliary' in UDC. Each of the species has its own distinctive connecting digit as shown below:

Species of Common Isolate	Connecting Digit
Form	(0---)
Geographical	(...)
Time	" . . . "
Point of view	.00

Language Isolates and Race and Nationality Isolates do not amount to Common Isolates though they are described as "Auxiliaries".

5.2. Basic Facet and Special Isolate Facets

The UDC provides also schedules of Special Isolate Facets. The isolates in any one such schedule is available for use in combination with a specified group of basic subjects only. UDC denotes these special isolates by the term 'Special (auxiliary) Subdivisions'. The following table gives their more specific names and their connecting digits.

Kind of Special Isolate	Connecting Digit
Special Generality Isolate	0
Analytical Division	-
Synthetic Division (Generally for Substances)	'(apostrophe)

5.3. Almost-Faceted Classification

Let us denote by the term 'Compound subject' a subject made of a basic subject and one or more isolate ideas. In spite of several schedules for the three varieties of special isolates provided by UDC for forming compound subjects, the major part of its main schedule is based on the 'Main Table' of DC. It, therefore, consists of not merely basic subjects but also hundreds of compound subjects. This schedule of basic and compound subjects has not been separated out into a short schedule of basic subjects and the respective schedules of special isolates needed for forming the different compound subjects given in the main schedule. Thus, the special isolate facets in UDC are only like veneer applied to the DC core of compound subjects. For this reason, UDC is described as "Almost-Faceted" instead of "Faceted".

6. VERSIONS 1 AND 2 OF CC: RIGIDLY-FACETED

CC is the first fully-faceted scheme designed for classification. Its schedule consists of:-

1. A short schedule of basic subjects without any admixture of compound subjects;
2. Six schedules of common isolates; and
3. Scores of schedules of special isolates for use in classifying the compound subjects going with the basic subjects-in general, one set of distinctive special isolates going with one basic subject. But all was not well in the early stages of its development. It was beset with notational rigidity. It came to light only as the number of facets in compound subjects increased. After the practice of depth classification began, the rigidity became serious. The slow overcoming of this rigidity is explained in Sec 62, 63, and 7 of this Paper.

6.1. Versions of CC

Viewed from the angle of provision of schedules of special isolate facets for the compound subjects going with the respective basic subjects, the following versions of CC may be recognised:-

1. Version 1.- Ed 1 (1933) to Ed 3 (1950);
2. Version 2.- Ed 4 (1952) to Ed 6 (I960); and
3. Version 3.- Forthcoming Ed 7. (This is being already brought into use since 1964 in the schedules for depth classification being published in the quarterly *Library science with a slant to documentation* and in the *Papers* of the Annual DRTC Seminars.)

6.2. Common Isolate Facets

CC provides for the representation of six species of common isolate facets in the class numbers of the subjects presenting them. In Ed 1 to 4 the term 'Common Isolate' was denoted by the term 'Common Subdivision'.

6.2.1. Anteriorising Common Isolate

One of the species of Common Isolates has no connecting digit. This species is called 'Anteriorising Common Isolate'. The first digit of its number is a Roman small. It is invested with anteriorising quality. For example,

'Ba Bibliography of mathematics' precedes - that is, is anterior to - 'B Mathematics'; and

'L45; 421m Periodical on pulmonary tuberculosis' precedes - that is, is anterior to - 'L45; 421 Pulmonary tuberculosis'. Documents represented by class numbers having an anteriorising common isolate number are Approach Documents - that is, documents embodying a special treatment of a subject, such as bibliography, glossary, cyclopaedia, history, biography, and standard of the host subject, which a reader would like to glance through before taking up the ordinary books on the host subject. Viewed from the angle of positive subjects, a subject with an anteriorising isolate has the same extension as the host subject itself. No other scheme provides for the Approach Document to a subject to precede the ordinary books on the subject. When this feature of CC was explained in the FID/CA meeting held in Belgrade in 1954, the engineers and the other professionals welcomed this feature and appreciated its value. In view of this I suggested at that meeting that the UDC also can secure this by declaring that the digit-pair "(0)" has anteriorising value.

6.2.2. Posteriorising Common Isolate

Each of the remaining five species of common isolates is deemed to be a manifestation of one and only one of one or other of the five fundamental categories - Personality, Matter, Energy, Space, and Time. Accordingly, each has its distinctive connecting digit as shown below.

SN	Kind of Common Isolate	Connecting Digit
1	Time	' (single inverted comma)
2	Space	. (dot)
3	Energy	: (colon)
4	Matter (Attribute and Material)	: (semi colon)
5	Personality	, (comma)

Because of the insertion of the connecting digit, a compound subject consisting of a host subject and a posteriorising common isolate can come only after the host subject. This explains the reason for each of these five species of common isolates being called 'Posteriorising Common Isolate'. For example,

'J381.44 Rice cultivation in India' succeeds - that is, is posterior to -'J381 Rice cultivation'.

The addition of a posteriorising common isolate decreases the extension of the host subject.

6.3. Special Isolate Facets

6.3.1. Version 1 of CC

The designing of CC began late in 1924. At that time experience was confined to the classification of macro subjects only. Even there, it was confined only to classification by DC. It was then only half a century after the design of DC. And yet, books embodying subjects with three or four facets had already appeared in abundance. These could not be given coextensive class numbers. There were only two ways of meeting the situation. One of them was to choose forcedly only one isolate facet for representation in the class number and omit the others. This forced choice and omission led to different practices in different libraries. Merrill's *Code for classifiers* (1928) gives a survey of such different practices. The second method was to represent all the facets in the class number, and freezing all the isolate numbers except the last one. This resulted in unhelpful sequence among subjects. Therefore came the feeling that the class number should be made to represent all the facets and at the same time freedom should be kept for the isolate numbers in all the facets, and not merely in the last facet, to be lengthened by the addition of digits. It was found that this could be managed if a connecting digit with ordinal value between those of '0'(zero) and "1" (one), could be inserted between two consecutive isolate numbers. The digit ":" (colon) was chosen for the purpose and invested with an ordinal value between those of '0' (zero) and '1' (one). After making this decision, the main entries in two printed classified catalogues then available in the Library of the School of Librarianship of the University College of London, - those of the Carnegie Library of Pittsburgh and of the Mitchell Library of Glasgow - were examined. The facets presented by the compound subjects were noted. Further, the facets not represented were also noted. This led to the concept of a facet formula of special isolates to be attached to each basic subject. A schedule of basic subjects was constructed. Schedules of special isolates were also constructed for each basic subject. On the basis of these provisional schedules, class numbers were constructed for a large assortment of subjects in the two catalogues mentioned above. Class numbers were also constructed similarly for the books announced in a few monthly issues of the *Publishers' circular.* In this way, the facet formula for each basic subject was made to have as many facets as were demanded by the books published till then. The subjects not presenting all the facets fell into two groups. In Group 1, only the end facet or two or more consecutive facets at the end of the facet formula were absent. These gave no difficulty. But in Group 2, one or more intermediate facets were absent. To avoid the formation of homonyms in the class numbers, each of the intermediate absent facets had to be represented in the class number by the connecting digit ':' (colon). This led to an ugly cluttering of consecutive ':' (colons) in the class numbers of a small percentage of subjects. It was felt that this was due to the rigidity caused by a predetermined facet formula to be conformed to by all the compound subjects going with a basic subject. Thus, Version 1 of CC was Rigidly-Faceted to a severe degree.

6.3.2. Version 2 OF CC

This severe rigidity of a pre-determined facet formula was all along throwing a challenge. A way of lessening the rigidity was found in 1949. It was made possible by the Postulate of Five Fundamental Categories and the provision of different con–necting digits for the isolates deemed to be manifestations of the different fundamental categories. This result was given in Vol 1 of the *Abgila.* The rigidity was further reduced in 1952 by the Postulate of Rounds and Levels. This result was given in Vol 2 of the *Abgila*.

6.4. Rigidly-Faceted Classification

The results of these Postulates were incorporated in Ed 4 (1952) of CC. Ed 6 (1960) still continues in the same state. In this version the rigidity disappeared in respect of Rounds. But it persisted in respect of Levels within a Round. For, the number and the succession of levels had to be pre-determined and the schedule of special isolates had to be provided for each one of them. If any intermediate level was absent in a subject, cluttering of connecting digits was necessary. Till 1963, it looked as if this rigidity could be removed, if and only if, a distinctive connecting digit could be improvised for each of any number of Levels in a Round. This was beyond practicability. Therefore, the rigidity of a pre-determined facet formula persisted. For this reason, Versions 1 and 2 of CC are described as 'Rigidly- Faceted'.

7. VERSION 3 OF CC: FREELY-FACETED

7.1. Removal of Rigidity in Respect of Levels

From 1963 onwards, an attempt was made to remove the persisting rigidity by work in the notational plane. The concept of old Octave Notation was replaced by the concept of the versatile Sector Notation. The first findings of the Sector Notation were published in the *Annals of library science* in 1963. A more productive set of findings were published in *Library science with a slant to documentation* in 1964. Sec HD4 of Ed 3 (1967) of the *Prolegomena to library classification* gives a list of 51 sectors.

These make possible to have 51 distinctive Levels within a Round. This may prove sufficient for the foreseeable future.

7.2. Superimposition of Isolates In [1P1]

A new methodology for the construction of depth schedules was established in 1963. Since then depth schedules have been constructed for the classification of compound subjects going with each of several basic subjects. On account of their great industrial importance, most of the schedules constructed relate to the basic subject Production Engineering. It has been found that the Universe of any particular Commodity - whole commodity - has to be classified on the basis of a very large number of Qualifiers. A Qualifier is a characteristic of division and classification that yields only groups and classes of whole commodities. For example, the Universe of Screws requires 17 qualifiers. The largest numbers of qualifiers, we have come across till now, is 221. This has been in the case of the Universe of Motor Vehicles. In these cases, the qualifiers themselves are to be represented by digits, as if they were isolates. Therefore, the qualifiers are called Quasi Isolates. Super-imposition of quasi- isolates - that is, the qualifiers - is the method used to represent a sub-universe of whole commodity derived on the basis of two or more qualifiers. This turned up as a serious new problem in the design of depth classification. But the Sector Notation meets the situation admirably without any trace of rigidity. When the number of qualifiers to be super-imposed exceeds 51, the 'qualifiers are represented not merely by the first digit of the sector but also by the later digits to the extent necessary. Here are five examples taken from Paper H by A Neelameghan, M A Gopinath, and P H Denton published in the June issue of this volume.

1. Motor car, Racing-Plastic body
   D93C1 , ZK1 -95

2. Motor car, Ford Mustang-Passenger transport-Petrol engine
   D93C1 ,(F=M) –ZB –XI

3. Motor car, Vauxhall Viva 1966-Petrol engine
   D936C1 ,(V=V=66) –XI
   –Unitized body construction–PVC Seat cover
   –9ZY –9t5
   —Rack and pinion steering
   –w8

4. Motor car, Van Dome's DAF–Amphibian–Marshy terrain
   D93C1, (V=D) –ZVP –Z5F
   –Mountainous terrain-Gradient climb 60%-Dry weight, 100 cwt
   –Z57 –Zz60 –ZuB10
   –Mean maximum speed 25 mph–Petrol engine–Four stroke
   –Zj25 –XI –M4
   –Two cylinder-Automatic transmission
   –L2 –zk6

The following is an extreme example requiring the superimposition of 100 quasi-isolates. The sequence of quasi-isolates is presented in a column to facilitate distinguishing groups of the quasi-isolates and sensing the helpfulness of the sequence of groups.

Grouping of quasi isolates by	Superimposed Isolate Terms and Numbers
	Motor car D93C1
Brand	–GT Bond –(GT=B)
Weight	–Laden weight 18·3 cwt-Kerb weight 15·3 cwt –ZyB18=3 –ZwB15=3 –Weight distribution on, rear axle 43.7% –ZsH43=7 –Weight distribution on front axle 56·3% –ZsB56=3
Dimension	–Overall length 13' 1 "–Overall width 5' –Zr13=1 –Zn5
	–Ground clearance 6' 7"–Overall height 4'5" –Zm6=7 –Zk4=5
Speed	–Maximum on top gear 15·8 mph –Zh4B15=8
Power supply	–Battery (12v–38 amp) –Zc10(b12–a38)

Engine	–Petrol engine–Maximum power 63 bhp at 5,800 rpm –X1 –S63A58 –Maximum torque 67 lb-ft at 3,500 rpm –P67A35 –Compression ratio 9 to 1–Cylinders 4 –N9 –L4 –Bore diameter 2·73"–Displacement 70 cu in –K2=73 –H70 –Stroke distance 3" per sec –G3 –Carburetor 2SU brand-Fuel Pump AC operated –CH2SU –CB66
Oil filter	–Full flow–Renewable –C8 –C1
Valve gear	–Overhead–Pushrod and rocker –BCB –BC1
Body	Double back-bone frame –9ZV –Fibre glass reinforced panel –9ZJ4
Seat	–PVC headlining –9s5
Suspension	–Rear (Independent swinging axle-Transverse leaf spring-Telescopic damper) –770(25-zW8-zS2) –Front (Independent Kingpin between double wishbones–coiled spring–Antiroll bar–Telescopic damper) –710(23-zWM-zS6-zS2)
Wheel	Wheel base 7'7.5"-Front and rear track 4' –zL7=7=5 –zJ4
Rim	–Pressed steel disc-Diameter 3' 5"–4-studfiixing –zC –zB3=5 –z94
Tyre	–Dunlop C41-Tubeless-Size 5·2–13 –z1D=C41 –zzU –zz5=2A13
Transmission	

Gear box	–Synchromesh type-Forward speed 4 –zxE -zu4
Gear ratio	–Reverse 15·4 to 1–Top 4·11 to 1–Third 5.73 to 1 –zt15=4 –zsE4=11 –zsD5=73 –Second 8·87 to 1–First 15·4 to 1 –zsC8=87 –zsB15=4
	–Hypoid bevel gear–Final drive 4·11 to –zr1 –zn4=1 –Disc-type single clutch-Dry-Diameter 6·25" –zfl–ze4 –zc6=25
Grouping of quasi isolates by	Superimposed Isolate Terms and Numbers
	-Hypoid bevel gear-Final drive 4.11 to 1 -zrl -zn4=l -Disc-type single clutch-Dry-Diameter 6-25" -zfl-ze4 -zc6=25"
Steering	-Rack and pinion-Steering wheel diameter 15" –w8 –u15 –Turning circles lock-to-lock 3·5 –r3=5 –Diameter of turning circles between curbs 25' –pJ25 –Diameter of turning circles between walls 28' –pC28
Brake	–Girling –kZG –Rear wheel brake (Drum diameter 7"– Shoe width 1·25"–Swept area 55 sq in) –kR0(M7–G1=25–D55) –Front wheel brake (Disc diameter 9"– Shoe width 1·25"–Swept area 144 sq in) –KQ0(N9–G1025–D144)
Safety provision	–Head light 50 watts –fH10(B50)
Windshield wiper	–Single speed–Self parking–Shock absorber –f1U –f1T –f1H

Comfort	–Heating facility-Fresh air ventilation –c44 –c31
	Single speed fan-interior carpet trimming –c123 –b54
Maintenance factor	–Fuel tank capacity 10 Imp gallons –aR10 –Cooling system oil 9·5 pints –aN9=5 –Engine sump oil 7 pints –aM7 –Oil change every 6,000 miles –aK60 –Final drive oil 1 pint –aG1 –Slip diflferential oil change every 12,000 mls –aF12 –Gearbox oil 1.5 pints –aC1=5 –Grease application 4 points every 6,000 miles –aB4B6
Tyre pressure	
Full load driving	–Rear 26 psi–Front 24 psi –za7H26 –a7B24
Fast driving	–Rear 26 psi–Front 24 psi– –a3H26 –a3B24
Normal driving	–Rear 22 psi–Front 22 psi –alH22 –alB20

Note.—The large number of quasi isolates presented by the subject in example 5 should not be taken as typical. But such a subject is rare. It is given to show only the capacity of Version 3 of CC to give co-extensive class number even to a very complicated subject. Normally, the number of quasi isolates presented by a subject is a few. In this connection *see* the following papers:—

1. Neelameghan (A) and Gopinath (M A). Pragmatic approach in the design of a depth classification schedule: A case study. (Lib sc. 2; 1965; Paper C).

2. Parthasarathy (V V). Combination of quasi isolates: A case study. (DRTC Seminar [Papers and proceedings]. 3; 1964; Paper E).
3. Raghavendra (M K). Refinement technique in the design of depth classification schedule: A case study. (DRTC Seminar [Papers and proceedings]. 3; 1964; Paper F).

While the rigidity due to pre-determined facet formula and that due to Levels in a Round took several years for removal, the discovery and removal of the rigidity in respect of superimposition were simultaneous in the development of Version 3 of CC.

7.3. Absence of Rigidity in Version 3 of 3 CC

As far as can be seen, Version 3 of CC imposes no predetermined number of facets for a compound subject. Nor does it impose a pre-determined number of isolates within a facet, that can be superimposed. They are left quite free. If a facet formula is given, in respect of any basic subject, in a simplified version of CC for the classification of macro documents, it is only as a remembrancer to an ordinary classifier about the possible facets likely to occur in the compound subjects. It should be strictly understood that it is not a case of pre-determination of facets. Indeed, it should now be clear that facets belong to compound subjects and not to basic subjects. A basic subject is itself only a facet in a compound subject.

7.4. Same Pattern of Facet Sequence in All Subjects

A compound subject has full freedom to have any number of facets. When the facets are separated out and identified in the idea plane, their sequence is determined for representation in the class number on the basis of Postulates and Principles for Facet Sequence. The roots of the sequence so determined run to the near-seminal level. Indeed, this sequence of the facets is in accordance with what may be called the Absolute Syntax of isolate ideas, naturally preferred by the majority of thinkers.

No rigidity is enforced on their sequence by the notational system. The sequence of facets imposed by the Principles for Facet Sequence happens in the idea plane itself and not in the notational plane. Unless the pattern of the sequence of facets is determined in the idea plane and it is the same in all compound subjects and it is according to stated Postulates and Principles, the sequence of the subjects themselves will prove unhelpful - indeed, it will be chaotic.

7.5. Freely Faceted Classification

Thus, Version 3 of CC forms a Freely Faceted Classification.

8. CONCERTED RESEARCH IN CLASSIFICATION AND COMPUTER

The name of a subject should be fed into the memory of the Computer used for document search, in the form of its class number individualising it on the basis of a Freely-Faceted Scheme for Classification, instead of its name in a natural language or even technical terminology. Then, the computer can give better service. It can avoid the omission of any relevant document or the inclusion of any irrelevant one. If a reader is not able *to* specify each of the later facets of his subject, the computer can present to him the main entries of all the documents answering to the facets he has specified. Thereafter, the computer can also be ordered to arrange the selected entries in a classified sequence. This will secure for the reader the opportunity for browsing, as the classified catalogue does, and thereby formulate his subject in precise terms in all its facets. This of course assumes that mistake would not have been made about the basic facet or about the isolate facets having the greatest bond strength. The Theory of Bond Strength is explained in Chap V of Ranganathan's *Descriptive account of the Colon Classification* (India, 1967) and (USA, 1965). Further, a separate computer can be kept for each basic subject and perhaps even for some compound subjects. Then the whole computer need not be worked for each search. This will increase the lifetime of the computer; this in turn will lead to a considerable economy. To make further improvements, continuing concerted research is necessary in the fields of Design of Classification and of Building the Computer. It is only when classified catalogue is constructed on the basis of a well-developed Freely Faceted Classification and the computer is developed so as to take into its memory the main entries of such a catalogue that the relative cost and viability of document retrieval with the classified catalogue and the computer respectively can be compared on a sound basis. So far as the time required by a reader for document retrieval is concerned, the difference would be negligible.

★★★

Is There a Library Profession ? (Musings on Library Service 2)

S. R. Ranganathan

National Research Professor in Library Science and Honorary Professor, Documentation Research and Training centre, Bangalore-3.

Abstract

After listing the attributes common to crafts and profession, the distinctive attributes of a profession are stated to be in high intellectual capacity, prolonged substantial university training, continuous improvement in methods of work, these being based on research and research itself based on postulated fundamental laws. The existence of the library profession is established on the basis of this set of distinctive attributes.

0. SCEPTICISM

Sceptics ask, "Is there a library profession? Is it possible?" To answer these questions, we must begin with the answer to the question "What is a profession?"

1. CRAFT AND PROFESSION

The term 'Profession' is an elusive one. According to the dictionary, it is "One's principal calling, vocation, or employment". Another meaning given is "The collective body of persons engaged in a Calling". The calling of a person may be anything from that of an Woodcutter, or a bone-setter, or a tribal chief at one end to a machine tool engineer, or an orthopaedic surgeon, or a judge of the High Court at the other end. No one would regard any of the first

Reprinted with permission from Library Herald, Vol 10(2-3), pp. 645-652, 1968.

three callings as a profession. Each of these would be denoted only by the term 'Craft'. At the same time everyone would regard any of the last three callings as a profession. The groups of the callings at the two extremes stand clearly apart. But, there is a continuum of callings at the two extremes. As we move onwards from the craft-end to the profession-end, it is difficult to say when we change over from "Craft" to "Profession". There is no clear boundary line. Further a craft of one period changes into a profession in a later period. What is the attribute to be acquired by a craft to get changed into a profession? This needs exploration.

2. NON-DIFFERENTIA BETWEEN CRAFT AND PROFESSION

The undermentioned attributes may be applicable to any calling in the continuum from craft to profession. Therefore, they do not provide differentia.

1. Owning special skill;
2. Giving a distinctive service to society;
3. Following a code of ethics in relation to the members of the calling itself and to the public served. The code is agreed upon by the members of the calling, whether written or not;
4. Collective organisation to advance and safeguard the economic interests of the members-say, trade union or guild in crafts, and association in Professions;
5. Provision for the special education of the entrants - be it in apprenticeship and or/formal education;
6. Knowledge of the basic sciences concerned. Even for a craft this is helpful; for example, in the nineteenth century Britain. Birckbeck gave such a knowledge to artisans and this was later continued by the Workers' Educational Association;
7. Status of the calling in the society at large. This may be a misleading attribute. For example, the calling of the

government bureaucracy and of politicians carries a high status today in the eyes of the public. Similarly, in the past, the calling of court officials and of even courtiers carried a high status in the eyes of the public. Again, an individual member of any calling can command a high status by virtue of his own personality, even if the status of the majority of the members of the calling is low; and

8. Salary level of the calling. This too may be as misleading as status. This is clinched by the saying. "The sorriest of trades and the noblest of professions". The attribute of salary level will have however, to be reckoned with so long as "currency civilisation" continues.

3. DIFFERENTIA BETWEEN CRAFT AND PROFESSION

The undermentioned attributes are special to a profession. They form the differentia between a profession and a craft.

1. The intellectual ability needed in the pursuit of a profession falls in the first quartile in the descending intellectual scale; it may also extend into the second quartile to some extent, but not into the third or the fourth. Moreover, the exclusive range of work of a profession would require specialisation of a high intellectual order in the appropriate subject complex;
2. After a twelve year period of general school education, professional education-that is education in the distinctive subject complex concerned-takes another five years. All the five years may be devoted to specialized education as in Engineering, Agriculture, and Medicine, or distributed over three years of liberal education and two years of specialised education as in Education and Law. Usually the period of specialized education is preceded by a pre-course apprenticeship and succeeded by a post-course apprenticeship for a specified period. The latter is generally

extended informally beyond the specified period in order to acquire sufficient depth and maturity;

3. In a craft, the improvement in the standard and techniques of service is made casually by trial and error. It is in homeopathic doses; and it is done at long intervals. On the other hand, in a profession the improvement is made continuously by systematic development research. It is further made in doses of large size;
4. Research usually makes a blending of empirical research and a *priori* research;
5. As a basis for a *priori* research, there is a set of Fundamental Laws-Hypotheses in natural sciences and Normative principles in social sciences. Such fundamental laws are only postulates. The epithets 'true' and 'false' are not applicable to them. Their value consists only in being helpful in carrying forward research in the discipline concerned. A calling gets confirmed as a profession only when it is based on such fundamental laws. Most callings in the area of pure natural sciences, some of the applied natural sciences and a few of the social sciences have reached confirmation in this way as a profession during the last two hundred years - and some of them only in recent years. It is not meant that the last two attributes mentioned in this section should be developed by each member of the profession. Many will merely put into practice with discretion and understanding the findings of research and be of help in developmental research. But a few will always engage themselves in research. These few form the spearhead of the profession.

4. WARNING

4.1. Semi-Professional

As auxiliary to each profession, there will be a large number of persons doing routine work distinctive to the profession, in accordance with the specification made by the profession from time to time. These should not be taken to be professionals. They may be called only semi-professionals. This term is used to distinguish them from the others doing for the profession general-office-routine work, such as correspondence work and book-keeping. In Medicine, for example, nurses do not count as professionals but only as semi-professionals. So also in Law, the clerks of the advocates, and the solicitors working for the professional are semi-professionals. Similarly, among the persons working in a library, the circulation assistants, the persons replacing books on the shelves, and those in charge of binding work are only semi-professionals and not professionals.

4.2. Help From Other Professions

A calling, using for its work to help, the machinery and the technique provided by some other profession does not become a profession if its own distinctive work does not qualify it to be a profession. For example, the calling of planers and shapers of metal pieces in accordance with the specification prescribed and the machine tools provided by the engineering profession does not form a profession; it is only a trade or a craft. So also, the calling of sweepers does not become a profession though it may use vacuum machinery invented and provided by the engineering profession. Similarly, the calling of librarians does not become a profession merely on the ground of its using electronic gadgets such as computers invented and produced by the engineering profession, or of its doing reprographic work using the inventions of the profession of technologists. This has to be stated because some librarians are claiming to be doing professional work of a high order on account of their using such new glamorous gadgets to the neglect of the distinctive work of the library profession! Library staff turning their attention to them belong neither to the library profession nor to the engineering profession nor to the technological profession. They can at best be taken as technicians or semi-professionals engaged by the library profession.

5. EXISTENCE OF THE LIBRARY PROFESSION

A library profession does exist to day, because it has all the differentia-attributes mentioned in Sec 4 of this paper.

1. Its research is now guided by the normative principles postulated as the Five Laws of Library Science. These laws are continuously opening up new areas for research. This marks the confirmation and the maturity of the profession;
2. A *priori* research based on the Five Laws, empirical research, and their blending are now steadily in progress both in response to specific demands and in anticipation of demand. Full-timed research workers also are just coming into existence either in universities or in special research institutes such as the DRTC of Bangalore;
3. Developmental research to meet the situations arising now and then is now being undertaken in some libraries also. Of course, when the problems for investigation increase in intensity or in magnitude, they are passed on to those in the profession engaged in full-timed or nearly full-timed research;
4. Improvement in library outlook; organisation, and techniques has now begun to flow steadily and in doses of appreciable size;
5. Professional librarians are now provided post-graduate professional education in their distinctive subject complex extending over nearly two years, in universities and university like bodies; and
6. There is no doubt today about the high intellectual ability needed in one aspiring to enter the library profession. This is essential as the commodity acquired, organised, and served by the library profession is intellectual commodity calculated to inform, educate, and inspire intellectuals and to provide intellectual entertainment to all. The incidence of the above mentioned attributes has begun to have its effect on the status and salary scale of library profession.

6. OBSTACLE IN THE PATH

The progression of the calling of librarians towards the stage of a profession has had to be slow. Many were the obstacles in the path. Some have been overall obstacles put in the path by the older professions. There is also the usual obstruction from the rank and file of the calling itself put against the intellectuals among them attaining the professional stage and themselves being left at the semi-professional stage. The last-lap-obstruction comes from some of the intellectuals themselves. Having slipped into the library profession along with the others and having taken possession of the concomitant worldly benefits, they turn Judas obstructing further progress and even denying the true differentia between craft and profession. Again some of the distinctive spheres of work of the profession had been usurped earlier by others; and these have had to be rescued. The overcoming of all such obstacles will be described in the later papers of this series.

★★★

Librametry and Its Scope

S. R. Ranganathan
National Research Professor in Library Science, India and Hon Professor, DRTG, Bangalore - 3.

Abstract

The term 'Librametry' was coined in 1948 at the Aslib Conference of the year in Leamington Spa. Illustrations of the use of the elements of statistical calculus are given in the determination of the strength of the library staff in the disposition of the circulation and the reference staff during the different hours of the day, in the organisation and development of national and state library systems, in the distinction between service libraries and dormitory libraries, and in the design of library buildings. Illustrations are also given in the use of operations research in the transfer of a big library from one building to another without closing the library to the public, and in the periodical changes in the sequence of the subjects in the stackroom to help the fulfilment of Law 3 of Library Science. Some illustrative areas are given for the application of librametry in library techniques such as book selection, classification, cataloguing, and in the use of electronic Doc-Finder. Lastly, the inclusion of the Elements of Statistical Calculus in the curiculum for library science is considered.

1. GENESIS OF THE TERM 'LIBRAMETRY'

In September 1948, I was working in Manchester as a member of the Faculty of the International Summer School on Public Libraries,

Reprinted with permission from Library Science with a slant to Documentation, 4(3), pp. 597-644, 1967.

conducted by IFLA and UNESCO. During that period, I received an invitation from the Aslib to attend its Annual Conference on 18 September 1948 at Leamington Spa. On account of delay of the train, I reached the Conference rather late. Mr. Henri LeMeister, the President of the Aslib, was in the chair and somebody was in the middle of his speech. It referred to library statistics now and then. LeMeister asked me to sit by his side on the platform and also to give my views on that speech. Unfortunately, I did not know the name of the speaker, nor the theme of his address in full. LeMeister furnished me with the necessary information. To my great delight and surprise, the speaker was Dr. Bernal, with whose work I was familiar. The term 'Librametry' came out for the first time in my remarks on Professor Bernal's speech [2]. I said that many of the matters connected with library work and service involved "large numbers".

Therefore, as the saying goes, the wood could not be seen on account of the trees. However a calculus had been developed to deal with phenomena involving "large numbers", in an incipient form in the nineteenth century and in full vigour in the twentieth century. That is Statistical Calculus. It had been already in use in diverse disciplines. Karl Pearson had introduced the term 'Biometry' early in the present century. The study of economics with the aid of statistical calculus had given rise to the term 'Econometry'. So also we have the term 'Psychometry'. It is necessary for us librarians to develop 'Librametry'. The Chairman and many of the members of the audience welcomed this suggestion. At the end of the meeting, Professor Bernal and myself rested for an hour on the sunny lawn of the Conference House, discussing the potentiality of Librametry.

1.1. Earlier Practice of Librametry though without that Name

Though the term 'Librametry' was coined by me only in 1948, I had been practising the application of the elements of statistical calculus to library problems since 1925. This was because I learnt statistical calculus when I was a student of mathematics during 1914 to 1916, and I had to teach mathematics, the erratic vicissitude in the percentage of successful candidates in the examination from year to year was the first to engage my thought. Professor P. V. Seshu Ayyar and myself collaborated in 1921 in going into this problem, on the basis of the marks-registers for the Intermediate examinations from 1911 to 1921, maintained by the University of Madras. We arrived at a formula for removing the annual idiosyncrasies, in terms of standard deviation and average [13]. It was later considered by the Hartog Committee on Examinations. After I became librarian in 1924, I saw many possible uses of the elements of statistical calculus in the day-to-day working of libraries, in the organisation of a library system, and in the development of library techniques. I also began to practice it.

2. LIBRAMETRY IN THE DAY-TO-DAY WORK OF A LIBRARY

2.1. Strength of Staff

From 1925, the number of volumes added and the number of visitors to the Madras University Library, and the number of volumes used in a year went on rising steadily. The curve of growth was fairly steep [5]. The steepness began to slacken only after 1936. The procurement of sanction for the additional staff necessary to cope with the increase of work, was a difficult affair. It was a matter of annual fight with the authorities. However, I was keeping detailed statistical data about the man-hours needed in a year for each item of work in the library. In 1947 when I was invited by the Indian Institute of Science (Bangalore) for advice on staff requirements, these statistical data enabled me to evolve a detailed staff-formula based on work-load and not on mere guess or sentiment [8]. This staff formula based on statistical data was found to be of help in several other libraries. The Library of the International Labour Office and the Library of the Swedish Railways were among them. In 1958, the University

Grants Commission of India adopted this formula [16], This has given relief to many libraries in the country. With the help of the modern facilities for time and motion study, the constants of the staff formula can be verified and fixed with precision.

2.2. Disposition of Staff

Another problem encountered in the Madras University Library in the earlier years was providing just the adequate staff-neither in excess nor in defect - in the Circulation and the Reference Sections, during different periods of the day. For this purpose, hourly statistics were maintained, from 1925 to 1930. An analysis of these figures brought out unerringly the pattern of the distribution of the density of work during the different periods of the day. This helped us to organise the hours of duty of the members of the Circulation and the Reference Sections in an efficient and equitable way. For example, from 7 to 10 am, one person was sufficient in each Section; from 10 am to 7 pm, two persons were necessary in the Circulation Section; from 10 am to 4 pm, two persons were necessary in the Reference Section; from 4 pm to 7 pm, three persons were necessary in it; and from 7 pm to 8 pm, one was sufficient in each Section. This disposition of the staff increased their productivity.

3. LIBRAMETRY IN THE ORGANISATION OF NATIONAL OR STATE LIBRARY SYSTEM

3.1. Viability of Independent Library Authority and of Rural Library

While writing my Library development plan for India [7] in 1950, I had to press into service the demographic and the financial statistical data to formulate a plan about population clusters and areas that would be viable to be made independent library units. A norm was also established for the viability of the minimum population of a locality to have a branch library. In the light of the increase in the cost of books and in staff salary during the last twenty years, the size of the viable units had to be increased. But in the establishment of branch libraries in the rural area, political and sentimental considerations often lead to uneconomical decisions. For example, under its Public Libraries Act (1948), the Tamil Nadu (Madras State) had 1057 rural branch libraries at the end of the year 1966 [1]. By now, it has increased still further. But statistical considerations would limit the number of such branch libraries to 802 [15]. If only the concerned people had a statistical sense and used it to arrive at decisions objectively, this would have been avoided.

3.2. Librametry in Relation to Service Libraries and Dormitory Libraries

In the past, each library was actuated by a hoarding sentiment. It often prided itself in the number of volumes it had. Law 1 of Library Science - "Books are for use" -- was not acted upon [4]. Nor were the authorities guided by the wise advice of our National Poet Rabindranath Tagore that "What makes a library big is not its size but its use" [3]. Hardly any library kept statistical data about the number of years for which a book continued to be of use. I kept such data in the Madras University Library for about twenty years. A good percentage of books went out of use in five years; a smaller percentage in ten years; and most of the books in twenty years. In the case of works of lasting value, new editions were brought out from time to time. Copies of such books in a library are usually worn out by legitimate use in about ten to twenty years; and they have to be replaced by new editions. If each library holds on to all the books that once got into it, it increases the cost of building and of maintenance without any real advantage. On the other hand, librametry would suggest that libraries should be grouped into service libraries and dormitory libraries. On the recommendation of its Documentation Committee, of which I was Chairman, the Indian Standards Institution, recommended in 1960 an upper limit for service libraries. For example, for a university library, according to its size, the upper limit recommended was 100,000 to 300,000. When the University of Calcutta applied for grant of a few millions of rupees to erect a new library building, so as to hold nearly a million volumes, a delegation of the Library Committee of the University Grants Commission, of which I was Chairman, went to the University for local enquiry. The Vice-Chancellor, Professor Siddhantha, and the University Architect (an Englishman) readily saw the wisdom in the indication of librametry and agreed that the volumes with a low and vanishing frequency of use - not used even once in three years - should be accommodated in a dormitory library in an easily accessible place well outside the city area, so that any of its books occasionally wanted may be brought over for use. But a professor insisted that all its 300,000 or 400,000 volumes were in active use; and that none of the books could be sent out to the dormitory collection. Thereupon, the members walked through the stackroom. The British architect put his little finger on the tops of the books in several places. The dust was a few millimeters' deep! This proved how unhelpful sentiments thrive, when a librametric sense is not developed.

3.3. Librametry and the Design of Library Building

Apart from the stackroom, the size of the reading room requires attention in the design of a library building. Each room -- be it a general reading room or a periodicals reading room or research reading room or a set of cubicles - has to be designed so as to accommodate readers during peak hours. In this, I got some ideas from the Probability and its engineering uses (1928) by Thornton C Fry. To decide the accommodation needed during peak hours, careful hourly data of the number of occupants should be kept and the trend should be determined. We kept such data in the Madras University Library from 1925 to 1933. By a forecast on the basis of these data, the size of the general reading room and of the periodicals reading room needed for about ten years was determined. Provision was also made for the other rooms to be brought into use in due course. The other rooms, that were not needed for immediate use by the library, were occupied by the University Office. By 1939, the two reading rooms in actual use by the Library were getting full on Sundays and other holidays. But, thereafter, the unexpected World War II reduced the number of readers. If the library had the anticipated normal growth in its readers, the other rooms occupied by the University Office should have been taken over by the Library for its use.

4. OPERATIONS RESEARCH IN LIBRARY WORK

4.1. Tranfer of Library from One Building to Another

In 1936, the Madras University Library had to be transferred from its temporary place in the Senate House to its buildings. It was the ambition of the staff not to close the Library to effect the transfer, except perhaps on the day of formal opening. To carry out this ambition, the method of Operations Research was adopted. The books were all bundled in units 1.5 feet high. Each bundle had a slip on its top. On it were entered the inclusive call numbers of the books in the bundle, the exact shelf plank into which the bundle will go in the new building, and also the number of books in the bundle likely to be in demand during the interim period, and, therefore, withdrawn from it. These withdrawn books were in open book-racks, as usual, in the old building, for use by readers. About a month before the opening of the new building, about 5,000 bundles had been gradually transferred to the new building in the sequence of the decreasing probability for the use of any book in that bundle. In the last three days, many of the books in current use also were transferred to the new building. With a band of volunteers brought by Sri S Chandrasekharan, then an honours undergraduate and now Union Minister for Public Health and Family Planning. All the 1,200 bays in the new stackroom had been fitted with bay guides in advance. Thus, it was possible to keep the Library closed only for ten hours on the opening day. Even on that day, the Library functioned for three hours after the opening.

4.2. Periodical Rearrangement of the Subjects in the Stackroom

It was found that Law 3 of Library Science - "Every Book its Reader" - could be better satisfied by a periodical reshuffling of the subjects in the stackroom. This reshuffling had to be done when the library was working in full swing and without any extra place for the temporary housing of the books in any subject. Here again, the paper work done on Operations Research was of help in the rearrangement of the subjects without any difficulty or confusion or inconvenience to readers.

5. LIBRAMETRY AND BOOK SELECTION

The subject-scatter of book selection and the subject allotment of book-fund are important factors in book selection. With the help of the histograms showing these two factors for each of a few years of the past and of what can be conjectured about the changes likely to disturb in the immediate future, the proportion suggested by these histograms, the problem is solved objectively, and with greater reliability than if it is done with unaided conjecture [6]. This was of much help in the Madras University Library. In the use of the histograms, some weightage or correction may have to be applied to some of them with circumspection. Two instances of this precaution are worth mentioning. It was found that psychology and education showed the highest frequency of use. This raised some doubt and to the detailed examination of the kind of books that were issued in these two subjects. It was found that the Psychology of sex by Havlock Ellis and the bound volumes of university question papers swelled the frequency of use in the two respective subjects. Therefore the frequencies, in these two subjects had to be modified.

6. LIBRAMETRY AND CLASSIFICATION

6.1. Absolute Syntex and Facet Syntax

One of the vital problems in library classification is the decision of the most helpful sequence of the Personality, Matter, Energy, Space, and Time facets in a compound subject. On the basis of flair and experience, I had formulated certain postulates in this matter. One of the postulates will arrange the facets in the sequence mentioned above. It is worth verifying the validity of the helpfulness of this postulate objectively. In my Valedictory Address to the Symposium on the "Foundation of Syntactic Relations in Classification" held in the University of Maryland in June 1966, I had suggested a statistical method of determining the Absolute Syntax, if any, governing the sequence of facets of the subject inherent in the human intellect-in-action as it is today. Then the helpfulness or otherwise of the facet syntax given by my postulate can be decided upon. This investigation should be made by a team of specialists in Epistemology Psychology, Linguistics, Reference Service, Design of Classification, and Statistical Calculus [11]. I had also suggested the precaution that should be taken in carrying out this investigation. The final findings by statistical calculus will enable the classificationist to base the design of classification scheme on a fairly firm foundation. The present wastage in discussing the problem based on opinions and sentiments can be avoided. I even suggested that this piece of work and statistical investigation should be provided for by a Foundation.

6.2. Long and Short of Class Number

6.2.1. Book Level

A trivial amusing opinion was rampant for a few years after the publication of Colon classification in 1933. It was generated and believed by naive "arm-chair" librarians that the Colon Class Number was much longer than the Decimal Class Number at the book level. In 1935, the question was statistically examined [14]. The finding was presented in table.

SN	Statistical Constants	CCN	DCN
1	Mode (most frequently occuring number of digits)	3.00	5.00
2	Medium (number of digits which is not exceeded by half of the class number)	4.00	5.00
3	Mean (the average number of digits in the class numbers)	4.80	5.80
4	Standard deviation (a measure of the spread of the range of the length of notation)	2.40	1.70
5	Correlation co-efficient between CC and DC.	0.56	

The figures in table speak for themselves about the great risk or grave mistake of more opinion while dealing with large numbers. Further, "the difference in the standard deviations of the Colon class Numbers and of the Decimal Class Numbers carried a message".

The Colon frequency curve is much more spread out and graduated than the Decimal Frequency curve. In other words, the Colon Class Number imitates more closely the variation of the "intension" of the subjects than the Decimal class Numbers. The latter leans towards artificiality. The steepness and the narrowness of the Decimal Frequency Curve showed that the Decimal class Numbers are unnaturally crowded within a narrow range of five digits.

6.2.2. Article Level

Again, in 1967 a similar statistical comparison was made of Colon Class Numbers and the Universal Decimal Class Numbers at the level of articles - that is, depth classification. The finding was as follows [10]

SN	Statistical Constant	CC	UDC
1	Mode	12	18
2	Median	12	17
3	Mean	12	18

The above table shows that the average number of digits in UDC Numbers is fifty per cent more than that in the CC Numbers.

7. LIBRAMETRY AND CATALOGUING

A library catalogue is a permanent record. Its value depends upon the consistent sequence of the entries. This depends upon the headings of entries being consistently chosen and rendered. This, in its turn, depends upon rigorous cataloguing rules. On the other hand, when I learnt cataloguing in 1924, in the University College (London), the Cataloguing Code used was the Anglo-American Code of 1908, which was far from being rigorous. The students would give different choices of heading and even for the same heading different renderings. The lecturer used to say that any of these different choices and renderings might be used. This was a puzzle to me. By 1934, I had designed a fairly rigorous Catalogue Code - the classified catalogue code, now in its fourth edition. Some librarians criticized that Code had gone into too many details and had denied freedom to individual cataloguers! I had to meet this critism by having recourse to statistical calculus. I mentioned about per factors which enter into the establishment of the catalogue entries for a book. If the rules allow freedom to every cataloguer to adopt his own style, the number of styles possible was shown to be 1,024. Therefore, the probability for consistency among the catalogue entries would be only one in 1,024, because a succession of cataloguers would contribute the entries in them, each following his own style. It is, therefore, impracticable to maintain uniformity of entries in a library catalogue and the catalogue of a growing library can hardly escape becoming a hotchpotch sooner or latter [12]. This finding of statistical calculus appears to have made some impact on the Anglo-American Code. For, its Edition 3 (1967) has more rigour than its Edition 1. And yet, it is not as rigorous as it should be; I attribute this to the statistical sense not having been brought to bear on the problem.

8. SAMPLING

Catalogue entries and class numbers have to be tested for their accuracy. The question is whether hundred per cent revision is necessary, or a sample revision would prove sufficient. Here, it should be the former. For, a mistake even in one class number or in one catalogue entry will cause difficulties. On the other hand, hundred per cent inspection will be unnecessary and too expensive and, therefore; sampling of lots will be sufficient in finding out the problems such as the period of active use of books or the opinion of readers about the efficiency of library service. In the cases where sampling is sufficient, how should the lot for sampling unit, the sampling plan, the sampling efficiency, and the sampling error, be determined? These problems have to be investigated and guiding principles should be established on the basis of a guide such as the Manual on basic principles of lot sampling published by the Indian Standards institution as its publication IS : 1548-1960, or some similar manual. This problem of sampling arises in many other areas of library work.

9. LIBRAMETRY AND ELECTRONIC DOC-FINDER

Another new problem has recently arisen. This has been caused by the "Wonder Sense" induced in the majority of librarians by electronic engineering. In the first flush of wonder, there is a tendency in the members of the library profession to swallow everything claimed by electronic engineering, even to the point of abdicating or minimising their own effort in classification and cataloguing. The problem of the extent to which the work of an electronic doc-finder would depend upon a sound system of classification and cataloguing, the minimum workload necessary to make the electronic doc-finder viable, the amount of noise and leakage should be investigated by statistically controlled experiments. The Cranfield experiment was the first of its kind. But it did not use a good individualising scheme for classification and cataloguing. The experiment should be repeated with a good scheme for classification and cataloguing and in conformity to the principles of sampling.

9.1. Statistical Calculus in Library Science Curriculum

The above are only examples of areas in library work leading themselves to the use of librametry. I am sure that a careful search will disclose more areas. We should consider from this point of view the desirability of acquainting librarians under training with the basic ideas of statistical calculus, the statistical outlook, and statistical awareness. In my teaching of library science during the last forty years, I had always given a statistical flavour, as it were, in the exposition of many problems. Is this sufficient desirable or necessary to give a few formal lessons on the Elements of Statistical Calculus biased to library practice and library science? This can be done only by a teacher who is proficient in statistical calculus and has the necessary knowledge of library science. Otherwise, the course is likely to become lopsided and forbidding. The time has come to decide this issue.

BIBLIOGRAPHIC REFERENCES

1 Sec 31 Annual Report, Madras Library Association. 29; 1967;32.

2 Sec 2 Aslib Proceedings. 1;1949; 103.

3 Sec 32 Rabindranath Tagore. What makes a library big ? (In library movement; a collection of essays by diverse hands. (Madras Lib Assoc, pub series,1) 1929. P 1-4).

4 Sec 32 Ranganathan (S R). Five laws of library science. Ed 1. (Madras Lib Assoc, pub series. 2) 1931. P 327.

5 Sec 21 -. -. -.P 326.
6 Sec 5 -. Library book selection. (Ranganathan series In lib sc. 16). Ed2.1966. PartE.
7 Sec 31 -. Library development plan: Thirty-year programme for India with draft library bills for the Union and the Constituent States. (Delhi, Univ pub, Lib sc series, 2) 1950.
8 Sec 21 --. Preface to library science. (Delhi Univ pub, Lib sc series, 1) 1948. Sec 7541.
9 Sec 621 -. Prolegomena to library classification. (Ranganathan series in lib sc, 20). Ed 3,1967, Sec SP5.
10 Sec 622 -.-.- Sec SQ3.
11 'Sec 61 -.-.-Sec XJ5.
12 Sec 7 --. Theory of Library catalogue. (Madras Lib. Assoc, pub series,7) 1938. P 21-34.
13 Sec 11 SESHU AYYAR (P V) and RANGANATHAN (S R). Memorandum on Educ rev. 28; 1922: 164-78) --. --. Statistical study of some examination marks. (J Ind Math Soc. 14;1922;43-5.-15;1923; 141-5).
14 Sec 62 Sivaraman (K M). Colon vs Decimal Classification - a statistical study of their notation. (Mod lib. 5; 1935;77-81
15 Sec 31 SUGRABEGUM (R) and RANGANATHAN (T). Rural Library System (Lib sc. 1;1964;Paper Q, Sec 73)
16 Sec 21 UNIVERSITY GRANTS COMMISSION (India). University and college libraries, containing the report of the Library Committee (1957). (Chairman : S R Ranganathan). 1965. Sec K4 and V2.

★★★

Unified View of Education and Library Work

S. R. Ranganathan

Abstract

Begins with the description of the revolt of the author against the method of teaching to which he was exposed sixty years ago as a student. It was all reading a text book or taking down dictated notes. While a student in Teachers' College in 1916, nothing more was suggested except the introduction of questions and answers and of the four Herbartian steps in the classroom. There was no worthwhile library in school or in college. On becoming lecturer in 1917, the author formed a classroom library and integrated library work and classroom teaching, resulting in individual instruction rather than mass lecturing. This produced a good result. This, he continued for all the six years till he became University Librarian. Since 1929, when he started the School of Library Science in Madras, he has been using this method all along. Now it is called student-centred, library-centred teaching instead of teacher-centred textbook-centred teaching. After forty six years of this practice, the South India Teachers' Union has started making controlled experiments on this method in fourteen high schools since 1963. The overall purpose of formal education is to increase self-educability in every adult, in order that he can continue his self-education forever with the aid of the public library system socialising books and making them available freely to one and all.

Reprinted with permission from Library Herald, Vol 10(2-3), pp. 703-710, 1968.

1. EDUCATION SIXTY YEARS AGO

I was a student in a college about sixty years ago. In those days only ten per cent who were at the top of the intellectual scale among the students of college going age used to take the college course. Our class was forty strong. The first ten were self-educables. Even the worst teaching could not kill out felt spirit of learning. The next ten were tolerable though susceptible to being inhibited by wrong methods of teaching. The remaining twenty were declared failures. It was little realized then that this declaration was against the teachers themselves rather than the students. There was a good deal of bullying and ridiculing of these unfortunate twenty students. This was most revolting to me, though I did not belong to their group. I used to say to myself quite often, "If ever I become a teacher...."

2. NO HELP IN THE TEACHERS' COLLEGE

After passing my M.A. examination, I spent one year in the Teachers' college learning the methods of teaching. There was precious little worth knowing. The only new terms I heard was the four Herbartian steps - even these only in the theory class. There was nothing of it in the actual teaching in the Model School attached to the College.

3. AT THE PRESIDENCY COLLEGE

The Presidency College was a very big institution teaching to the highest standards. Each Department had its own library. But it appears to have been organized that way more for administrative convenience rather than for academic reasons. For, the departmental library would be open only on two or three days in a week for a short while for charging and discharging books. Anyhow, I started using this library in the same way in which I used the classroom libraries in the smaller colleges. The result was equally good. There was *esprit de corps* among the students. There was no highbrow and lowbrow among them. I could help each student according to his own needs. The students would themselves help one another very freely. My own colleagues were excellent friends. Within two years they saw the change in the spirit of the students. They too were willing to fall in line with this method of teaching. But just at that time I was appointed as the Librarian of the University.

4. OBSERVATION IN THE UNITED KINGDOM

The first year after my appointment as University Librarian was spent in UK, obstensibly to study library science in the University College, London. But my interest in teaching and the generous outlook of the members of the Faculty in that University made it possible for me to observe the teaching in some schools and colleges. I found that the educational institutions had good libraries and that they were well used by the students. But, I did not find any correlation between classroom work and library work.

5. BACK TO MADRAS

I returned to Madras in 1925. After putting the Library of the University in some order, as a preliminary measure, I started a Library School. In this School also I used my method of teaching. Taking advantage from my position as University Librarian and as an old student of the Teachers' College, I used to spend one hour each week in the Teachers' College speaking to the students on School Library Work. This somehow caught the attention of the older teachers in the State. In about four years, in response to their request the Universiry of Madras asked me to give a series of lectures and demonstrations on School Library Work to headmasters and teachers in service. This went on for a few years. To support my method of teaching work, I began to import books on Education, particularly from USA. I found an extraordinary book of 1899 in this collection; it was the—*School and society* by John Dewey—that masterpiece. I also found books containing jargons like Pedagogy of Individual Instruction, Project Method, Dalton Plan, and so on.

6. JOHN DEWEY INTRODUCED INTO MADRAS

My old colleagues of the Madras Teachers' Guild were introduced to John Dewey's book and to the other books. But the old conservatism was too hard to break. Except for about half a dozen enthusiasts nobody else cared for any change. No doubt, the Teachers' College had begun to speak of Pedagogy of Individual Instruction, Project Method, and so on; but all this was only in the verbal plane—nothing whatever in action.

6.1. Solace from John Dewey

This was, no doubt, very disappointing to me. The idea did not catch in Madras till I retired from there. But I received solace in 1950. In that year I met John Dewey in New York. Eversince, I knew his *School and society*, he had become my hero. When I went to him, he surprised me by his intimate knowledge of my book *School and college libraries* (1942). We settled down to compare notes.

Dewey: – Thought I had my vision in the 1890's, I do not think that the idea has as yet permeated into many of the institutions even in my country.

Myself: – I am surprised to hear this. But it is a solace to me. For, although I started along similar lines in 1917, and although my book was written in 1942, it has not at all permeated anywhere in our country.

Dewey:– You know that it takes more than a century for my new idea to get accepted even by a few.

Myself:– I now realize it, sir. Any emotion-free intellectual stuff appears to have little permeability

Dewey:– That is well put.

The monagenarian and myself had a hearty laughter.

Dewey:– I am glad that we have met. You must come and spend some days in my country house before you leave for India.

6.2. Ray of Hope

In 1962, a ray of hope appeared. Two of my old colleagues of the Teachers' Guild, who were still active though retired from salaried work, wrote to me that they would like to start the new method of teaching which we have had some decades earlier. Later, they brought with them to me a few young teachers. We spent six weeks together in initiating and demonstrating to them the Student-Centred, Library-Centred Teaching. Messrs Natarajan and Srinivasachari were determined to push this through. By way of abundant caution they started with a few controlled experiments. Every year the result was assessed. As usual, the younger people—both teachers and students—plumped for this method. The rigid old teachers continued their cynical views. In spite of it, fourteen schools have by now been brought under this scheme. In this scheme, there is hardly any substantial difference between classroom work and library work. The classroom is used to stimulate curiosity and interest in the students in stated areas of subject determined partly by the curriculum and partly by the moods of the students. The teachers play a great part in this. They also enjoy it. For, their experience with one set of students is totally different from the experience with another set; and as the saying goes, "Variety is the spice of life". The true function of the teacher in the classroom is to throw the leaven at the time in the right way and then leave the ferment to work among the students each in the way most helpful to him. Once this is done, self-education begins in the library—of course, the teachers and the librarian withdrawing into the background, but ever ready to give help at the right moment. This is the productive unification of education and library work in the formal institutions for education.

7. LONG-RANGE BENEFIT

What is described in Sec 6.2 is only a short-range benefit of the unification of classroom work and library work. This is only a means to a larger end. In fact, it is the larger end that is paramount. Education is not a process that ends sharply on leaving the school or college. It is a life-long process. It goes on growing all through adult life. In adult life, it is impossible for everybody to sit in a classroom and be taught by a teacher. Education will have to be self-education. The source for self-education is environment going into one's experience. To-day, a vital element in that environment is the intellectual deposit of the great thinkers of the past and the present. These intellectual deposits are available in pellets called 'Books'. Modern society is keen in every citizen continuing the self-education without end. To facilitate this, modern society socialises books. It collects them in libraries for free services to all. To use the public library system so built and maintained, the self-educability of every citizen should be well cultivated before leaving school or college. This is the higher social purpose of the unification of education and library work.

BIBLIOGRAPHICAL REFERENCES

1. Dewey John : *School and society*. 1899.
2. Ranganathan S R : *Organization of libraries*. Ed 3. 1963. Oxford University Press, Madras.
3. Ranganathan S R : *School and college libraries*. 1942. Madras Library Association.
4. SITU Council of Education Research. *Library as an effective instrument of learning in secondary schools*. 1964.
5. Library centred teaching (Project Report 1964-65). 1965.

★★★

Index

★ ★ ★